THE
SPECIAL EDUCATION
SOURCEBOOK

A Teacher's Guide to Programs, Materials, and Information Sources

Michael S. Rosenberg, Ph.D.
and Irene Edmond-Rosenberg, M.P.A.

WOODBINE HOUSE   1994

Cover illustration & design: Lili Robins

Library of Congress Cataloging-in-Publication Data

Rosenberg, Michael S.
   The special education sourcebook : a teacher's guide to programs, materials, and information sources / Michael S. Rosenberg and Irene Edmond-Rosenberg.
      p. cm.
   Includes bibliographical references and indexes.
   ISBN 0-933149-52-2 : $21.95
   1. Special education—United States—Handbooks, manuals, etc.
2. Special education—United States—Directories. I. Edmond-Rosenberg, Irene.
II. Title.
LC3981.R67 1994   94–21554
371.9′0973—dc20   CIP

Manufactured in the United States of America

10 9 8 7 6 5 4 3 2

To our great sources of love and guidance,
our parents

Vera and Harry Rosenberg
Mary and Robert Edmond

Table of Contents

section I : *Introduction*

Why a Special Education Sourcebook?

Decades of educational research have confirmed several suspicions long held by many professional educators. First, diversity rather than homogeneity characterizes most classrooms. Be it in a general or special education setting, students differ considerably along a number of dimensions, including achievement level, motor development, learning style, and social competence (to name just a few). Clearly, in today's schools, there are no "regular" or "typical" classrooms or students. Second, and perhaps most importantly, *all students,* regardless of their unique differences, can regularly experience success when their teachers are able to make certain relevant instructional accommodations. Teachers who are able to (a) recognize and assess students' special learning needs, and (b) access and apply the variety of successful approaches, strategies, and materials available for the classroom are most likely to have students who achieve academic success. We are indeed fortunate that researchers, curriculum developers, test developers, and advocates for children and youth, as well as general and special education teachers, have made great strides in developing strategies for meeting the unique needs of students with special learning needs. The knowledge and technology for delivering "individualized instruction" to diverse groups of students exist and can be applied in both general or "mainstream/inclusive" settings as well as in more restrictive "pull-out" special education environments.

Still, schools are busy places that consistently place great demands on teachers. Larger class sizes and increased noninstructional responsibilities tend to limit the discretionary time available to those in the classroom—time that could be used to seek out and evaluate novel programs for the many students who experience difficulty with traditional instructional methods. We have entered an era in which society expects educators to be more than just "conveyors of academic content." They are to teach values, social skills, problem-solving, citizenship, and higher-order thinking skills. Moreover, they are to ensure that the wide variety of learners in their classrooms master the skills necessary for a successful transition to the post-school world.

Fortunately, most dedicated, professional educators typically take it upon themselves to seek out practical methods for meeting the diverse needs of students in their classrooms. We have been told by a number of teachers that information about new resources is often acquired through discussions with peers, mailing lists from vendors, and the "inheritance" of materials from others. Although this is often a rewarding process, the scope of materials gathered this way can be limited by the style and interests of the person sharing the information (or by not being "in the loop" with certain vendors). We have designed this **Special Education Sourcebook** to provide a broad array of resource materials that can offer a more comprehensive view of "what is out there." Our goal was to provide educators with comprehensive annotated listings describing available resources for recognizing, understanding, and meeting the challenges of students who have special needs. With a reader-friendly and logically sequenced organizational structure, the **Sourcebook** should be seen as a guide for securing additional information associated with successful special education practices.

Our primary target audience for the **Sourcebook** is the large number of special and general education teachers who educate students with special needs. Clearly, these groups of professionals will benefit from the listings of resources centering on the understanding of specific handicaps as well as the descriptions of curricular content-based resources and materials. Our secondary target audiences for the **Sourcebook** include parents of students with special needs and the students themselves. We believe that citations dealing with advocacy groups, legislation, support groups, and postsecondary school alternatives will be of special interest to these individuals.

How The Sourcebook Is Organized

Quite frankly, we were overwhelmed with both the quantity and quality of information related to the education of students with special education needs. In just one decade, there has been an incredible growth in the range and variety of resources available to students with disabilities and their teachers. Those who teach students with learning problems no longer need to "make do" with one curriculum guide or "make the most of" a specific material or kit because it is the only one available that comes close to addressing the assessed needs of the students. Today, there are large numbers of publishers, organizations, and advocacy groups that market materials for all types of individual learning styles and situations that can make instruction and habilitation challenging. Special education and its related professional areas have an established knowledge base with a correspondingly large number of resource materials, curricular alternatives, and instructional materials that can be either used directly, or adapted, for the benefit of learners with special needs. In our attempt to come to grips with the massive amounts of materials available for inclusion in the **Sourcebook**, we thought long and hard as to what would be the most useful organizational structure. We also consulted with a number of teachers, preservice student-teachers, related service personnel, parents, and teacher educators, asking how *they* would organize the wide array of resources. Finally, we reviewed other sourcebooks to see how they were organized. In the end, we determined that the **Sourcebook** would contain six major sections—this brief introductory narrative section and five broad content-based sections: **General Special Education; Understanding Specific Disabilities; Early Childhood Special Education and Emerging Academic Competence; Promoting Academic, Social, and Functional Competence;** and **Partnerships for Lifelong Success.**

This **Introduction** is designed to set the stage for the **Sourcebook** by describing how it was conceptualized and developed. More importantly this section explains how the **Sourcebook** is organized and how to best use the material in an efficient and effective manner. The second section, **General Special Education,** details resources that (a) provide a general overview of special education and children with disabilities, (b) define the process of special education, (c) address the policy and legal issues associated with special education, including Individual Education Plan (IEP) development, and (d) explore the range of available and possible service delivery options (i.e., where students are educated).

The third section, **Understanding Specific Disabilities,** details resources that will help educators understand the specific disability conditions they often encounter in the classroom. For ease of reference, the section is subdivided into the following subsections: **Mild to Moderate Learning and Behavioral Disabilities** (containing separate sections for Learning Disabilities (LD), Attention Deficit Disorders (ADD), Emotional Disturbance/Behavioral Disorders, and Category Free Conceptualizations); **Mental Retardation; Sensory Disabilities** (Visual Impairments, Hearing Impairments, and Deaf-Blindness); **Communication Disorders; Physical Disabilities; Traumatic Brain**

Injury and Health Impairments; Multiple Disabilities; and **Autism.** Each of the sections and subsections begins with a brief narrative that defines the disability condition and highlights critical definitional issues. *It is emphasized, however, that we should focus our attention on what children can do rather than on the label that is often assigned to them.*

Section Four, **Early Childhood Special Education and Emerging Academic Competence,** focuses on resources that describe successful early intervention programming and resource materials that can be used in teaching infants and toddlers with special needs.

Section Five, **Promoting Academic, Social, and Functional Competence,** is the largest section in the **Sourcebook** and focuses on resources related to teaching and the development of specific skills. General information, specific assessment devices, commercially developed materials, and curriculum guides are reviewed. To organize the wide range of skills taught by educators, a number of subsections are used: **Assessment, Academic Skills and Strategies, Social Competence and Self-Esteem, Functional Competence,** and **Technology in Special Education.** A further subdivision of the **Academic Skills and Strategies** section allows for easy reference to reading, spoken and written language, mathematics, social studies, and science resources. Similarly, the **Social Competence and Self-Esteem** section is divided into sections highlighting materials that assist in (a) the development of classroom management skills, and (b) the design of instructional programs for promoting social competence and self-esteem.

Section Six, **Partnerships for Lifelong Success,** contains resources related to (a) transitions to the world of work and postsecondary educational alternatives, and (b) collaborative consultation with parents, fellow educators, and related service professionals. An Appendix listing the addresses and phone numbers of the companies that produce or distribute the materials listed concludes the **Sourcebook.**

Types of Resource Materials Found in the Sourcebook

Under each of the major subheadings noted above, resource materials are organized by "type," and listed in American Psychological Association (APA) style.

This means that for books, the initial reference is by author and publication date, followed by the title, the city and state where the book is published, and, finally, the name of the publishing company. Within each section, books are listed in alphabetical order according to the authors' last names. For curriculum materials, periodicals, and multimedia materials, listings are in alphabetical order by resource title. Similarly, organizations are listed in alphabetical order according to the name of the organization.

Within each section, books are presented first. **Generic Textbooks,** typically used in preservice and inservice coursework, are merely listed and dates of publication are omitted as new editions always seem to be forthcoming. **Resource Books** come next. These are books that are not designed exclusively to supplement college coursework, and tend to be narrower in focus than textbooks. **Multimedia** resources, which include videotapes, slides, and audio materials, are also described briefly. **Periodicals** include professional journals, magazines, and newsletters. Each entry contains a description of the typical content of the periodical and how to get more information (i.e., address and phone number). Similarly, **Organizations,** including clearinghouses, government agencies, and advocacy groups, are listed alphabetically and described with relevant information for contact.

In entries involving instructional materials, two major types of resources are highlighted. The category **Curriculum Guides/Comprehensive Programs/Kits** refers to the large number of programmatic "package" materials that are connected or sequenced based on specific themes, competencies, and/or grade levels. Many of these materials come in attractive kits and contain detailed teacher directions, curricular scope and sequence charts, and a variety of student practice materials. These materials are often the centerpiece of a teacher's instructional procedures. The category **Instructional Materials/Toys** refers to the large number of useful instructional materials that are used to supplement instruction. These materials are typically more focused in their stated goals and allow for depth rather than breadth of coverage. In some cases where producers market an especially large number of such materials, we have simply listed the producer and described the types of materials described in their catalog.

In the area of **Technology**, we have supplemented our listing of printed resources with a listing of vendors of assistive technology and software. The overwhelming amount of hardware and software currently available precluded any adequate description of the materials available from each vendor. To find out more about a particular vendor's software, contact them directly at the address given in the **Sourcebook.**

The Process Used in Developing The Sourcebook

Our first step in acquiring the materials for review was to develop a comprehensive listing of (a) publishers and other producers of disability-related materials, and (b) relevant organizations and government agencies. When this listing was complete, over 400 letters requesting catalogs, sample materials, and/or descriptions of available services were sent. Several months later, thanks to the good graces of the producers and organizations, our home and offices resembled warehouses—filled with boxes and containers of all shapes and sizes. All materials relating to the stated intent of the **Sourcebook** were reviewed. Outdated materials and those deemed to be of little use to our target audiences were set aside. In those cases of doubt (to include or not include...that is the question), the material was included. In many cases we sampled the materials received; in those cases where only catalogs were sent, we made use of all available descriptions to determine whether materials were suitable. Review forms were completed and coded for inclusion in the appropriate sections.

In addition to the materials gathered in response to our mailing, the **Sourcebook** includes materials (often older, but tried-and-true) either used in special education classes at the Johns Hopkins University, or recommended by colleagues in the special education field and by the special education teachers who reviewed the book for usefulness and comprehensiveness.

Making Informed Decisions about the Utility of Resources

The resources listed in this sourcebook are provided in a nonevaluative format. It is our belief, however, that a most important process in the selection of a particular resource is a thorough and systematic evaluation. Polloway and Patton (1993) suggest that resource materials be evaluated based on: **Publication and Cost; Physical Properties; Content;** and **Instructional Properties.**

When considering publication and cost (most vendors will provide cost of materials when you follow-up for more information), it is recommended that you consider the reputation of the publisher and determine how current the materials are. To the best of your ability, you should also objectively determine if the cost of the material is reasonable compared to alternatives in the marketplace. When evaluating physical properties of resources, look for high quality materials and workmanship in the production process and ensure that resources used by children will appeal to their aesthetic sense. For resources designated for young children or those with severe disabilities, take special care to ensure that there are no potential hazards (sharp endings on objects, small pieces, etc.) associated with product use.

The content of the resource is best evaluated by considering whether the use of the resource is consistent with one's instructional goals and objectives. For example, teachers considering a specific math material should determine whether the approach of a particular curriculum developer is consistent with the student's IEP, learning style, and assessed needs, as well as the educational philosophy currently being employed during math instruction. It is equally important to ensure that materials are (a) free of biases that are misleading or unacceptable to students, teachers, and members of the community, and (b) reflect the contributions and perspectives of our diverse population. Finally, consider the instructional properties of the resources. Specifically, consider the pedagological features of a particular resource. Is a study guide included with a text? Does the reading kit contain a pre- and post-assessment? Does the video contain a facilitator's guide? Is the material produced in a motivating fashion? These are all features that should be considered in evaluating the appropriateness of a particular resource.

Some Important Caveats, Limitations, and Thank-You's

Although there is an enormous amount of material listed and reviewed in the **Sourcebook**, we are sure that we have not included all that could be included. We were limited by (a) the responses to our mailings, and (b) our awareness of available materials. Certainly, there are enough resources available for teachers and related service personnel to get critical questions answered. Nonetheless, we invite users of the **Sourcebook** to forward descriptions of resources that we may have missed. We will try to include these materials, if suitable, in future editions. Several Reference Review Forms can be found in Appendix B.

We also invite users to provide feedback on the organization of the **Sourcebook**. Specifically, we would welcome comments regarding such factors as ease of use, frequency of use, and currency of resources listed. Appendix B contains review forms that can be photocopied and mailed to us care of Woodbine House.

Prices for materials are not given, as many publishers and other producers raise their prices almost yearly. The **Sourcebook** is not intended to be an order catalog, but rather a guide to identifying and locating appropriate resources. For information on price and availability of any materials that interest you, contact the producer at the address given in Appendix A. Most companies listed have catalogs or other written product information available free of charge.

Finally, we would like to acknowledge the assistance of a number of people who have assisted in the development of this resource. Faculty, graduate students, and support staff at Johns Hopkins University, including Elana Rock, Steve Wilkens, Stacey Newbern, and Sharon Lampkin, assisted in the organization and review of materials. We appreciate all of their input. The reviewers, Donna Myer, Kathy Porter, and Cay Holbrook, provided insightful feedback as to the organization and "user-friendliness" of the **Sourcebook,** and provided additional resources for inclusion. We thank them for their efforts and encouragement. Finally, we wish to express our gratitude to Susan Stokes, our editor at Woodbine House. Susan kept us on task and was an excellent and understanding resource at all times throughout this project.

Reference

Polloway, E. A., & Patton, J. A. (1993). *Strategies for teaching learners with special needs*. New York: Merrill/Macmillan.

section II : *General Special Education*

This section details resources that provide a general overview of the characteristics, history, and organization of remedial and special education. In organizing this wide array of useful materials, we subdivided this "General" section into 3 subsections: (1) What is Special Education?; (2) Legal Aspects, Policy Initiatives, and IEP Development; and (3) Service Delivery Systems.

What Is Special Education?

Special education is typically defined as the individually planned and systematically monitored arrangement of physical settings, special equipment and instructional materials, teaching methodologies, and other interventions designed to assist children with exceptionalities to achieve the greatest possible self-sufficiency and success in school and the community (Heward & Orlansky, 1992). Special education is also a collaborative enterprise that requires an active commitment from a variety of professionals who come from a number of diverse professions. Consequently, agreeing on what actually constitutes "special education" is a challenging, if not impossible, task. Obviously, teachers, occupational therapists, physical therapists, speech-language pathologists, psychologists, and physicians view the needs of students with disabilities through their own "professional perspectives."

Most agree, however, that special education is about *teaching* students whose unique abilities or needs necessitate changes in how instruction is delivered. This does not mean that all special education must be provided in separate settings away from the general population by those with extraordinary credentials. The truth is that close to two-thirds of all children with disabilities receive much of their education in general education classrooms with the support of an interdisciplinary team of professionals who share the responsibility of ensuring that each child with a disability learns despite his or her special needs. Thus, most general education teachers deliver some form of special education to their students through the usual process of adapting instruction to meet the unique needs and learning styles of their students.

The relationships among the many individuals involved in these team efforts are not always smooth. Many problems are the result of uncertainty as to how special education and rehabilitative services fit within the context of general education practices. Special education appears to be in a perpetual state of redefinition, trying to grab hold of the most effective means of working collaboratively to teach those with special needs. Many of the resources that follow review the rich history of special education and address the variety of ways we have attempted to "get a firm grip" on what special education actually is and who children with special needs actually are.

AVAILABLE RESOURCES

Introduction to Special Education/Exceptional Children Textbooks

Perhaps the most time-efficient way to get a comprehensive overview of special education and exceptional children would be to consult an introductory text typically used in initial college coursework. At last count there were approximately 38 such books of varying style and formats available. These books are updated and revised frequently in order to reflect the rapidly changing field. A number of supplements (instructor's manuals, students study guides, overhead transparencies) are also made available for individuals who will teach introductory courses.

Regardless of the variety of extras that may be provided, the majority of these books tend to follow a similar framework and include broad-based information on (a) the definition of special education; (b) the history and legal aspects of special education; (c) service delivery alternatives; (d) the characteristics of children with disabilities; and (e) specific issues related to successful programming. Some of the more popular and organized efforts are listed below. Consult the individual publishers for the most recent edition.

Books

Blackhurst, A. E., & Berdine, W. H. *An introduction to special education.* New York, NY: HarperCollins.

Bullock, L. M. *Exceptionalities in children and youth.* Boston: Allyn & Bacon.

Cartwright, G. P., Cartwright, C., & Ward, M. *Educating special learners.* Belmont, CA: Wadsworth.

Hallahan, D., & Kauffman, J. *Exceptional Children: Introduction to special education.* Boston: Allyn & Bacon.

Hardman, M., Drew, C., Egan, W., & Wolf, B. *Human exceptionality.* Boston: Allyn & Bacon.

Haring, N. G., & McCormick, L. *Exceptional children and youth.* New York, NY: Merrill/Macmillan.

Heward, W. L., & Orlansky, M. *Exceptional children.* New York, NY: Merrill/Macmillan.

Kirk, S. A., & Gallagher, J. J. *Educating exceptional children.* Boston: Houghton Mifflin.

Meyen, E. L. *Exceptional children in today's schools.* Denver: Love Publishing.

Meyen, E. L., & Skrtic, T. M. *Exceptional children and youth: An introduction.* Denver: Love Publishing.

Morse, W. C. *Humanistic teaching for exceptional children.* Syracuse, NY: Syracuse University Press.

Patton, J., Blackbourn, J., Kauffman, J., & Brown, G. *Exceptional children in focus*. New York, NY: Merrill/Macmillan.

Smith, D. D., & Luckasson, R. *Introduction to special education: Teaching in an age of challenge*. Boston: Allyn & Bacon.

Smith, R., Neisworth, J., & Hunt, F. *The exceptional child: A functional approach*. New York, NY: McGraw-Hill.

Suran, B. G., & Rizzo, J. *Special children: An integrative approach*. Glenview, IL: Scott, Foresman.

Ysseldyke, J., & Algozzine, B. *Introduction to special education*. Boston: Houghton Mifflin.

Resource Books: General Special Education/Exceptional Children

Anderson, W., Chitwood, S., & Hayden, D. (1990). *Negotiating the special education maze: A guide for parents and teachers*. Rockville, MD: Woodbine House.

> Although this text examines the special education process primarily from the parent's perspective, it also includes useful information for teachers, including step-by-step strategies for developing appropriate IEPs, tips on improving parent-teacher communication, and requirements of federal laws.

Batshaw, M. L., & Perret, Y. M. (1992). *Children with disabilities: A medical primer*. Baltimore, MD: Paul H. Brookes.

> An easily understood, illustrated review of childhood development and the wide range of disabilities which can occur. Chapters cover the basics of genetics and what can go wrong, as well as prematurity, inborn errors, nutritional problems, mental retardation, vision, hearing, communication disorders, attention deficit disorders, learning disabili-

ties, autism, cerebral palsy, spina bifida, seizure disorders, and traumatic brain injury.

Browne, S., & Stern, N. (1985). *With the power of each breath: a disabled women's anthology*. Pittsburgh, PA: CLEIS.
> A feminist anthology documenting the experiences of over 65 disabled women.

Carballo, J. B., et al. (1990). *Survival guide for the first-year special education teacher*. Reston, VA: CEC.
> A practical guide for first-year special education teachers, written by veteran teachers who love the profession. Topics include organizing the classroom, record keeping, managing stress, and working with parents, administrators, and colleagues.

Ferguson, P. M., Ferguson, D. L., & Taylor, S. J. (1992). *Interpreting disability: A qualitative reader*. New York, NY: Teachers College Press.
> A book of interpretive research methods that juxtaposes stories and results from applied research. The book deals with disabilities such as autism and Down syndrome and addresses topical issues such as mainstreaming.

Marozas, D., & May, D. (1990). *Issues and practices in special education*. White Plains, NY: Longman.
> Utilizing current literature, case studies, and classic literature, this text stimulates conversation on critical issues (e.g., withholding treatment from severely disabled newborns, AIDS, etc.) in the field.

Park, L. D. *How to be a friend to the handicapped: A handbook and guide*. New York, NY: Vantage Press.
> This guide is a reference manual for those who live and work with people with disabilities. The handbook includes thoughts on handling common daily experiences that provide challenges for the handicapped, such as using automobiles, selecting pets, sporting events, or fitness.

Paul, J. (1983). *The exceptional child: A guidebook for churches and community agencies*. Syracuse, NY: Syracuse University Press.

> Practical advice on exceptionalities is presented for the non-specialist in clear, jargon-free language. This edited volume contains chapters on families of children with disabilities as well as suggestions for community-based educational, recreational, and pastoral programming.

Perske, R. *Hope for the families: New directions for parents of persons with retardation or other disabilities. Circles of friends: People with disabilities and their friends enrich the lives of one another. New life in the neighborhood: How persons with retardation or other disabilities can help make a good community better*. Nashville: Abingdon.

> A series of beautifully illustrated self-help and case-study stories to assist parents, families, and the disabled person herself in her role and rights as a productive and needed member of society.

Stainback, W., & Stainback, S. (1992). *Controversial issues confronting special education: Divergent perspectives*. Boston: Allyn & Bacon.

> Using a pro-con format, current issues facing the field of special education are addressed in this edited volume. Major themes debated include service delivery systems, assessment procedures, classroom management techniques, research practices, and the theoretical underpinnings of the special education profession.

Weinstein, G. R., & Pelz (1986). *Administrator's desk reference on special education*. Gaithersburg, MD: Aspen.

> A book designed for school administrators that addresses the basics of special education and includes topics such as legal and policy issues, administrative issues, and overviews of the various disability conditions.

Westling, D., & Koorland, M. (1988). *The Special Educator's Handbook*. Boston, MA: Allyn & Bacon.

> This handbook gives practical advice on many areas and skills necessary for a successful career in special education. Beginning with tips for procuring a teaching position, the

book gives strategies for organizing classrooms, planning schedules, establishing relationships, planning individualized instruction, using behavior management techniques, utilizing administrators, and other essential skills. Beginning teachers will find a wealth of "survival tips" on using audiovisual and instructional materials, managing field trips, reducing stress, performing noninstructional duties, and dealing effectively with parents. In all, this is an easy-to-read, comprehensive resource which would be most helpful to inservice or beginning teachers.

Multimedia

American Disability Channel (ADC). San Antonio, TX: ADC.

ADC is a telecommunications cooperative that works with national and local disability organizations to disseminate information. A number of local cable companies provide programming from the channel.

Disabilities and Special Education Film and Video Rental Service. Bloomington, IN: Indiana University Audio Visual Center.

A large and diverse collection of films and videos are available to all recognized schools, institutions, and organizations throughout the United States. Approximately 200 holdings on *all* facets of special education are available. Write or call for the descriptive catalog of holdings and rental procedures.

"Educating Peter." (1992). Port Chester, NY: National Professional Resources, Inc.

This Oscar-winning documentary follows Peter, a young boy with Down syndrome, through his first year in a classroom with normally developing peers. At first, Peter and his classmates have great difficulty adjusting to one another, but as everyone's understanding and social skills grow, he becomes an accepted member of the class.

An Exceptional Child Video Series. Princeton, NJ: Films for the Humanities, Inc.

> Series deals with seven exceptional children, specifically their schooling and their families, to see what can be learned from their experiences. Each of the seven tapes is approximately 26 minutes.

"Regular lives." Reston, VA: CEC.

> A 30-minute documentary showing the inclusion of students with mental and physical disabilities into regular education community life. Tape comes with fact sheets and a guide for conducting discussions.

Resources Geared Specifically for Children and Youths

Friedberg, J. B., Mullins, J. B., & Sukiennik, A. W. (1991). *Portraying persons with disabilities: An annotated bibliography of nonfiction for children and teenagers*. New Providence, NJ: R.R. Bowker.

> A selective reading guide for young people (preschool to high school) that allows readers to learn about people with disabilities. The bibliography describes and evaluates over 300 nonfiction titles published between 1980 and 1991.

Living with Disabilities. Chicago: Society for Visual Education.

> This series of filmstrips and tapes, designed for upper primary to intermediate students, focuses on eight children who, despite having disabilities, live their lives like other children their age. The objectives of the series include: (a) defining the term disability, (b) presenting children with disabilities as having full and active lives, and (c) promoting understanding of these children. Specific disabilities illustrated in the four programs are visual impairments, hearing impairments, epilepsy, cerebral palsy, Down syndrome, and spina bifida.

Magination Press Books for Children. New York, NY: Magination Press Books.

> Magination Press specializes in picture books about therapy for children and their families. Written by child psychiatrists and other professionals who work with children, the stories deal with the treatment of serious behavioral, psychological, social, and medical problems. Each book confronts a different dilemma and is intended primarily for children experiencing the problem to read with and without their parents. Professionals and educators will also find these books valuable. Noteworthy titles include, but are not limited to: *Robby really transforms: A story about grown-ups helping children; Otto learns about his medicine: A story about medication for hyperactive children; Julia, mungo, and the earthquake: A story for young people about epilepsy; Ignatius finds help: A story about psychotherapy for children, Putting on the brakes: Young people's guide to understanding attention deficit hyperactivity disorder; Wish upon a star: A story for children with a parent who is mentally ill; Russell is extra special: A book about autism for children;* and *Cat's got your tongue: A story for children afraid to speak.*

Moulton, G., & Van Der Voo, A. *Insight Books*. San Diego: Wright Group.

> A series of 12 books about disabled children for children. In all of the books, the characters are people first, and people with disabilities second. These attractive, easy-to-read books are generally 12-15 pages in length with large and colorful illustrations. Titles (and the corresponding disability) include: *Peter* (asthma), *My best friend* (epilepsy), *My Father* (multiple sclerosis), *My cousin Tom* (deaf), *Emma* (CP), *My friend Andrew* (spina bifida), and *Dan, my new neighbor* (muscular dystrophy).

Robertson, D. (1992). *Portraying persons with disabilities: An annotated bibliography of fiction for children and teenagers.* New Providence, NJ: R.R. Bowker.

> A selective bibliography of 473 annotated entries (picture books through junior novels published between 1982 and 1991) that will enable students, librarians, counselors, parents, and educators to take a closer, more intimate look at physical, mental, and emotional impairments.

Wilmor Distribution Center Books. Williamsport, PA: Wilmor.

> The Wilmor Distribution Center offers a wide variety of children's literature from many publishing houses. The stories focus on coping with disabilities and on how people with disabilities can and do function in society. Titles include: *The gift of the girl who couldn't hear*; *Why I'm already blue*; *My friend Leslie*; *Mandy*, and *A guide dog goes to school*.

Periodicals

Disability, Handicap, & Society is a quarterly international journal providing a focus for debate on issues such as human rights, discrimination, policy, and practices. **Write:** Carfax Publishing, P.O. Box 2025, Dunnellon, FL 32630.

ERIC Digests are short reports (1,000-1,500 words) that provide a basic introduction, overview, and pertinent references on topics of prime interest to the broad educational community. Digests can come singly or in specially prepared comprehensive thematic flyer files (e.g., policies and procedures, cultural diversity, etc). **Write:** ERIC Clearinghouse on Handicapped and Gifted Children, 1920 Association Drive, Reston, VA 22091-1589.

Exceptional Child Education Resources is a quarterly abstract of all book and journal literature in special education. It is available both in hard copy and as an on-line library database. **Write:** Council For Exceptional Children, 1920 Association Drive, Reston, VA 22091-1589.

Exceptional Children, published by the Council for Exceptional Children, has the largest circulation of all special education periodicals. It contains comprehensive, in-depth research and discussion articles pertaining to all aspects of the development and education of students with disabilities. Journal is received with CEC membership. **Write:** Council For Exceptional Children, 1920 Association Drive, Reston, VA 22091-1589.

Exceptionality is the official journal of the Division for Research of CEC. The journal is devoted to the publication of original research and research reviews pertaining to individuals of all ages and disabilities. A variety of different disciplines are featured including education, medicine, psychology, and sociology. **Write:** Lawrence Erlbaum Associates, Inc., Journal Subscription Department, 365 Broadway, Hillsdale, NJ 07642.

The Journal of Special Education, published quarterly, provides research articles and scholarly reviews by expert authors in all areas of special education. Features include critical commentaries, integrative reviews, special thematic issues, and intervention studies. **Write:** The Journal of Special Education, PRO-ED, 8700 Shoal Creek Boulevard, Austin, TX, 78758-6897.

KALEIDOSCOPE: International Magazine of Literature, Fine Arts, and Disability, published by United Cerebral Palsy Services for the Handicapped, is an informative, entertaining, literary magazine rather than a venue of information related to rehabilitation, advocacy, or independent living. Through various types of artistic expression (fiction, nonfiction, art, poetry), people are able to understand the experience of disability. **Write:** KALEIDOSCOPE, 326 Locust Street, Akron, OH 44302-1876 or **Phone:** (216) 762-9755.

Special Educational Needs Abstracts is a quarterly information service which provides access to a wide range of sources (e.g., conference papers, reports, etc.) for parents and professionals concerned with the educational needs of children and adults with disabilities. **Write:** Carfax Publishing, P.O. Box 2025, Dunnellon, FL 32630.

Advocacy, Support Groups, Organizations, Clearinghouses, and Government Agencies

American Council on Rural Special Education (ACRES) is a rural "community" at the national level, working to improve services to individuals with disabilities who reside in rural areas. The organization publishes **Rural Special Education Quarterly,** a professional journal, and **RuraLink,** a newsletter. A number of other useful publications and information regarding national conferences can be received from the organization. **Write:** Dr. Joan Sebastian, ACRES, Department of Special Education, University of Utah, 124 Milton Bennion Hall, Salt Lake City, UT 84112 or **Phone:** (801) 581-8442.

Council for Exceptional Children (CEC) is a large professional organization dedicated to advancing the quality of education for all children with disabilities and improving the conditions under which special educators work. The organization has a number of special interest divisions (e.g., Division for Learning Disabilities, etc.), described in later sections, and a number of publications and member services. A number of topical conferences and an annual international meeting are also sponsored by CEC. The organization also sponsors lobbying and advocacy activities. Members receive two journals, **Exceptional Children** and **Teaching Exceptional Children** as well as access to a wealth of information from the Divisions and the CEC/ERIC Clearinghouse. **Write:** Council for Exceptional Children, 1920 Association

Drive, Reston, VA 22091-1589 or **Phone:** (703) 620-3660.

Council of Administrators of Special Education (CASE), a division of CEC, promotes professional leadership by providing opportunity for study of common special education administrative and supervisory concerns and a means of communicating about them. The division publishes a journal, **CASE In Point,** twice a year, and the **CASE Newsletter,** five times a year. **Write:** CASE. CEC, 1920 Association Drive, Reston, VA 22091-1589 or **Phone:** (703) 620-3660.

The **Division of International Special Education and Services (DISES)** of CEC addresses the need for better liaison with persons concerned with providing services to individuals with disabilities throughout the world. DISES works to facilitate exchanges throughout the world and publishes a yearly monograph and the **DISES Newsletter. Write:** DISES, CEC, 1920 Association Drive, Reston, VA 22091-1589 or **Phone:** (703) 620-3660.

ERIC Clearinghouse on Handicapped and Gifted Children is a national clearinghouse that provides information on all aspects of the education and development of students who have disabilities or who are gifted. Services include on-line searches, document abstracts, meetings, conferences, and the publication of bibliographies, directories, monographs, and research summaries. **Write:** ERIC Clearinghouse, Council for Exceptional Children, 1920 Association Drive, Reston, VA 22091-1589.

The **HEATH Resource Center** is a national clearinghouse which collects and disseminates information about disability issues in postsecondary education. The center identifies and describes educational and training opportunities as well as promotes and recommends strategies for the full participation by individuals with disabilities in postsecondary programs. HEATH publishes a newsletter three times a year as well as a host of other resource papers, monographs, and directories. **Write:** HEATH, One Dupont Circle, Suite 800, Washington, DC 20036 or **Phone:** (800) 544-3284.

National Center for Youth with Disabilities/National Resource Library maintains and disseminates information about adolescents with chronic illnesses and disabilities. Services include on-line searches, conferences, topical publications, and information dissemination. **Write:** University of Minnesota Hospital and Clinic, 420 Delaware St., Minneapolis, MN 55455. **Phone:** (800) 333-6293.

The **National Clearinghouse for Professions in Special Education** encourages individuals to seek careers in the various fields related to the education of children and youth with disabilities. The Clearinghouse collects, synthesizes, and disseminates information regarding career opportunities, personnel supply and demand, and personnel preparation programs for increasing the supply of qualified professionals serving individuals with disabilities. **Write:** National Clearinghouse for Professions in Special Education, Information Center, c/o Council for Exceptional Children, 1920 Association Drive, Reston, VA 22091 or **Phone:** (703) 264-9475/(703) 620-3660 (TDD).

The **National Council on Disability** is an independent federal agency comprised of 15 members appointed by the President and confirmed by the Senate. It is charged with addressing, analyzing, and making recommendations on issues of public policy which affect people with disabilities. The National Council distributes a free newsletter, **FOCUS,** and welcomes requests for copies of policy papers. **Write:** National Council on Disability, 800 Independence Ave., SW, Suite 814, Washington, DC 20591 or **Phone:** (202)267-3846/(202)267-3232(TDD).

National Information Center for Children and Youth with Disabilities (NICHCY), one of the Clearinghouses mandated by Congress, provides free information to educators, parents, caregivers, advocates, and others concerned with assisting children and youth with disabilities become participating members of the community. Services include personal responses to questions, referrals to other organizations, prepared information packets, and technical assistance to families and professional groups. NICHCY publishes a **News Digest, A Parent's Guide,** and a **Transition Summary. Write:** NICHCY, P.O. Box 1492, Washington, DC 20013-1492 or **Phone:** (800) 695-0285 (Voice or TDD).

The **National Organization on Disability (NOD)** promotes the fuller participation of Americans with disabilities in all aspects of community life. Its primary program is the Community Partnership Program, a network of 2000 towns, cities, and counties nationwide. NOD undertakes many different activities to improve attitudes toward people with disabilities; to expand educational and employment opportunities; to eliminate physical barriers; and to expand participation in religious, cultural, and recreational activities. NOD publishes a quarterly newsletter, **REPORT. Write:** NOD, 910 16th St., NW, Suite 600, Washington, DC 20006 or **Phone:** (202)293-5960/(202)293-5968 (TDD).

The **Sibling Information Network** is an organization established for families and professionals who are interested in the welfare of individuals with disabilities and their families, especially siblings. Available to its members are resources including a quarterly newsletter, a bibliography of children's literature, a bibliography of relevant journal articles, a listing of audiovisual materials, and descriptions of support services. **Write:** Sibling Information Network, The A. J. Pappanikou Center on Special Education and Rehabilitation, 991 Main Street, East Hartford, CT 06108. **Phone:** (203) 282-7050.

The **Teacher Education Division (TED)** of CEC promotes the development of more effective programs for professional preparation of special education practitioners. The division sponsors a yearly conference and publishes a journal, **Teacher Education and Special Education,** quarterly, and the **TED Newsletter** three times a year. **Write:** TED, CEC, 1920 Association Drive, Reston, VA 22091-1589 or **Phone:** (703) 620-3660.

The **U.S. Department of Education, Office of Special Education and Rehabilitative Services (OSERS)** maintains a clearinghouse of information regarding federal activities involving children and youth with disabilities. OSERS disseminates a great deal of programmatic information resulting from funded research and model demonstration projects as well as useful brochures, monographs, and position papers. A periodic journal, **OSERS News in Print,** is also produced by the agency. **Write:** U.S. Department of Education, Office of Special Education and Rehabilitative Services, Clearinghouse on Disability Information, Room 3132, 330 C Street, SW, Washington, DC 20202-2524 or **Phone:** (202) 732-1241.

The **U.S. Government Printing Office (GPO)** publishes a large number of subject-specific bibliographies that list publications related to disabilities, special education, and the professionals who work with individuals with disabilities. Specific subject bibliographies include: The Handicapped, Mental Health, and Elementary and Secondary Education. These documents listed in the bibliographies are prepared by officers or employees of the government and are available for a modest charge. **Write:** GPO, Superintendent of Documents, 710 North Capitol Street, Washington, DC 20402.

Legal Aspects, Policy Initiatives, and IEP Development

Legislation (laws and regulations) and litigation (court cases) have, and probably will continue to influence how, when, and where special and remedial education services are delivered to students with disabilities. Undoubtedly, every teacher, administrator, related service provider, and staff professional will come into contact with **The Individuals with Disabilities Education Act (IDEA)** of 1991, which amended P.L. 94-142, the Education of All Handicapped Children's Act originally passed in 1975. P.L. 94-142 changed the course of education for individuals with special needs (Rosenberg, O'Shea, & O'Shea, 1991). Prior to this landmark legislation, many children with disabilities were being excluded from schools, or served inadequately in educational and clinical settings, as well as being misdiagnosed and misclassified due to biased assessment procedures.

The legal mandates concerning special education have daily impact on how students with disabilities are educated. For the most part, the law states that all children, regardless of the type or severity of their disability, shall receive a free and appropriate public education. Specifically, the law requires that (a) all children placed in special education programs have an individualized education program (IEP); (b) accurate, nondiscriminatory assessment procedures guide educational planning and placement; (c) students be placed in the least restrictive environment (LRE)—that is, a student should be removed from the regular educational environment only when his or her disability prevents education in the general education environment from being satisfactorily achieved; (d) due process of law guides all aspects of special education placement and programming; and (e) parents or surrogates be actively involved in the planning and implementation of their child's educational program.

One of the more tangible legal aspects related to the education of students with disabilities is the IEP. The IEP is the written document which articulates the specific plan of action for educating an individual student identified as having a disability. The law is quite precise regarding what an IEP should include and who is to participate in its development. Each IEP must include: (a) a statement of present educational performance levels; (b) annual goals to be achieved by the end of the school year; (c) short-term objectives noted in observable and measurable terms; (d) a statement of special services needed; (e) an initiation date and expected duration of services; (f) a description of the extent to which the child will participate in general education programs; (g) a listing of individuals responsible

TABLE 1

SPECIAL EDUCATION LEGISLATION: P.L. 94-142 AND RECENT AMENDMENTS

P.L. 94-142 (1975)	Bill of Rights for elementary and secondary students with handicaps. Required that a free appropriate education (FAPE) be provided in the least restrictive environment with corresponding parents' rights and due process protection.
P.L. 98-199 (1983)	Amendments emphasized planning for transition services for secondary students and authorized training and provision of information to parents and volunteers through parent training and information centers.
P.L. 99-457 (1986)	Amendments to P.L. 94-142 mandated special education and related services to children with disabilities, ages 3 to 5, and created a discretionary early intervention program to serve children from birth through age 2.
P.L. 101-476 (1990)/ P.L. 102-119 (1991)	Renamed "Education of All Handicapped Children Act" (EHA), the "Individuals with Disabilities Education Act" (IDEA), and amended the definition of children with disabilities (formerly handicaps) by adding children with autism and traumatic brain injury. The provision of therapeutic recreation, assistive technology, social work services, and rehabilitation counseling were added as related services, and the definition of IEP was expanded to include a statement of needed transition services.

for implementing the program; (h) criteria to assess whether objectives are being met; and (i) beginning at age 14, a statement of needed transition services.

The IEP is to be developed at a specific multidisciplinary meeting at which a number of participants are given the opportunity to provide relevant input. By law, individuals required to attend include: (1) the child's teacher; (2) a representative of the local school district (other than the teacher) knowledgeable of district special education procedures; (3) a member of the evaluation team who can discuss, interpret, and explain all test results; (4) the child's parents or guardian; and (5) when appropriate, the child him- or herself. Other professionals such as physical therapists, physicians, speech-language therapists, and attorneys may also attend if deemed necessary.

Unfortunately, some teachers view the IEP process as an arduous task that adds little to their instructional program. In fact, many educators have expressed frustration at the mountains of paperwork that must be completed to comply with this dreaded chore. However, the IEP is a true opportunity for cooperative planning, monitoring, and revising of educational approaches. If used as a living and working document, as opposed to paperwork that is merely completed and filed away, the IEP can serve as the focal point that organizes and coordinates all services delivered to students with disabilities. An "IEP use strategy" can provide a more organized workplace for educators and clinicians, as well as ensuring that educational goals are being regularly pursued.

Clearly, the legal mandates protecting students with disabilities pose strong challenges for all educators. As all involved in education will be involved actively in implementing the IDEA standards, it is critical that we remain current. Table 1 illustrates how recent amendments have affected the landmark legislation of P.L. 94-142.

AVAILABLE RESOURCES: Legal Aspects/Policy/IEP

Books

Note: A number of resources contain useful chapters or devote some coverage to legal and policy aspects of special education as well as IEP development and evaluation. For example, many of the books noted in the "What Is Special Education?" section contain at least a chapter on the litigation and legislation relevant to special education practices. Resources noted below, however, go beyond the typical cursory coverage and are devoted exclusively to legal and/or policy issues. A separate section is provided for resources devoted exclusively for the understanding and development of IEPs.

Castellani, P. (1987). *The political economy of developmental disabilities.*
> The political, economic, and social forces influencing the growth and changing structure of services for individuals with disabilities are examined in this provocative text.

Ekstrand, R. E., Edmister, P., & Riggin, J. (1989). *Preparation for special education hearings: A practical guide to lessening the trauma of due process hearings.* Reston, VA: CEC.
> Guide assists in the presentation of various aspects relating to a due process hearing. Also presented are strategies for dealing with posthearing reactions.

Gallagher, J. J., Trohanis, P. L., & Clifford, R. M. (1989). *Policy implementation and PL 99-457: Planning for young children with special needs.* Baltimore: Paul H. Brookes.

> Edited volume that addresses the many significant issues associated with the implementation of Part H of P.L. 99-457, the legislative initiative which focuses on meeting the needs of infants and toddlers with disabilities and their families.

Goldman, C. D. (1991). *Disability rights guide.* Kansas City: Westport.

> A guidebook which provides "practical solutions to problems affecting people with disabilities." The book covers state and federal laws and practical approaches to such issues as employment, accessibility accommodations and barriers, housing, education, and transportation, as well as attitudinal barriers and misconceptions faced by those with disabilities.

Rothstein, L. F. (1990). *Special education law.* White Plains, NY: Longman.

> A comprehensive overview of special education law complete with interpretations and explanations. Special features include appendices that contain a listing of terms, special education regulations, and major developments in the field.

Sage, D. D., & Burrello, L. C. (1986). *Policy and management in special education.* Boston: Allyn & Bacon.

> A concise overview of issues confronting school administrators regarding the delivery of special education services.

Shrybman, J. A. (1982). *Due process in special education.* Gaithersburg, MD: Aspen.

> Comprehensive text which details P.L. 94-142 and Section 504. Special emphasis is placed on describing the "special education process" and the procedures typical of due process hearings.

Skrtic, T. M. (1991). *Behind special education: A critical analysis of professional culture and school organization.* Denver: Love.

> This three-part, ten-chapter text proposes a new configuration for school organization that allows for both the excellence of general education and the equity goals of special education.

Tucker, B. P., & Goldstein, B. A. (1992). *Legal rights of persons with disabilities: An analysis of federal law.* Horsham, PA: LRP Publications.

> A comprehensive analysis of federal rights of persons with disabilities. Educators will be especially interested in chapters dealing with (a) the structure and procedures of IDEA, (b) Section 504, (c) discipline, and (d) IEPs. For those interested, future updates and revisions at an additional cost are provided periodically.

Turnbull, H. R. (1990). *Free appropriate public education: The law and children with disabilities (3rd edition).* Denver: Love Publishing.

> The book addresses how the nation's public schools have dealt with the challenge and opportunity of educating students with disabilities. Six principles of special education, law—zero reject, nondiscriminatory classification, individualized education, least restrictive placement, due process, and parent participation, are detailed and common objections to these principles are addressed.

Weber, M. C. (1992). *Special education law and legislation treatise.* Horsham, PA: LRP Publications.

> A comprehensive and thorough overview of the variety of elements of special education law. Topics include the numerous issues addressed by IDEA, due process hearings, and factors related to eligibility for special services. Written in a style that will allow for meaningful interpretations by parents and educators, as well as lawyers.

Weintraub, F. J., Abeson, A., Ballard, J., & LaVor, M. L. (1977). *Public policy and the education of exceptional children*. Reston, VA: Council for Exceptional Children.
Although dated, this edited volume remains a definitive document on how public policy affects the lives of exceptional children. This comprehensive volume examines the (a) varying rights that advocacy groups have won for exceptional children, (b) varying avenues available for public policy changes, (c) techniques an advocate needs to change systems, and (d) professional rights and responsibilities of those involved in special education. This is a classic text that reflects our legislative and legal heritage.

Periodicals

The Arc Government Report, published semi-monthly by The Arc National Headquarters, provides information on important legislative, regulatory, funding, and public policy issues affecting individuals with mental retardation and other disabilities.

The National Disability Law Reporter, from LDR Publications, is a compilation of (a) major federal statutes, (b) federal and state judicial decisions, and (c) summaries of news and legislative activities affecting persons with disabilities. Available information is provided in a three-binder set and the NDLR is updated 24 times a year.

Special Education Report, available from Capitol Publications Inc., is an independent biweekly news service concerning legislation, regulation, and funding of programs for children and youth with disabilities. Typical features include litigation updates, state progress reports, easy- to-read-summaries of laws, regulations, and proposals, as well as early notice of available grant monies.

Advocacy, Support Groups, and Government Agencies

The Children's Defense Fund (CDF), an advocacy group which focuses on the rights of children, is typically involved in addressing legal and policy issues that affect the well-being of *all* children. **Write:** 122 C Street, NW, Washington, DC, 20001

The Roeher Institute, Canada's national institute for the study of public policy affecting individuals with an intellectual impairment and disability, has two major goals: (1) to identify and anticipate future trends that will support the presence, participation, self-determination, and contribution of persons with an intellectual impairment in their communities; and (2) to foster the exchange of ideas leading to new ways of thinking about disabilities. The Institute conducts, sponsors, and publishes research and engages in a wide variety of dissemination activities. **Write:** The Roeher Institute, York University, 4700 Keele Street, North York, ON M3J 1P3. **Phone:** (416) 661-9611.

IEP RESOURCES

Books Bragman, R. (1992). *How to develop individualized transition plans*. Indian Rocks Beach, FL: Phillip Roy.

> A resource to assist in the development of IEPs for transitioning from school to work and community life. In addition to suggestions for determining the needs of students with mild and moderate disabilities, materials appropriate for implementation of specific objectives are provided.

Fiscus, E., & Mandell, C. (1983). *Developing individualized education plans*. St. Paul, MN: West Publishing.

> The objective of this text is to provide detailed information of the content required in IEPs as well as the principles and practices that guide the application of that content. Specific

chapters are included on (a) assessing present levels of performance, (b) organizing the IEP committee meeting, (c) developing annual goals and short-term objectives, and (d) evaluating and monitoring the IEP.

Strickland, B. B., & Turnbull, A. P. (1990). *Developing and implementing individualized education programs.* Columbus, OH: Merrill/Macmillan.

> A comprehensive resource/text designed to assist educators in acquiring the skills necessary for successful IEP development. The book is organized into three major sections: (1) procedural guidelines for IEP development; (2) mechanics of IEP development; and (3) implementation of the IEP. The target audience for this resource is the practitioner who is responsible for IEP development and implementation.

West, L. L., et al. (1992). *Integrating transition planning into the IEP Process.* Reston, VA: CEC.

> A practical guide for incorporating transition planning into the IEP process. Sample IEPs that include transition planning are included.

Service Delivery Systems: How Special Education Services Are Delivered

Service delivery systems are the formal mechanisms by which educational services are provided to students. For students with disabilities, IDEA requires that, to the maximum extent appropriate, educational services should be provided in the *least restrictive environment* (LRE). However, what constitutes the least restrictive environment is relative; what is appropriate for one student is not always appropriate for another. Consequently, decisions as to the when and where of educational placement for students with disabilities are not easy and sometimes tend to be contentious.

In general, most school systems provide a wide range or *continuum of services* for students with disabilities. The continuum ranges in both degree and type of service available for an individual learner. A typical continuum begins with regular classroom placement, a least restrictive placement in which a student receives prescribed educational programs with the general education teacher, and ranges to increasing levels of restrictiveness such as periodic pull-out resource placements, full-time special classes, special day schools, and full-time residential facilities. Figure 1 illustrates one such continuum, the Cascade of Educational Services.

As noted by Rosenberg et al. (1991), there are several key assumptions inherent in the full continuum approach to providing educational services. First, it is assumed that a variety of options are available to meet the specific educational needs of individual students. Second, it is assumed that the majority of students are to be served in the lower portions of the continuum, otherwise known as the least restrictive environment. Finally, and perhaps most importantly, it is assumed that placement within a particular level of the continuum is not permanent. Students should have the opportunity to move between levels of the continuum based on their changing levels of educational performance. The greatest emphasis should be on returning students to less restrictive environments, with movement to more restrictive settings occurring only when necessary.

The attempt to educate students in the least restrictive environment has resulted in the widespread use of "mainstreaming" (or "integration"). Although the term mainstreaming does not appear in P.L. 94-142 or IDEA, the concept has generated considerable controversy, discussion, and debate. According to Heward and Orlansky (1992), much of the contention is due to confusion as to what mainstreaming actually is. For example, some people view mainstreaming as placing

Figure 1

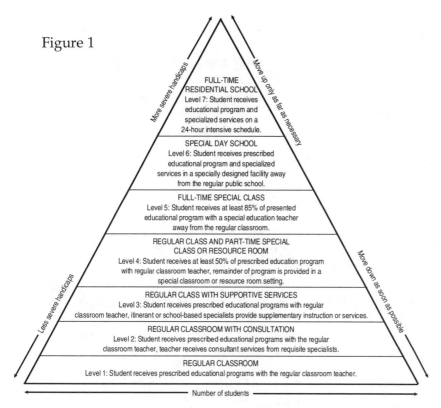

FULL-TIME RESIDENTIAL SCHOOL
Level 7: Student receives educational program and specialized services on a 24-hour intensive schedule.

SPECIAL DAY SCHOOL
Level 6: Student receives prescribed educational program and specialized services in a specially designed facility away from the regular public school.

FULL-TIME SPECIAL CLASS
Level 5: Student receives at least 85% of presented educational program with a special education teacher away from the regular classroom.

REGULAR CLASS AND PART-TIME SPECIAL CLASS OR RESOURCE ROOM
Level 4: Student receives at least 50% of prescribed education program with regular classroom teacher, remainder of program is provided in a special classroom or resource room setting.

REGULAR CLASS WITH SUPPORTIVE SERVICES
Level 3: Student receives prescribed educational programs with regular classroom teacher, itinerant or school-based specialists provide supplementary instruction or services.

REGULAR CLASSROOM WITH CONSULTATION
Level 2: Student receives prescribed educational programs with the regular classroom teacher, teacher receives consultant services from requisite specialists.

REGULAR CLASSROOM
Level 1: Student receives prescribed educational programs with the regular classroom teacher.

More severe handicaps

Move up only as far as necessary

Less severe handicaps

Move down as soon as possible

Number of students

Cascade of educational services. (Adapted from Deno, E. (1970). Special education as developmental capital. *Exceptional Children, 37,* 235; and Reynolds, M.C. (1962). A framework for considering some issues in special education. *Exceptional Children, 28,* 368.)

all students with disabilities into general education classrooms with little or no additional support or resources. Others believe that mainstreaming can mean completely segregated placements as long as the students with disabilities have some opportunity to interact with nondisabled peers in a few activities (e.g., lunch, recess, etc.). Although it is beyond the scope of this *Sourcebook* to detail the many conceptualizations of mainstreaming, it is generally accepted that mainstreamed students are "those for whom the least restrictive alternative includes activities in regular education classrooms" (Bauer & Shea, 1989).

Recently, there has been discontent with traditional LRE and mainstreaming practices. As noted by the National Association of State Boards of Education (NASBE, 1992), traditional mainstreaming practices have "left many students with fragmented educations and feelings that they neither belong in the general education classroom nor the special education classroom" (p. 10). Many mainstreaming opportunities are chosen for organizational convenience and scheduling purposes rather than educational needs. Consequently, many students perform poorly in the mainstreamed classes in which they are placed. As a result, NASBE, among others, has called for the creation of an *inclusive delivery system* that would fully include students rather than merely mainstream them. With this model, included students would, to the maximum extent possible, receive their educational services in the general education classroom with appropriate in-class support. Other features of the inclusive system include: (a) the school becoming the center of community activity, (b) a greater emphasis on community-based instruction, and (c) classrooms in which a variety of professionals work with students in response to individual needs.

Clearly, how we can best deliver needed special education services to students with disabilities will continue to dominate the professional dialogue. Fortunately, there are many excellent resources that can assist us in enhancing existing systems as well as in developing new approaches.

AVAILABLE RESOURCES
Mainstreaming/Integration Texts

As with Introductory texts, the most comprehensive and time-efficient means of gathering material on service delivery alternatives and procedures to promote and ensure appropriate "least restrictive placements" would be to consult a text on mainstreaming, integration, or inclusion. In general these texts: (a) operationalize the concept of LRE, integration, and/or inclusion, (b) discuss the legal aspects of such activities, and (c) provide strategies for integrating or mainstreaming students with a full range of disability conditions. A number of the more prominent texts are listed below.

Books

Chalmers, L. (1992). *Modifying curriculum for the special needs students in the regular classroom*. Moorhead, MN: Practical Press.

Choate, J. S. (1993). *Successful mainstreaming: Proven ways to detect and correct special needs*. Boston: Allyn & Bacon.

Gaylord-Ross, R. (1989). *Integration strategies for students with handicaps*. Baltimore, MD: Paul H. Brookes.

Lewis, R. B., & Doorlag, D. H. (1991). *Teaching special students in the mainstream*. Columbus, OH: Merrill/Macmillan.

Mann, P. H., Suiter, P. A., & McClung, R. M. (1992). *A guide for educating mainstreamed students.* Boston: Allyn & Bacon.

Meier, F. E. (1992). *Competency-based instruction for teachers of students with special learning needs.* Boston: Allyn & Bacon.

Saland, S. J. (1990). *Effective mainstreaming.* Columbus, OH: Merrill/Macmillan.

Schultz, J. B., Carpenter, C. D., & Turnbull, A. P. (1991). *Mainstreaming exceptional students: A guide for classroom teachers.* Boston: Allyn & Bacon.

Stainback, S., & Stainback, W. (1991). *Curriculum consideration in inclusive classrooms.* Baltimore, MD: Paul H. Brookes.

Stainback, S., Stainback, W., & Forest, M. (1989). *Educating all students in the mainstream of regular education.* Baltimore, MD: Paul H. Brookes.

Resource Books

Biklen, D. (1992). *Schooling without labels: Parents, educators, and inclusive education.* Philadelphia: Temple University Press.

An examination of families whose children with disabilities are full participants in family life. The author illustrates how the principles of full inclusion that are successful in family units can be extended to promote full integration in schools.

Giangreco, M., Cloninger, C., & Iverson, V. (1992). *Choosing options and accommodation for children (COACH): A guide to planning inclusive education*. Baltimore, MD: Paul H. Brookes.

> The authors provide a practical assessment and planning process for the inclusion of students with disabilities in general education classrooms, utilizing the latest advancements in the field. Instructions and easy-to-follow forms assist educational teams as they identify the content of students' educational programs, incorporate programs into a general education setting, and pursue family-valued outcomes.

Goodlad, J. I., & Lovitt, T. (1993). *Integrating general and special education*. New York, NY: Merrill/Macmillan.

> An edited volume that addresses how and how much to integrate and/or merge general and special education. Each of the contributors is a well-known scholar in school restructuring efforts and has considerable first-hand experience in service delivery for students with disabilities. Issues addressed include (a) financing a comprehensive service delivery plan, (b) curriculum considerations, and (c) the roles and responsibilities of teachers and principals.

Lipsky, D. K., & Gartner, A. (1989). *Beyond separate education: Quality education for all*. Baltimore, MD: Paul H. Brookes.

> Classic edited volume which advocates the restructuring of schools so they are inclusive and effective for all students. Specific educational and societal adaptations are both described and advocated.

Lloyd, J. W., Singh, N., & Repp, A. C. (1991). *The regular education initiative*. Sycamore, IL: Sycamore.

> Edited text which provides a comprehensive view of the regular education initiative and related calls for reform in the delivery of services to students with disabilities.

Sailor, W., Anderson, J., Halvorsen, A., Doering, K., Filler, J., & Goetz, L. (1989). *The comprehensive local school*. Baltimore, MD: Paul H. Brookes.

> The comprehensive local school model is detailed along with specific strategies that can help promote the development of a unified educational delivery system for all students with disabilities.

Stainback, W., & Stainback, S. (1990). *Support networks for inclusive schooling: Interdependent integrated education*. Baltimore, MD: Paul H. Brookes.

> An edited volume that focuses on how school personnel can develop a network of formal and informal supports when developing inclusive educational environments. Topics include peer tutoring, collaborative consultation, and mainstreaming assistance teams.

Sternberg, L., Taylor, R., & Schilit, J. (1986). *So you're not a special educator: A general handbook for educating handicapped children*. Springfield, IL: Charles C. Thomas.

> This text addresses questions about the school- aged special education population and includes discussions concerning assessment, labeling, planning educational programs, procedures and dilemmas, teaching methods, mandates and laws, and a selection of suggested readings.

Villa, R. A., Thousand, J. S., Stainback, W., & Stainback, S. (1992). *Restructuring for caring and effective education*. Baltimore, MD: Paul H. Brookes.

> An edited handbook in which school restructuring efforts are described with special emphases given to the specific processes necessary for educating heterogenous student populations.

Periodical

Inclusion Times, a newsletter published four times per year, focuses on issues and specific strategies for serving children and youth in general education and other inclusive learning environments. Highlighted are program descriptions, research reviews, and resource listings. **Write:** National Professional Resources, 25 South Regent St., Port Chester, NY 10573 or **Phone**: (800) 453-7461.

References

Bauer, A. M., & Shea, T. M. (1989). *Teaching exceptional students in your classroom.* Boston: Allyn & Bacon.

Heward, W. L., & Orlansky, M. D. (1992). *Exceptional children* (4th edition). New York, NY: Merrill/Macmillan.

National Association of State Boards of Education (1992). *Winners all: A call for inclusive schools.* Alexandria, VA: Author.

Rosenberg, M. S., O'Shea, L., & O'Shea, D. (1991). *Student teacher to master teacher: A handbook for preservice and beginning teachers of students with mild and moderate handicaps.* New York, NY: Macmillan.

section III : *Understanding Specific Disabilities*

This section details resources that allow for an understanding of the specific disability conditions that educators may encounter when providing services to students with special educational needs. In general, the primary focus of this section is on the characteristics, causes, and general treatment approaches associated with each of the disability conditions. (Materials addressing methods for assessing and treating deficiencies in specific academic or developmental areas are housed in Sections 4 6.) This section is organized as follows: (a) mild to moderate learning and behavioral disabilities (i.e., learning disabilities [LD], dyslexia, attention deficit disorders [ADD], and emotional disturbance/behavior disorders [ED/BD]); (b) mental retardation; (c) sensory disabilities (i.e., visual and hearing impairments); (d) communication disorders; (e) physical disabilities; (f) health impairments; (g) autism; and (h) multiple disabilities and traumatic brain injury (TBI).

Although the massive amounts of resource information available have been categorized by disabilities, it should be cautioned that all children are individuals and that there is as much heterogeneity within categories as there is between them. Specifically, not all students identified as having a particular disability will behave, function, or perform academically in an identical fashion. As noted by Blankenship and Lilly (1981), using categories tends to invite overgeneralization in the education and treatment of individual students. When a student carries a certain label, the label sets certain expectations in the minds of others. When the expectations are based on beliefs associated with the label rather than the specific strengths and weaknesses of the individual, the label can be detrimental to the individual.

Consequently, readers are advised not to "overgeneralize" from the valuable resources within these categorical sections.

Mild to Moderate Learning and Behavioral Disabilities

Generally speaking, students identified as having mild to moderate learning and behavioral disabilities experience lower levels of success on academic tasks and have greater difficulty in social situations than their nondisabled peers. In most instances, these students are not identified until they enter school. The beginning of school is the time when professional educators typically evaluate children's abilities in meeting age- and grade-appropriate expectations. Children who differ significantly from these norms in terms of behavior, language acquisition, motivation, and academic achievement are those most often identified as having mild to moderate learning and behavioral disabilities. The categories most frequently associated with mild to moderate handicaps are **learning disabilities (LD), attention deficit disorders (ADD),** and **emotional disturbance/behavior disorders (ED/BD).**

LEARNING DISABILITIES (LD)

Simply put, students who are identified as LD have difficulty in learning. These students have average to above average intellectual ability (as measured by standardized intelligence tests), yet they perform below what would be expected on measures of academic achievement. For example, a student who falls within the average range on an intelligence test would typically be expected to achieve at grade level. A learning disability is suspected if there is a significant discrepancy between actual achievement and the expectation for achievement as indicated by the intelligence test.

Students with learning disabilities are a heterogenous group who *may* experience the following problems: attention deficits, memory problems, a lack of coordination, perceptual disorders, listening problems, orientation difficulties, below average academic performance, inefficient learning strategies, motor skill difficulties, and poor social skills. It is important to remember that students identified as

LD are a diverse group. Often these students perform well in certain academic areas, while in others their performance is lower. Some are quiet and well-behaved; others are hyperactive, distractible, and impulsive. Some students with LD appear to have perceptual problems and experience letter, numeral, and word reversals; others respond well to written stimuli yet have problems following oral directions.

The disorder "specific learning disability" is formally defined by IDEA as:

> a disorder in one or more of the basic psychological processes involved in understanding or using language, spoken or written, that may manifest itself in an imperfect ability to listen, think, speak, read, write, spell, or do mathematical calculations. The term includes such conditions as perceptual disabilities, brain injury, minimal brain dysfunction, dyslexia, and developmental aphasia. The term does not apply to children who have learning problems that are primarily the result of visual, hearing, or motor disabilities, of mental retardation, or of environmental, cultural, or economic disadvantage.

This definition has been criticized widely and continues to spark emotional debates among professionals in the field. As noted by Rosenberg et al. (1991), some critics have argued that the definition needs to be broadened so that *any* child not achieving to his or her potential can receive special education services. Such a conceptualization would not rely on causal explanations nor exclude those who may have other disability conditions. Other critics have tried to narrow the definition of LD and have remained steadfast in their belief that all underachievers are not learning disabled. These individuals believe that LD is just one possible cause of underachievement and are confident that specific interventions geared to specific learning disabilities can improve academic and behavioral performance.

AVAILABLE RESOURCES: LD

Generic Textbooks

Ariel, A. (1993). *Education of children and adults with learning disabilities*. New York, NY: Merrill/Macmillan.

Bender, W. (1992). *Learning disabilities: Characteristics, identification, and teaching strategies*. Boston: Allyn & Bacon.

Gearheart, B., & Gearheart, C. (1989). *Learning disabilities: Educational strategies.* New York, NY: Merrill/Macmillan.

Hallahan, D. P., Kauffman, J. M., & Lloyd, J. (1985). *Introduction to learning disabilities.* Boston: Allyn & Bacon.

Lovitt, T. C. (1989). *Introduction to learning disabilities.* Boston: Allyn & Bacon.

Mercer, C. (1992). *Students with learning disabilities.* New York, NY: Merrill/Macmillan.

Reid, D. K. (1988). *Teaching the learning disabled: A cognitive developmental approach.* Boston: Allyn & Bacon.

Resource Books

Academic Therapy Publications. *Directory of facilities and services for the learning disabled.* Novato, CA: Author.
  The yearly directory is a list of schools, clinics, and clinicians who provide assessment and direct services for people with mild-moderate learning disabilities. The nationwide listings include educational journals, allied organizations, college guides, sources of specialized materials, special education software publishers, educational clearinghouses, and complete addresses with telephone numbers.

Brown, F. R., Aylward, E., & Keogh, B. K. (1992). *Diagnosis and management of learning disabilities: An interdisciplinary/lifespan approach.* San Diego: CA: Singular.
  An edited text that focuses on the diagnosis and management of learning disabilities with a concise interdisciplinary perspective. Specific topics in the text include such crucial subjects as the early identification of learning disabilities in preschool children by nontraditional methods (that is, other than by "significant discrepancy") and the transition from school to post-school experiences.

Cardoni, B. (1990). *Living with a learning disability*. Carbondale, IL: Southern Illinois University Press.

> An insider's view of what it is like to live with a learning disability. The book, written for teachers, parents, and individuals with LD, is a practical resource which focuses on (a) socialization skills and disabilities; (b) labeling; (c) legal issues; (d) college; and (e) life outside of school.

Clark, D. (1988). *DYSLEXIA: Theory & practice of remedial instruction*. Timonium, MD: York Press, Inc.

> Teachers and other professionals working with dyslexic individuals can utilize this text to acquire knowledge needed to make informed decisions about the many methods of instruction for dyslexic students. It examines recent research on the psychology of reading and reading development and the nature of dyslexia; remedial instruction; and remedial programs designed specifically for students with dyslexia.

Cummings, R., & Fisher, G. (1993). *The survival guide for teenagers with LD* (learning differences)*. Minneapolis: Free Spirit.

> A self-help book for teenagers with LD that helps in the understanding of LD and provides strategies for promoting success in school and preparing for the transition to life as an adult.

Duane, D., & Gray, D. (1991). *The reading brain: The biological basis of dyslexia*. Timonium, MD: York Press, Inc.

> Based on the latest research, this edited text focuses on the biological aspects of reading disability—the anatomy of a dyslexic person's nervous system—to allow the reader a better comprehension of the neurobiology of reading ability. It reviews topics such as the heritability of dyslexia, the identified chromosomes, the application of Magnetic Resonance Imaging, a classification of learning attention disorders, a neurobehavioral definition, and other related topics.

Dunn, K. & Dunn, A. (1993). *Trouble with school: A family story about learning disabilities*. Rockville, MD: Woodbine House.
> In this illustrated book, Allison Dunn and her mother take turns telling their side of story of discovering and dealing with Allison's learning disability. The dual narrative captures the thoughts and feelings typical of a family faced with a child's learning disability, and helps to underscore how a child and parent experience this situation differently.

Feldman, W. (1990). *Learning disabilities: A review of available treatments*. Springfield, IL: Charles C. Thomas.
> This book is designed for professionals and parents of learning disabled children seeking a better understanding of the available treatments. The various treatment programs are presented to assist the reader in determining the best course of treatment for the particular child with the learning disability.

Gaddes, W. H. (1985). *Learning disabilities and brain function*. New York, NY: Spring-Verlag.
> An informative text that addresses relationships among brain functions and the learning disabilities of childhood and adolescence.

Gallico, R., Burns, T., & Grob, C. (1991). *Emotional and behavioral problems in children with learning disabilities*. San Diego, CA: Singular.
> Teachers and mental health professionals are provided with a concise text on the interrelationship between learning disabilities and emotional disturbance. Case studies show how theory, diagnosis, and treatment actually work with children in school settings.

Griffiths, A. (1978). *Teaching the dyslexic child*. Novato, CA: Academic Therapy.
> Designed for the general public and written by a teacher of dyslexic children, this easy-to-read volume describes and defines dyslexia. The author also presents parental perspectives on the disorder, myths about dyslexia, and methods of

effective instruction with specific suggestions for how "you" can help.

Huston, A. M. (1992). *Understanding dyslexia: A practical handbook for parents and teachers*. Lanham, MD: University Press of America.

A practical and common sense approach to defining and diagnosing dyslexia is provided in this text. Suggestions for teaching students with dyslexia are provided for both parents and teachers.

Janover, C. (1988). *Josh: A boy with dyslexia*. Burlington, VT: Waterfront Books.

An adventure story for kids ages 8 11 that shares the fears, tragedies, and triumphs of a boy with LD. Section in the back of the book contains facts about LD and a list of resources for parents and teachers.

Martin, A. (1988). *Yours turly, Shirley*. New York, NY: Holiday House, Inc.

Shirley, a fictional fourth-grader with dyslexia, struggles with her feelings of inferiority as she compares herself to her intellectually gifted older brother and newly adopted Vietnamese sister.

Murphy, S. T. (1992). *On being LD: Perspectives and strategies of young adults*. New York, NY: Teachers College Press.

This book reveals the experiences of people labeled learning disabled and the adaptive and compensatory strategies they typically employ. The author seeks to broaden the perspectives of those who study the concept of LD and those charged with treating the problem.

Osman, B. (1982). *No one to play with: The social side of learning disabilities*. Novato, CA: Academic Therapy Publications.

A book dedicated to the painful issues of social learning disabilities that explores how children with LD often experience enormous unhappiness due to their inability to make friends. The book also contains an extensive bibliography on topics such as family relationships, the social side of school, friendship building, adolescence, and adult learning difficulties.

Pennington, B. (1991). *Diagnosing learning disorders: A neuropsychological framework*. New York, NY: Guilford.

> This text provides a classification system of learning disorders in children, reviews the research supporting such a system, and provides a usable, practical guide for practitioners who diagnose and treat these children.

Stevens, S. (1991). *Classroom success for the learning disabled*. Winston Salem, NC: John F. Blair.

> Suggestions on recognizing the student with LD are provided as are general strategies for adapting instructional procedures. A fictional account of a typical student with LD, "Al," is provided which allows readers to witness the student's struggles in school.

Waldron, K. A. (1992). *Teaching students with learning disabilities: strategies for success*. San Diego, CA: Singular.

> The practical concerns explored in this book include information on how (a) teachers of students with LD can create a positive atmosphere and still take charge, (b) students become motivated, (c) collaborative systems between regular and special educators can be more effective, and (d) interactions with parents can be more meaningful.

Weller, C., Crelly, C., Watteyne, M., & Herbert, M. (1992). *Adaptive language disorders of young adults with learning disabilities*. San Diego, CA: Singular.

> Since difficulty with adaptive language is so prevalent in young adults with learning disabilities, the authors believe it should be the main focus of language intervention. This text focuses on characteristics of adaptive language, assessment strategies for identifying adaptive language difficulties, teaching strategies for different types and severity levels of adaptive language difficulties, and suggestions on building curriculum.

Multimedia

"Children learn differently." Novato, CA: Academic Therapy Publications.
> A 30–minute video that illustrates the characteristics of students with learning disabilities.

LD and Dyslexia Video Series. Princeton, NJ: Films for the Humanities, Inc.
> A series of video programs which explore the characteristics and intervention techniques available for students with LD and Dyslexia. Titles include: **"Learning disabilities"; "Just another stupid kid"; "Dyslexia: Diagnosis and prognosis";** and **"Dyslexia: Disabled or different."**

Periodicals

Journal of Learning Disabilities, published ten times per year by PRO-ED, is a multidisciplinary journal containing articles on practice, research, and theory related to LD. **Write:** PRO-ED, 8700 Shoal Creek Blvd., Austin, TX 78758 or **Phone:** (512) 451–3246.

LD Forum, published by the Council for Learning Disabilities, is a magazine dedicated to disseminating information on "best practices" to practitioners who deliver services to students with LD. Specific topical areas include: assessment, behavior management, collaboration, instructional design, transition, and technology. **Write:** Council for Learning Disabilities, P.O. Box 40303, Overland Park, KS 66204–4303 or **Phone:** (913) 492–8755.

Learning Disabilities Research and Practice, published by the Division for Learning Disabilities of CEC, is a forum for presentation of current research in the field of LD and a vehicle for dissemination of information important to practitioners in the field.

Learning Disability Quarterly, published by the Council for Learning Disabilities, highlights original, applied research articles that involve students with LD. Integrative reviews and papers advancing theories and pertinent issues are also published. **Write:** Council for Learning Disabilities, P.O. Box 40303, Overland Park, KS 66204–4303 or **Phone:** (913) 492–8755.

Their World, a publication for the National Center For Learning Disabilities, is a clear and jargon-free exploration of issues facing individuals with LD and their families. Each issue contains special features (i.e., social and emotional dimensions of LD, creative environments) authored by leaders in the field as well as listings of valuable resources.**Write:** NCLD, 99 Park Avenue, New York, NY 10016 or **Phone:** (212) 687–7211.

Organizations

Center for Educational Research on Dyslexia conducts research on dyslexia and provides a network in which researchers can collaborate and disseminate their findings. The Center also provides technical assistance and training to school districts and organizations. **Write:** Center for Educational Research on Dyslexia, San Jose State University, One Washington Square, San Jose, CA 95192 0078 or **Phone:** (408) 924–3700.

Council for Learning Disabilities (CLD) is a national organization dedicated solely to professionals working with individuals with LD. Members receive two publications, **LD Forum** and **Learning Disability Quarterly,** which present the latest research in the field and how the research can be translated into practice. The organization also sponsors yearly international and regional conferences. **Write:** CLD, P.O. Box

40303, Overland Park, KS 66204 or **Phone:** (913) 492–8755.

Division for Learning Disabilities (DLD) of CEC promotes improved services, research, and legislation for those with LD. The organization publishes both the **Learning Disabilities Research and Practice** quarterly and the **DLD Times** newsletter three times per year. **Write:** DLD, CEC, 1920 Association Drive, Reston, VA 22091 or **Phone:** (703) 620–3660.

Learning Disabilities Association, Inc. (LDA). Formed by a group of concerned parents, LDA, with its national and local affiliates, offers information, referral, and legislation services. It also offers school program development services available to school systems in planning and implementing programs for early identification and diagnosis, as well as remediation in resource and special education classroom situations. The Learning Disabilities Association works with educators and correctional authorities to develop comprehensive approaches to education and employment. **Write:** 4156 Library Road, Pittsburgh, PA 15234.

National Center for Learning Disabilities (NCLD) is a national organization dedicated to assisting those with the hidden handicap of LD to live self-sufficient, productive, and fulfilling lives. Services provided by NCLD include raising public awareness and understanding, national information and referral, education programs and products (including the publication **Their World**), and legislative advocacy. **Write:** NCLD, 381 Park Avenue South, Suite 1420, New York, NY 10016 or **Phone:** (212) 545–7510.

The **Orton Dyslexia Society** is an international non-profit organization committed to the advancement of the study and treatment of specific language disabilities, or developmental dyslexia. The organization sponsors research and shares up-to-date information about advances in the field. The organization publishes a quarterly journal, **Perspectives on Dyslexia,** and a yearly compendium, *Annals of dyslexia*. **Write:** The Orton Dyslexia Society, Chester Building, Suite 382, 8600 LaSalle Rd., Baltimore, MD 21204–6020 or **Phone:** (800) ABCD-123.

Time Out To Enjoy, Inc. is a nonprofit organization designed to (a) educate the public about LD, (b) provide support to adults with LD, and (c) collect and provide resources for adults with LD. The organization publishes a newsletter entitled **Not for Children Only. Write:** Time Out To Enjoy, P.O. Box 1084, Evanston, IL 60204 or **Phone:** (312) 444–9484.

ATTENTION DEFICIT DISORDER (ADD)

Unlike many of the disability conditions described in this section, attention deficit disorder (ADD) lacks a single, universally accepted definition. Most professionals, however, adhere to the criteria for diagnosing ADD given in the *Diagnostic and Statistical Manual of Mental Disorders*, the authoritative guide for identifying mental disorders. (Readers should note that the fourth edition of this handbook, the DSM-IV, was published in 1994.) For a student to be considered to have ADD, three conditions must be met. First, at least eight of the following 14 symptoms must be present:

(1) fidgets with hands or feet, or squirms in seat;

(2) difficulty remaining seated when required to do so;

(3) easily distracted by extraneous stimuli;

(4) difficulty awaiting turn in games or group situations;

(5) blurts out answers to questions before they have been completed;

(6) has difficulty following through on instructions from others (not due to oppositional behavior or failure of comprehension);

(7) difficulty sustaining attention in tasks or play activities;

(8) often shifts from one uncompleted activity to another;

(9) difficulty playing quietly;

(10) often talks excessively;

(11) often interrupts or intrudes on others;

(12) often does not seem to listen to what is being said to him or her;

(13) often loses things necessary for tasks or activities at school or at home;

(14) often engages in physically dangerous activities without considering possible consequences (not for the purpose of thrill seeking).

Second, the symptoms identified from above must be present for six months or longer. Finally, the symptoms must be present before the student is seven years of age. As observed by Wodrich (1994), students with ADD are at-risk for a number of secondary problems including behavior problems, school learning problems, and a variety of interpersonal social problems.

AVAILABLE RESOURCES: ADD

Resource Books

Barkley, R. *Attention deficit hyperactivity disorder: A handbook for diagnosis and treatment.* New York, NY: Guilford.

> Text provides a comprehensive analysis of the history of ADHD, its primary symptoms, theories of its nature, associated conditions and etiologies, developmental course and outcome, and family context. The text describes the nature and diagnosis of ADHD, its assessment, and treatment.

Johnston, R. B. (1991). *Attention deficits, learning disabilities, and Ritalin: A practical guide.* San Diego, CA: Singular.

> The author addresses many misguided opinions and misconceptions surrounding the use of Ritalin—problems and pitfalls in diagnosis and treatment, expectations, limitations, and precautions. He also demystifies medical considerations of Attention Deficit Hyperactivity Disorder

(ADHD) and learning disabilities in refreshingly nontechnical language aimed at parents, teachers, and practitioners.

Quinn, P., & Stern, J. (1991). *Putting on the brakes: Young people's guide to understanding Attention Deficit Hyperactivity Disorder (ADHD)*. New York, NY: Magination Press.
> Written for children ages 8–13, this slim book clearly explains the nature and treatment of attention deficit disorders. The authors include many suggestions to help young people handle their symptoms and their emotions about their disorder.

Reif, S. F. (1993). *How to reach and teach ADD/ADHD children*. Reston, VA: CEC.
> This resource provides practical answers to a variety of questions and issues that typically challenge teachers of students with attention problems. Strategies for teaching organization and study skills as well as selected content areas are provided.

Wender, P. (1987). *The hyperactive child, adolescent, and adult: Attention Deficit Disorder through the lifespan.* New York, NY: Oxford University Press.
> Designed for parents, this text explains symptoms, diagnosis, and treatment of attention deficit disorders from childhood through adulthood.

Wodrich, D. L. (1994). *Attention deficit hyperactivity disorder: What every parent wants to know*. Baltimore, MD: Paul H. Brookes.
> A straightforward and clearly presented guide to understanding what ADD is and what type of treatment alternatives are available. Case studies and helpful checklists are included in this very readable volume.

Multimedia

Barkley, R. **"ADHD: What do we know?"** and **"ADHD: What can we do?"** video programs. New York, NY: Guilford.

> These two videos can be used with parent-support groups and as training tools for teachers. The videos present current scientifically based information about the causes of ADHD and the range of managment techniques that can be used at home and in the classroom. Each of the two videos comes with a complete professional package that can be used in group settings such as in-service training or seminars.

Copeland, E. D. (1989). **"ADHD/ADD video resource for schools—Attention disorders: The school's vital role."** Port Chester, NY: National Professional Resources.

Goldstein, S., & Goldstein, M. (1990). **"Educating Inattentive Children."** Port Chester, NY: National Professional Resources.

> Two videos that outline the educator's role in serving students with attention deficits. Information is provided regarding the identification of attentional problems as well as alternative interventions.

NPR Videos. Port Chester, NY: National Professional Resources.

> NPR markets a number of useful videos pertaining to ADD and "thinking skills." **"Educating inattentive children,"** for example, is a two-hour video designed for in-service use. Write for their descriptive catalog.

Organization

Children with Attention Deficit Disorders (CHADD) is a nonprofit organization that was started by parents of children with Attention Deficit Disorders and by professionals who work with such children. The objectives of CHADD include (a) maintaining support groups for parents, (b) providing a forum for continuing education, (c) being an information resource, and (d) ensuring that the best educational experiences are available to children with ADD. The organization sponsors conferences and assists in the development of local chapters. **Write:** CHADD, 499 Northwest 70th Avenue, Suite 308, Plantation, FL 33317 or **Phone:** (305) 587–3700.

Periodical

The **ADHD Report,** published six times per year by National Professional Resources, is a newsletter written for practitioners, educators, and researchers who require up-to-date information on clinical practices involving individuals with ADHD. **Write:** National Professional Resources, 25 S. Regent St., Port Chester, NY 10573 or **Phone:** (800) 453–7641.

EMOTIONAL DISTURBANCE/ BEHAVIOR DISORDERS

Emotional Disturbance/Behavior Disorders (ED/BD) is a category of disability that is easier to recognize than it is to define. There is a general agreement that there is a condition associated with emotional and/or behavioral difficulties, yet there is little agreement as to how to define (or even name) this condition. Currently, IDEA uses Bower's (1969) definition to identify students with such problems. Briefly, the term "serious emotional disturbance" means a condition with one or more of the following characteristics over a long period of time and to a marked degree that adversely affects a child's educational performance:

(1) An inability to learn which cannot be explained by intellectual, sensory, or health factors;

(2) An inability to build or maintain satisfactory interpersonal relationships with peers and teachers;

(3) Inappropriate types of behavior or feelings under normal circumstances;

(4) A general pervasive mood of unhappiness or depression; or

(5) A tendency to develop physical symptoms or fears associated with personal or school problems.

The term includes schizophrenia, yet does not apply to children who are socially maladjusted unless it is determined that they possess a serious emotional disturbance.

It should be noted that dissatisfaction with the definition of ED/BD is widespread and it is quite possible that a new definition will be included in a future reauthorization of special education law. Whatever formal definition is to be adopted, it is clear that operationally, students identified as having ED/BD will exhibit a diverse set of behaviors. At one extreme, these students may engage in high rates of acting out, aggressive behaviors; at the other extreme students may be extremely withdrawn with low rates of social interaction. In characterizing the range of behaviors associated with ED/BD, Rosenberg, Wilson, Maheady, and Sindelar (1992) have used the terms high incidence behavior disorders and low incidence behavior disorders to differentiate the types of behaviors that general and special educators tend to deal with on a daily basis. These high incidence behavior disorders can include hyperactive behavior (overactivity, distractibility, and impulsivity), aggression, rule-breaking/delinquency, and social withdrawal. Low incidence behavior disorders tend not to be observed by most educators and include the variety of psychotic behaviors exhibited by relatively few children and youth in the general population. These behaviors can include extreme social withdrawal, self-stimulatory behavior, and self-injurious behavior, as well as delusional thinking and behavior.

AVAILABLE RESOURCES: ED/BD
Generic Textbooks

There are a number of generic textbooks that focus on the diagnosis, characteristics, and treatment of ED/BD. In general, these texts provide individual sections or chapters on various facets relating to ED/BD including (a) definition and characteristics, (b) assessment, and (c) alternative methods for promoting prosocial behavior. Some of the more popular texts are listed below.

Coleman, M. C. (1992). *Behavior disorders: Theory and practice*. Boston: Allyn & Bacon.

Cullinan, D., Epstein, M., & Lloyd, J. (1983). *Behavior disorders of children and adolescents*. Boston: Allyn & Bacon.

Epanchin, B., & Paul, J. (1987). *Emotional problems of child-hood and adolescence: A multidisciplinary perspective.* New York, NY: Merrill/ Macmillan.

Kauffman, J. (1993). *Characteristics of behavior problems of children and youth: an educator's introduction.* New York, NY: Merrill/ Macmillan.

Morgan, D., & Jenson, M. (1988). *Teaching behaviorally disordered students: preferred practices.* New York, NY: Merrill/Macmillan.

Morse, W. C. (1985). *The education and treatment of socio-emotionally impaired children and youth.* Syracuse, NY: Syracuse University Press.

Paul, J., & Epanchin, B. (1991). *Educating emotionally disturbed children and youth: Theories and practices for teachers.* New York, NY: Merrill/Macmillan.

Peschel, E., et al. (1992). *Neurobiological disorders in children and adolescents.* San Francisco: Jossey-Bass.

Reinhert, J., & Huang, A. (1987). *Children in conflict: Educational strategies for the emotionally disturbed and behaviorally disordered.* New York, NY: Merrill/Macmillan.

Rosenberg, M., Wilson, R., Maheady, L., & Sindelar, P. (1992). *Educating students with behavior disorders.* Boston: Allyn & Bacon.

Shea, T., & Bauer, A. (1987). *Teaching children and youth with behavior disorders.* Boston: Allyn & Bacon.

Resource Books

Kelly, E. J. (1992). *Conduct problem/emotional problem interventions: A holistic perspective*. East Aurora, NY: Slosson.

> A text that explores intervention procedures which go beyond strictly mechanical and experimental approaches. The holistic approach explored is presented in a practical fashion designed to facilitate mainstreaming and collaborative efforts.

Nelson, C. M., & Pearson, C. A. (1991). *Integrating services for children and youth with emotional and behavioral disorders*. Reston, VA: CEC.

> Text provides a solid rationale and guideline for interagency collaborative programming in the delivery of services to students with ED/BD.

Wisconsin Department of Public Instruction (1990). *Education assessment of emotional disturbance: An evaluation guide*. Milwaukee, WI: Author.

> Developed in response to numerous requests for assistance in evaluating the needs of children and youths who are emotionally disturbed, this is a practical guide for screening and identifying such students. The guide contains information on the legal requirements for identifying and placing ED students by defining emotional disturbance and presenting evaluation techniques. More than 100 sample instruments, interview forms, and reports assist in defining the roles of various professionals in the assessment process. This is a valuable guide for ED teachers, school administrators, and social service professionals.

Multimedia

Understanding Child Variance Video Tape Series. By W. Morse and J. Smith. Reston, VA: CEC.

> A series of videotapes that explore the variety of theoretical models associated with the study and education of students with ED/BD. The individual tapes or the complete set are available and are accompanied by a trainer's guide.

Periodicals

Behavioral Disorders, published four times a year by the Council for Children with Behavioral Disorders of CEC, presents reports of original investigations and theoretical papers which relate to the education of children with emotional and behavioral problems. **Write:** CCBD, 1920 Association Drive, Reston, VA 22091–1589.

Beyond Behavior, published three times a year by the Council for Children with Behavioral Disorders of CEC, provides a source of analysis and commentary on issues concerning behavior of children and adolescents in our schools. The magazine also seeks to broaden the impact of research on practice and to lend support and affirmation to those who work with children and youth who are troubled and troubling. **Write:** CCBD, 1920 Association Drive, Reston, VA 22091–1589.

Child and Adolescent Mental Health Care (formerly Comprehensive Mental Health Care), published three times per year by Springer Publishing Co, is a multidisciplinary journal concerned with current thinking and research on the diagnosis, treatment, and habilitation of children and adolescents with developmental disabilities, psychiatric disorders, or multiple handicaps. **Write:** Springer Publishing Co., 536 Broadway, New York, NY 10012–9904 or **Phone:** (212) 431–4370.

Journal of Emotional and Behavioral Disorders, published quarterly by PRO-ED, is an international, multidisciplinary journal that offers articles on research, practice, and theory related to individuals with emotional and behavioral disorders and the professionals who serve them. **Write:** PRO-ED, 8700 Shoal Creek Blvd., Austin, TX 78758 or **Phone:** (512) 451 3246.

Journal of Emotional and Behavioral Problems, published by National Education Service, is a new journal designed for practitioners who work with children and youth who have emotional or behavior problems. The journal highlights practical and rejuvenating ideas that are multidisciplinary in nature. **Write:** JEB-P, National Educational Service, 1610 W. Third St., P.O.Box 8, Bloomington, IN 47402–0008 or **Phone:** (800) 733–6786.

Organizations

The **Council for Children with Behavioral Disorders (CCBD)** pursues quality educational services and program alternatives for children and youth with BD, advocates for their needs, and emphasizes research and professional growth as vehicles for better understanding of BD. CCBD publishes **Behavioral Disorders,** a journal, and the **CCBD Newsletter** quarterly. **Beyond Behavior,** a magazine devoted to commentary, is published three times per year. **Write:** CCBD, CEC, 1920 Association Drive, Reston, VA 22091 or **Phone:** (703) 620–3660.

The **National Alliance for the Mentally Ill Children and Adolescents Network (NAMI CAN)** is a nationwide network for serving children and youth with severe and chronic mental illness, particularly those who have, or are suspected of having, a neurobiological disorder. **NAMI CAN News,** the organization's newsletter, is published four times per year. **Write:** NAMI CAN, 2101 Wilson Blvd., Suite 302, Arlington, VA 22201 or **Phone:** (703) 524–7600.

Mild to Moderate Disabilities (MMD): Category-Free Conceptualizations

Even though the use of categorical referents is the common, more traditional means for describing students with mild to moderate disabilities, many educators have found it beneficial to employ a category-free classification system (Rosenberg, O'Shea, & O'Shea, 1991). This perspective puts greater emphasis on a student's behavioral functioning rather than factors used to either include or exclude a student from a particular category. Problem behaviors most typical of students with mild to moderate disabilities **may** fall into any of the following generic domains: academic underachievement, sensory and perceptual processing problems, perceptual-motor problems, attention deficit problems, memory deficits, receptive and expressive language problems, overactivity, impulsivity, poor peer relationships, and deficient social/emotional skills.

AVAILABLE RESOURCES: MMD
Generic Textbooks

Gearheart, B., DeRuiter, J., & Sileo, T. (1986). *Teaching mildly and moderately handicapped students*. Boston: Allyn & Bacon.

Henley, M., Ramsey, R., & Algozzine, R. (1993). *Characteristics of and strategies for teaching students with mild disabilities*. Boston: Allyn & Bacon.

Mercer, C., & Mercer, A. (1993). *Teaching students with learning problems*. New York: Merrill/Macmillan.

Retish, P., Hitchings, W., Horvath, M., & Schmalle, B. (1991). *Students with mild disabilities in the secondary school*. White Plains, NY: Longman.

Schloss, P., Schloss, C., & Smith, M. (1990). *Instructional methods for adolescents with learning and behavior problems*. Boston: Allyn & Bacon.

Smith, D. D. (1989). *Teaching students with learning and behavior problems*. Boston: Allyn & Bacon.

Resource Book

Waller, M. B. (1993). *Crack-affected children: A teacher's guide*. Thousand Oaks, CA: Corwin Press.
  This text relates the experiences of 63 teachers who discovered methods for dealing with the behaviors of students affected by crack. This is a practical resource with many teacher-based tips and techniques.

Periodical

Educating At-Risk Youth, a monthly newsletter published by National Professional Resources, Inc., contains information on issues such as drop-out prevention, substance abuse, incarcerated youth, and other risk factors.

Organizations

Association of Educational Therapists (AET) is a professional organization that seeks to regulate professional training and to promote professional practice among educational therapists. AET is an association of independent educational therapists (tutors) who work primarily with students with mild and moderate disabilities. The organization's publication, **The Educational Therapist,** is published three times annually and typically contains articles on (a) conducting tutorials, (b) types of disabilities, (c) organizational skills, (d) specific language learning disabilities, and (e) reports on research in the field. AET sponsors an annual conference in Los Angeles, local study groups, and specialized intensive workshops, as well as producing tapes of workshops and conferences. **Write:** AET, P.O. Box 946, Woodland Hills, CA 91365 0946 or **Phone:** (818) 778 3850.

Practical Allergy Research Foundation produces a variety of educational materials which discuss how unsuspected sensitivities to pollen, dust, molds, pets, foods, or chemicals can cause changes in physical wellness, as well as in the behavior, activity, and learning ability of some children. Each tape or book emphasizes selected aspects of these problems. Selected book and video titles include: *Is this your child? Discovering and treating unrecognized allergies; How you can recognize unsuspected allergies; Make the connection - What causes allergies and what you can do about it; Clues to predict possible allergies; Why an environmentally clean classroom.* The author of all materials is Doris J. Rapp, M.D., Pediatric Allergist. **Write:** Doris J. Rapp, M.D., Environmental Allergy Center, 2757 Elmwood Avenue, Buffalo, NY 14217 or **Phone:** (716) 875–5578.

Mental Retardation (MR)

According to IDEA, mental retardation is formally defined as significantly subaverage general intellectual functioning existing concurrently with deficits in adaptive behavior and manifested during the developmental period that adversely affects a child's educational performance. Until recently, students meeting these criteria were usually diagnosed as having a level or degree of mental retardation based on level of intelligence (as measured by IQ scores). Typically, students with scores between 55 and 69 on standardized intelligence tests were considered to have mild mental retardation; students with scores between 40–54 were considered to have moderate mental retardation; scores between 25–39 indicated severe retardation; and scores below 24 indicated profound retardation.

Using this classification system, the large majority of individuals with MR (approximately 85 percent) fell into the mildly retarded range and were believed able to master academic skills up to about the sixth grade level and to learn job skills well enough to support themselves independently or semi-independently (Heward & Orlansky, 1992). Students with moderate retardation comprised approximately 7–10 percent of those identified as mentally retarded, and were believed to benefit from highly individualized instruction in those skills necessary for successful community integration (e.g., daily living skills, self-care skills, basic work skills, and a functional vocabulary). Students with severe and profound mental retardation make up approximately 3–6 percent of those identified as MR and were believed to typically require intensive instruction in self-care and basic communication skills. Still, as noted by Heward and Orlansky (1992), recent advances in instructional technology helped students with severe and profound mental retardation acquire skills previously thought beyond their capability—to the point of being semi-independent adults able to live and work in the community.

In 1992, the American Association on Mental Retardation developed a new system for classifying mental retardation. Rather than using levels of measured intelligence, this new system is based on an individual's unique strengths, weaknesses, and needs for special supports. As noted by Kozma and Stock (1993), the intent of this new classification system is to describe more accurately the variability in the way different people with similar IQ scores can function. It also recognizes that people with mental retardation can move from one classification to another as they develop new skills and become more independent. The new system classifies individuals with MR by the amount of support or help that is needed across four dimensions related to success in their environment (i.e., intellectual and adaptive skills; psychological and emotional considerations; physical/health/etiology considerations; and environmental considerations). For each of these dimensions, the four intensities of support are:

Intermittent: Not requiring consistent support, yet needing support on a short-term basis (e.g., due to a job loss or an acute medical crisis).

Limited: Requiring time-limited (yet not intermittent) support consistently over time (e.g., time-limited job training or transitional supports for the school-to-work period).

Extensive: Requiring regular support (e.g., daily) in some environments and not time-limited (e.g., long-term job support and long-term home living support).

Pervasive: Requiring constant, high-intensity support across environments. Supports typically involve more staff members and intrusiveness than do extensive or time-limited supports, and may be of a potential life-sustaining nature.

In general, individuals with MR *may* exhibit specific weaknesses in communication, self-care, home-living, social skills, community use, self-direction, health and safety, functional academics, and leisure skills (Luckasson et al., 1992).

AVAILABLE RESOURCES: MR
Generic Textbooks

Drew, C., Logan, D., & Hardman, M. (1992). *Mental retardation: A life-cycle approach.* New York, NY: Merrill/Macmillan.

Luftig, R. (1987). *Teaching the mentally retarded student: Curriculum, methods, and strategies.* Boston: Allyn & Bacon.

Patton, J., Beirne-Smith, M., & Payne, J. (1990). *Mental retardation.* New York, NY: Merrill/Macmillan.

Snell, M. (1993). *Instruction of students with severe disabilities.* New York, NY: Merrill/Macmillan.

Westling, D. (1986). *Introduction to mental retardation.* Boston: Allyn & Bacon.

Resource Books

Kleinfeld, J., & Wescott, S. (1993). *Fantastic Antone succeeds! Educating children with FAS/FAE*. Anchorage, AK: University of Alaska Press.

> An edited volume in which strategies for handling educational and behavioral problems associated with fetal alcohol syndrome or fetal alcohol effects are presented.

Levine, K., & Wharton, R. (1993). *Children with Prader-Willi syndrome: Information for school staff*. Roslyn Heights, NY: Visible Ink Incorporated.

> This brief booklet presents characteristic behavioral and learning problems associated with Prader-Willi syndrome and then suggests specific approaches to deal with these problems in the classroom.

Luckasson, R., et al. (1992). *Definition and classification in mental retardation*. Washington, DC: AAMR.

> Comprehensive manual that provides valuable insight into the new definition and classification system used to conceptualize mental retardation. The manual and workbook present the (a) new definition of mental retardation; (b) outline the three-step process of diagnosis, classification, and identification of intensities of support; (c)explain how to apply the new definition with appropriate forms; and (d) provide case studies that demonstrate how to implement the definition.

Plumridge, D., & Hylton, J. (1989). *Smooth sailing into the next generation: The causes and prevention of mental retardation*. Saratoga, CA: R & E Publishers.

> A resource manual geared toward young readers, their parents, and teachers which provides specific information about the *preventable* causes of mental retardation. Issues addressed include young maternal age; family planning; the use of prescription drugs, street drugs, and alcohol; and parental health care before and after conception.

Pueschel, S. (1990). *A parent's guide to Down syndrome: Toward a brighter future.* Baltimore: Paul H. Brookes.
> This guide, also available from the publisher in a Spanish edition, covers developmental issues from birth through adolescence. Included are chapters on integration and curricular needs.

Schopmeyer, B., & Lowe, F. (1992). *The fragile X child.* San Diego: Singular Publishing Group.
> Written primarily for occupational and speech-language therapists, this book contains sections on the genetics and medical aspects of fragile X syndrome, as well as on developmental and behavioral characteristics and therapeutic interventions.

Smith, R. (1993). *Children with mental retardation: A parents' guide.* Rockville, MD: Woodbine House.
> This guide includes information relevant to all children with mental retardation, whether or not they have a diagnosed syndrome or condition. It is intended to provide parents with an introduction to their child's medical, therapeutic, and educational needs and covers topics such as family adjustment, daily care, special education, and legal rights. Helpful sections for teachers include those on behavior management, setting goals, and teaching self-help skills, and how mental retardation affects cognitive processes such as attention, memory, abstract thinking, as well as other areas of development.

Stark, J., Menolascino, F., Albarelli, M., & Gray, V. (1987). *Mental retardation and mental health.* New York, NY: Springer-Verlag.
> An edited text that explores the problems associated with the delivery of mental health services to individuals with mental retardation. Specific recommendations for improved service delivery are provided.

Sternberg, L., Ritchey, H., Pegnatore, L., Wills, L., & Hill, K. *A Curriculum for profoundly handicapped students: The Broward County Model Program*. Austin, TX: PRO-ED.

> With this step-by-step text, teachers are provided with a sensible approach to teach and measure the progress of their students with profound handicaps, establish reasonable instructional goals, and select skills—gross motor, fine motor, cognitive, receptive communication, expressive communication, social/affective—that can be taught in small groups and determine how to set up a classroom.

Stray-Gundersen, K.(1986). *Babies with Down syndrome: A new parents' guide*. Rockville, MD: Woodbine House.

> Intended as an introduction to Down syndrome for parents, this book includes information on the nature and causes of Down syndrome, the effects on cognitive skills and other areas of development, medical issues, family and daily care issues, and early intervention.

Trainer, M. (1991). *Differences in common: Straight talk on mental retardation, Down syndrome, and life*. Rockville, MD: Woodbine House.

> The author draws on her personal experience as a mother of a child with Down syndrome in this collection of more than 50 essays. A wide range of issues is explored, including family adjustment, public attitudes, mainstreaming, and independence.

Periodicals

American Journal on Mental Retardation, published by the American Association on Mental Retardation (AAMR), is a scientific and archival journal reporting original contributions to knowledge on MR. For the most part, research studies and analytical reviews of the literature are published. **Write:** AAMR, 1719 Kalorama Road, N.W., Washington, DC 20009 or **Phone:** (800) 424–3688.

Education and Training in Mental Retardation, published by the Division on Mental Retardation and Developmental Disabilities of the Council for Exceptional Children, publishes research and critical reviews of the literature on the education and welfare of persons who are retarded. Major emphases of the journal are identification and assessment, educational programming, training, prevention, community understanding, and legislation. **Write:** MRDD, Council for Exceptional Children, 1920 Association Drive, Reston, VA 22091.

Journal of Autism and Developmental Disabilities, published quarterly by Plenum, provides research reports, integrative literature reviews, and successful program descriptions relating to individuals with autism and other developmental disabilities. **Write:** Plenum Publishing Corp., 233 Spring St., New York, NY 10013.

Journal of the Association for Persons with Severe Handicaps (JASH), published quarterly by The Association for Persons with Severe Handicaps, presents data-based articles, commentary, and book reviews that focus on the full range of knowledge necessary to serve individuals with severe handicaps. **Write:** JASH, 7010 Roosevelt Way, N.E., Seattle, WA 98115 or **Phone:** (206) 523–8446.

Mental Retardation, published by the American Association on Mental Retardation, typically highlights critical summaries, descriptions of successful programs, and research studies involving individuals with mental retardation. **Write:** AAMR, 1719 Kalorama Road, N.W., Washington, DC 20009 or **Phone:** (800) 424–3688.

Organizations

American Association on Mental Retardation (AAMR) is an interdisciplinary association of professionals and concerned individuals in the field of mental retardation. The association promotes the well-being of individuals with MR and supports those who work in the field. Activities include the publication of books and journals (**American Journal on Mental Retardation**), national conferences, and advocacy. **Write:** AAMR, 1719 Kalorama Road, N.W., Washington, DC 20009–2683 or **Phone:** (800) 424–3688.

The **ARC** (formerly the Association for Retarded Citizens) is dedicated to improving the lives of children and adults with mental retardation. Through its national office and local chapters, the ARC supports research and education concerning the prevention of mental retardation in infants and young children. ARC has several informational publications (booklets, pamphlets, and books) and videos on research, employment, prevention, family, and organizational issues. The national organization publishes a newsletter, **The ARC,** six times a year, and the **Government Report,** semi-monthly. **Write:** The ARC, National Headquarters, 500 E. Border Street, Suite 300, P.O. Box 300649, Arlington, TX 76010 or **Phone:** (817) 261–6003.

The **Association for Persons with Severe Handicaps (TASH)** is an organization of a diverse group of individuals (teachers, parents, therapists, etc.) concerned with all aspects of severe disabilities. The organization has long advocated for the inclusion of individuals with severe handicaps and disseminates much needed information on policies and intervention techniques. **Write:** TASH, 29 Susquehanna Ave., Ste. 210, Baltimore, MD 21204 or **Phone:** (410) 828–8274.

The **Division on Mental Retardation and Developmental Disabilities (MRDD)** of CEC promotes professional growth and research to advance programs for persons with MR. The division sponsors conferences and publishes a quarterly journal, **Education and Training in Mental Retardation,** and a newsletter, **MRDD Express,** three times per year. **Write:** MRDD, CEC, 1920 Association Drive, Reston, VA 22091 or **Phone:** (703) 620–3660.

The National Down Syndrome Congress (NDSC) seeks to create a national climate in which all persons recognize and embrace the value and dignity of persons with Down syndrome. The organization is the national clearinghouse for Down syndrome information and provides a number of services including (a) the NDSC journal published 10 times per year, (b) the NDSC Hotline (800–232–NDSC) for access to information, (c) an annual convention, and (d) the coordination of advocacy activities and local parent networks. **Write:** 1605 Chantilly Rd., Atlanta, GA 30324 or **Phone:** (800) 232–NDSC.

The **National Fragile X Foundation** provides information about fragile X syndrome, one of the leading genetic causes of intellectual disabilities. It publishes a newsletter, and supports research into diagnosis, treatment, and education of individuals with fragile X. **Write:** 1441 York St., Suite 215, Denver, CO 80206 or **Phone:** (303) 333–6155.

The **National Organization on Fetal Alcohol Syndrome (NOFAS)** publishes a newsletter and sponsors workshops, conferences, and awareness campaigns on issues related to Fetal Alcohol Syndrome. **Write:** NOFAS, 1814 H Street, N.W., Suite 710, Washington, DC 20006 or **Phone:** (800) 66–NOFAS.

The **Prader-Willi Syndrome Association** distributes publications on Prader-Willi syndrome and a newsletter. The national organization oversees local chapters that provide support and information. **Write:** 6490 Excelsior Blvd., Suite E-102, St. Louis Park, MN 55426 or **Phone:** (612) 926–1947.

Williams Syndrome Association publishes a newsletter and brochures on Williams syndrome, and supports research. **Write:** P.O. Box 3297, Ballwin, MO 63022–3297 or **Phone:** (314) 227–4411.

Sensory Disabilities

When speaking of students with sensory disabilities, we are referring to students who have visual and/or auditory problems which affect the delivery of educational services. We first present resources related to visual impairments and then hearing impairments. Note that resources helpful in assisting students with the multiple disability deaf-blindness can be found throughout this "Sensory Disability" section. Resources specific to deaf-blindness alone are found at the end of this section.

VISUAL IMPAIRMENTS

According to IDEA, a visual impairment (including blindness) is an impairment in vision that, even with correction, adversely affects a child's educational performance. Surprisingly, only about 15 percent of those identified as legally blind have no useable vision. Thus, it has been recommended (e.g., American Federation for the Blind, 1987) that terms of greater precision be used to describe individuals with visual impairments. Terms having this added precision include **low vision** (a level of vision that allows enhancements of functional vision yet is still accompanied by some problems associated with visual planning and execution of tasks); and **blind** (reserved for only those who have no useable sight). Typically, many students who are blind or partially sighted can have success with the same educational programming as their nondisabled peers. What is generally required, however, are: (a) modifications and adaptations in the mode of instructional delivery, (b) adaptations of instructional materials, (c) specialized instruction in orientation and mobility skills, and (d) assistance in acquiring and using assistive devices. Not surprisingly, approximately 86 percent of students who are considered legally blind (visual acuity of 20/200 or less in better eye after correction or a visual field of less than 20 degrees) attend regular public schools (American Printing House for the Blind, 1987).

AVAILABLE RESOURCES: VI
General Textbooks

Ashcroft, S. A., Henderson, F., Sanford, L. D., & Koenig, A. J. (1991). *New programmed instruction in braille.* Nashville, TN: SCLARS Publishing.

Jacobson, W. H. (1993). *The art and science of teaching orientation and mobility to persons with visual impairments.* New York, NY: American Foundation for the Blind.

Jose, R. T. (1983). *Understanding low vision.* New York, NY: American Foundation for the Blind.

Levack, N. (1991). *Low vision: A resource guide with adaptations for students with visual impairments.* Austin, TX: Texas School for the Blind and Visually Impaired.

Scholl, G. T. (1986). *Foundations of education of blind and visually handicapped children and youth: Theory and practice.* New York, NY: American Foundation for the Blind.

Welsh, R. L., & Blasch, B. B. (1980). *Foundations of orientation and mobility.* New York, NY: American Foundation for the Blind.

Resource Books

American Foundation for the Blind (1993). *AFB directory of services for blind and visually impaired persons in the United States.* New York, NY: Author.
> State-by-state listings of local, state, regional, and national services (schools, agencies, information services, etc.) for individuals with visual impairments. Available in a hardback book and electronic format (IBM DOS compatible).

American Foundation for the Blind (1990). *Sources of products for blind and visually impaired persons.* New York, NY: Author.
> The Foundation provides a comprehensive listing of manufacturers of products often needed by individuals with visual impairments and blindness. The listing is available in large print and on PC compatible diskettes.

Flax, M. E., Golembiewski, D. J., & McCauley, B. L. (1993). *Coping with low vision*. San Diego, CA: Singular.

> This text is a self-help guide and resource manual specially published in large-type format for partially sighted people and their families. It is designed to answer the many questions that arise when an individual is diagnosed as having low vision. The authors provide useful information on low vision along with many helpful suggestions for coping with this condition.

Harley, R., Truan, M., & LaRhea, D. (1988). *Communication skills for visually impaired learners*. Springfield, IL: Charles C. Thomas.

> The authors address numerous topics including the historical perspectives of the visually impaired; reading readiness; approaches to readiness instruction; assessment of reading skills; identifying the visually impaired with learning problems; teaching techniques; writing and learning skills; and current technology and instructional materials for visually impaired learners.

Leary, B., & vonSchnaden, M. (1982). *"Simon Says" is not the only game*. New York, NY: American Foundation for the Blind.

> Professionals throughout the United States contributed to this collection of more than 100 games and songs designed to provide a fun way to teach concepts to students with visual impairments.

Loumiet, R., & Levack, N. (1992). *Independent living: A curriculum with adaptations for students with visual impairments*. Austin, TX: Texas School for the Blind and Visually Impaired.

> In this guide, information is provided on assessment, teaching and evaluation of social skills, leisure skills, and daily living skills for students who are visually impaired.

Mangold, S. S. (1982). *A teacher's guide to the special educational needs of blind and visually handicapped children.* New York, NY: American Foundation for the Blind.

> This text provides information on the adaptation of curriculum (e.g., science, communication skills, self-esteem) for students with visual impairments. One chapter addresses the need for classmates of students with VI to be aware of such impairments.

National Braille Press. *Catalog of resources.* Boston: Author.

> The National Braille Press publishes a catalog listing many services, publications, and books available to individuals with visual impairment. The catalog contains a brief description of the use of the materials and abstracts of the books and publications which can be ordered from Braille Press.

National Braille Press. *Just enough to know better.* Boston: Author.

> A user-friendly book that introduces the Grade 2 braille code. Written in both print and braille, the book contains contractions and a number of practice activities.

Olmstead, J. E. (1991). *Itinerant teaching: Tricks of the trade for teachers of blind and visually impaired students.* New York, NY: American Foundation for the Blind.

> A guide to providing itinerant services for teachers of students with visual impairments. This book addresses diverse aspects of itinerant teaching including scheduling; production and adaptation of curriculum and materials; and sources of information, materials, and equipment.

Resources for Rehabilitation (1990). *Living with low vision: A resource guide for people with sight loss.* Lexington, MA: Author.

> This resource is a large print, comprehensive directory designed to assist individuals with sight loss to locate needed services, products, and publications in order to keep working and enjoying life. Specific chapters are devoted to children and those with both sight and hearing loss.

Rogow, S. M. (1988). *Helping the visually impaired child with developmental problems: Effective practice in home, school, and community*. New York NY: Teachers College Press.

> This book focuses on visually impaired children who are developmentally delayed or who have additional developmental handicaps. The premise of this book is that interaction with people and the environment is essential to effective learning and personal growth.

Torres, I. & Corn, A. (1990) *When you have a visually handicapped child in your classroom: Suggestions for teachers*. New York, NY: American Foundation for the Blind.

> This 56 page resource gives practical suggestions to regular classroom teachers attempting to include a student with a visual impairment in his or her classroom. Topics include detection of eye problems, social integration of the student with a visual impairment, orientation and mobility, and suggestions for inclusion of technology into the classroom curriculum.

Trief, E. (1992). *Working with visually impaired young students: A curriculum guide for birth-3 year olds*. Springfield, IL: Charles C. Thomas.

> This text tackles the challenge and purpose of the early identification and treatment of the visually impaired. Also included in the text is a curriculum model to early intervention; a review of the literature; and behavioral objectives for each developmental level. This guide provides a practical hands-on curricular approach for parents and educators of the visually impaired that allows the young children to make the transition from a specialized center-based or home-based program into the mainstream.

Willoughby, D., & Duffy, S. L. (1989). *Handbook for itinerant and resource teachers of blind and visually impaired students*. Baltimore: National Federation of the Blind.

> This comprehensive and practical 54 chapter handbook provides an overview of resources and procedures for dealing with the education of blind and visually impaired students. Topics include teaching braille, characteristics of

students with visual impairments, orientation and mobility, placement options, general classroom arrangements, and daily living skills. This handbook is almost like an encyclopedia of all one should know when teaching kids with visual impairments.

Wisconsin Department of Public Instruction (1990). *A guide to curriculum planning in education for the visually impaired.* Milwaukee, WI: Author.

This resource suggests adaptations for all subject areas and provides information on specialized classes for students with VI, such as "Orientation and Mobility," "Daily Living Skills," and "Low Vision." The guide also provides background information on identification and assessment, psychosocial development, general considerations, and the early childhood of these students.

Materials/Multimedia/Assistive Devices

Ann Morris Enterprises Catalog. East Meadow, NY: Ann Morris Enterprises.

This company offers a catalog of products for people with vision losses. It is available in large print, audio cassette, IBM and Apple format disk, and in braille. Catalog items include audible accessories; canes and accessories; computer software; general merchandise; housewares; medical accessories; and writing accessories.

Children's Braille Book Club. Boston: National Braille Press.

This resource is a book-of-the-month club for books in a print-braille format. The Press also publishes a number of useful resources, such as *A braille primer for sighted parents.*

DVS Home Videos. St. Paul, MN: DVS Home Video.

DVS markets a number of movies for those with visual impairments. The movies are described by the Descriptive Video Service without interfering with the movie's dialogue or sound effects.

Exceptional Teaching Aids. Castro Valley, CA: Exceptional Teaching Aids.

> Exceptional Teaching Aids provides a wide range of educational products for students with visual impairments. A catalog highlights holdings in the areas of math, science, reading, brailling, mobility, sports, recreation, art, and life skills.

Howe Press Twin-Vision Books. Watertown, MA: Perkins School for the Blind.

> The Howe Press markets a number of twin-vision books made from the original print books with braille added to the print pages (or clear plastic sheets). Many traditional favorite stories are available.

Instruction Manual for Learning to Read Braille by Sight. Louisville, KY: American Printing House for the Blind.

> A thorough instructional series that introduces the letters, contractions, and rules of the braille code. Practice exercises and answer keys are provided.

LS&S Materials and Devices. Northbrook, IL: LS&S Group.

> This company specializes in products for the visually impaired. A catalog contains over 60 pages of all types of assistive devices, books, software, and tapes.

MaxiAIDS Resources. Farmingdale, NY: MaxiAIDS.

> MaxiAIDS markets a number of assistive devices including talking dictionaries and multispeed tape recorders. Write or call for a catalog.

"Oh, I see." New York, NY: American Foundation for the Blind.

> This video provides an introduction to visual impairments for regular classroom teachers, classroom peers of students who are visually impaired, and school staff. It is a helpful tool to develop classroom modifications and adaptations.

"Reach out and teach: Meeting the training needs of parents of visually and multiply handicapped young children." By Kay Ferrell. New York, NY: American Foundation for the Blind.

> Designed as a guide for parents, this program contains a handbook, parent workbook, and slide/tape presentation that demonstrates step-by-step training in such areas as gross and fine motor development, daily living skills, communication skills, and concept development.

Seedlings Twin-Vision Books. Livonia, MI: Seedlings.

> Seedlings markets a variety of twin-vision books in which print type is rewritten onto braille paper.

The Reading Edge. Peabody, MA: Xerox Imaging Systems

> The Reading Edge scans books, recognizes text, and converts the text to synthesized speech in seconds. This tool is flexible enough to read virtually any type of printed document and requires no previous computer experience. Full marketing materials are available by writing or calling.

Periodicals

Journal of Vision Rehabilitation is a multidisciplinary publication that brings together original work in the theory and practice of vision rehabilitation from a number of disciplines including optometry, ophthalmology, rehabilitation, psychology, and education. **Write:** Media Periodicals, 2440 "O" Street, Suite 202, Lincoln, NE 68510 1185.

Journal of Visual Impairment and Blindness, published ten times per year by the American Federation for the Blind, is a scholarly journal for professionals and researchers. Typical features include articles on research and practice, commentary, book and media reviews, and a calendar of coming events. The journal is published in inkprint, braille, and cassette editions.

RE:view (formerly Education of the Visually Handicapped), published quarterly by the Association for
Education and Rehabilitation of the Blind and Visually Impaired, includes practical articles, original research, interviews, and other features of interest to
teachers of students with visual impairments. Twice
per year the journal publishes listings of current literature on blindness, visual impairment, and deaf-
blindness. **Write:** Association for Education and
Rehabilitation of the Blind and Visually Impaired,
206 N. Washington Street, Alexandria, VA 22314.

Organizations

American Council of the Blind (ACB) promotes effective participation of blind people in all aspects of society. The organization acts as a national clearinghouse
for information, publishes **The Braille Forum,** and
provides legal assistance, scholarships, and program
development support. **Write:** ACB, 1155 15th St.,
N.W., Suite 720, Washington, DC, 20005 or **Phone:**
(800) 424–8666

American Foundation for the Blind (AFB) is a leading
national resource for people who are blind or visually impaired, the organizations which serve them,
and the general public. Among its many activities,
AFB provides consultation services, technical assistance, and houses a number of libraries and information centers. The organization publishes a number of
publications including the **Journal of Visual Impairment and Blindness,** as well as marketing a number
of products for individuals with vision problems. For
a complete listing of services and free catalogs, **Write:**
AFB, 15 West 16 Street, New York, NY 10011 or
Phone: (800) 232–5463.

American Printing House for the Blind (APH), the world's largest company devoted solely to producing products for individuals who are visually impaired, publishes and distributes a wide variety of materials for individuals with visual impairments. For example, the Printing House publishes a large catalog of large-type books and a most useful catalog of instructional aides, tools, and supplies. **Write:** APH, P.O. Box 6085, Louisville, KY 40206–0085 or **Phone:** (800) 223–1839.

Association for Education and Rehabilitation of the Blind and Visually Impaired (AER) promotes all phases of education and work for blind and visually impaired persons of all ages. The organization operates a job exchange and reference information center, and cooperates with colleges and universities in the delivery of conferences and workshops. The organization publishes 3 periodicals: **AER Report, Job Exchange Monthly,** and **RE:View. Write:** AER, 206 North Washington St., Suite 320, Alexandria, VA 22314 or **Phone:** (703) 548–1884.

The **Division on Visual Handicaps (DVH)** of CEC promotes appropriate educational programs for individuals who have visual handicaps and seeks to provide a greater understanding of their concomitant conditions. The division publishes a newsletter, the **DVH Quarterly. Write:** DVH, CEC, 1920 Association Drive, Reston, VA 22091 1589 or **Phone:** (703) 620–3660.

The **National Association for the Visually Handicapped (NAVH)** is a non-profit, national organization devoted solely to the partially seeing. NAVH represents those people who are not totally blind—individuals who do not require braille, guide dogs, or canes—but, even with the best corrective lenses, do not have adequate vision. NAVH is a pioneer in the production of large print books, which it distributes free. NAVH serves as a consultant to commercial publishers, produces and distributes large print newspapers, and maintains a free large print loan library. NAVH provides counsel and advice to adults, parents, and children; public education; professional education; visual aids; information on suitable lamps; and information and referrals. **Write:** NAVH, 22 West 21st Street, New York, NY 10010.

The **National Federation of the Blind** is a large organization of blind individuals that emphasizes the rights and capabilities of people who are blind. The organization seeks to involve blind people in education and employment and sponsors a number of activities and publications for parents and teachers. The Federation's magazine, **Future Reflections,** offers practical guidance for parents raising a blind child. **Write:** National Federation of the Blind, 1800 Johnson St., Baltimore, MD 21230.

The **National Library Service for the Blind and Physically Handicapped** administers a national library service that provides reference materials, braille and recorded books, and magazines on free loan to anyone (eligible residents of the United States or American citizens living abroad) who cannot read standard print because of visual or physical disabilities. **Write:** 1291 Taylor Street N.W., Washington, DC 20542 or **Phone:** (202) 707–5100; (202) 707–0744 TDD.

Recording for the Blind (RFB) is a nonprofit organization that serves people with a print disability—blindness, low vision, learning disabilities, or physical impairments that affect reading. RFB's core services include a free library of recorded books and a recording service for any new titles. An additional service is a listing of books on a computer diskette. Contact them for a catalog subscription. **Write:** RFB, 20

Roszel Road, Princeton, NJ 08540 or **Phone:** (609)–452 0606.

HEARING IMPAIRMENTS

According to IDEA, "hearing impairment" is defined as an impairment in hearing, whether permanent or fluctuating, that adversely affects a child's educational performance. This is in contrast to **deafness,** which is an impairment so severe that a child is unable to use hearing to understand speech, with or without amplification, although it may be possible to perceive some sounds. A child who is considered **hard-of-hearing** would require special adaptations (i.e., amplification, auditory training, etc.) for the successful delivery of educational services, yet it is possible for such a child to benefit from speech and other auditory stimulation. Hearing impairment and deafness are often categorized as being either **congenital** (present at birth) or **adventitious** (acquired later in life). Moreover, there are two general classes of hearing loss: **conductive** and **sensorineural.** A conductive loss, affecting the intensity or loudness of sound, is usually caused by interference with the transmission of sound from the outer to the inner ear. This interference can be caused by birth defects such as incomplete or malformed auditory canals, an illness or disease that leaves fluid or debris in the ear, or even an excessive build-up of earwax. A sensorineural loss affects the intelligibility and clarity of sounds and it is typically the result of damage to parts of the middle and inner ear or a lack of functioning of the auditory nerve.

Although we should be careful when making generalizations about the characteristics of individuals with hearing impairments, it is clear that the effects of a hearing impairment can be complex and pervasive. As noted by Heward and Orlansky (1992), hearing children tend to acquire their vocabulary, knowledge of grammar, idiomatic expressions, and other aspects of verbal behavior by listening to others. As a result of limited exposure to verbal communication, children with hearing impairments often have significant language deficits and tend to lag behind their hearing peers in academic achievement.

AVAILABLE RESOURCES: HI
Generic Textbooks

> Luetke-Stahlman, B., & Luckner, J. (1991). *Effectively educating students with hearing impairments.* White Plains, NY: Longman.

Luterman, D. M. (1986). *Deafness in perspective*. San Diego: College Hill.

Moores, D. F. (1987). *Educating the deaf: Psychology, principles, and practices*. Boston: Houghton Mifflin.

Paul, P., & Quigley, S. (1990). *Education and deafness*. White Plains, NY: Longman.

Vernon, M., & Andrews, J. (1990). *The psychology of deafness: Understanding deaf and hard-of-hearing people*. White Plains, NY: Longman.

Resource Books

Baker-Shenk, C., & Cokely, D. (1980). *American Sign Language: A teacher's resource text on grammar and culture*. Washington, DC: Gallaudet University Press.
> Written for teachers with minimal knowledge of linguistics, this guide explains the grammar and structure of American Sign Language. A description of the Deaf community in the United States is included.

Bess, F. (1988). *Hearing impairment in children*. Timonium, MD: York Press, Inc.
> This edited text emphasizes a multidisciplinary approach to the study of hearing loss in children. Emphasis is placed on the management of hearing-impaired children; review of current knowledge; new approaches to assessment; parental role and services; and a comprehensive discussion of amplification for children.

Bornstein, H., Saulnier, K., & Hamilton, L. (1983). *The comprehensive Signed English dictionary*. Washington, DC: Gallaudet University Press.
> This illustrated volume has over 3,100 signs used in the Signed English system. In addition, there is a section which provides a general description of the Signed English system.

Bornstein, H. (1990). *Manual communication: Implications for education.* Washington, DC: Gallaudet University Press.

> This edited volume describes the sign systems commonly used in the education of deaf students: American Sign Language, Pidgin Sign, Signed English, Signed Exact English, and Cued Speech.

Bornstein, H., & Saulnier, K. *The Signed English starter.* (1984). Washington, DC: Gallaudet University Press.

> Targeted at beginners, this guide contains 940 basic signs used in Signed English, arranged topically. Practice exercises are included.

Bowe, F. (1991). *Approaching equality.* Silver Spring, MD: T. J. Publishers.

Bowe, F. (1986). *Changing the rules.* Silver Spring, MD: T. J. Publishers.

Hairston, E., & Smith, L. (1983). *Black and deaf in America: Are we that different.* Silver Spring, MD: T. J. Publishers.

Walworth, M., Moores, D. F., & O'Rourke, T. J. (1992). *A free hand: Enfranchising the education of deaf children.* Silver Spring, MD: T. J. Publishers.

Woodward, J. (1982). *How you gonna get to heaven if you can't talk with Jesus.* Silver Spring, MD: T. J. Publishers.

> These five books offered by T. J. Publishers spotlight deafness, sign language, and deaf culture. They discuss public laws which guarantee special education programs for deaf children, the effectiveness of ASL, personal accounts of the struggle for equal rights, and the relationship between deaf culture and hearing society.

Christensen, K., & Delgado, G. (1993). *Multicultural issues in deafness.* White Plains, NY: Longman.

> This is a collection of papers which provides information on how to best serve the special needs of deaf students from diverse populations including African-Americans, Hispanics, Native Americans, and Asian/Pacific Island Americans.

Gannon, J. (1981). *Deaf heritage: A narrative history of deaf America.* Silver Spring, MD: National Association of the Deaf.

> This resource is a comprehensive, multi-faceted history of the population of individuals with hearing loss. This 480–page volume chronicles historical events and individuals and can serve as an in-depth view of deaf culture. A companion student text and workbook is also available.

Kluwin, T. N., Moores, D. F., & Gonter-Gaustand, M. (1992). *Toward effective public school programs for deaf students: Context, process, & outcomes.* New York, NY: Teachers College Press.

> This issues-oriented edited text uses new data to define the complex issues involved in the public education of deaf children. The authors recommend possible courses of action for organizing effective public school programs. Specifically, chapters deal with how different deaf constituencies have unique needs; how the family contributes to and makes demands on the school system; how, based on some criteria, deaf children are succeeding; and how, using other criteria, they are losing out.

Luterman, D., & Ross, M. (1991). *When your child is deaf: A guide for parents.* Timonium, MD: York Press, Inc.

> Parents of newly diagnosed hearing-impaired children can use this guide to understand the impact of a hearing impairment to the parenting process and to review current audiological procedures, amplifying systems, educational philosophies, coping mechanisms, and lists of helpful organizations.

Martin, D. (1991). *Advances in cognition, education, and deafness.* Washington, DC: Gallaudet University Press.

Moores, D. F., & Meadow-Orlans, K. P. (1990). *Educational and developmental aspects of deafness.* Washington, DC: Gallaudet University Press.

> These are two edited volumes that address specific issues involved in the education and development of deaf individuals. Topics in the Martin volume, a collection of papers and presentations from the Second International Symposium on Cognition, Education, and Deafness, include (a)

cognitive assessment, (b) language and cognition, (c) neuroscientific issues, and (d) cognitive intervention programs. The Moores & Meadow-Orlans volume zeros in on issues surrounding the deaf child in school and at home.

O'Rourke, T. J. (1973). *A basic course in manual communication: (Student and teacher manuals)*. Silver Spring, MD: National Association for the Deaf.

These materials, published by the National Association for the Deaf, are geared toward teaching basic sign language. The first book teaches signed English while the other teaches American Sign Language. This curriculum includes conversationally relevant signs, fingerspelling, grammatical sign principles, and background, cultural, and linguistic information related to deaf people and sign language.

Ross, M. (1990). *Hearing-impaired children in the mainstream*. Timonium, MD: York Press, Inc.

This edited text reviews the components involved in helping hearing-impaired students become appropriately mainstreamed from the elementary years to the college level. Components include the audiological evaluation, effective IEPs, exemplary public and private programs, staff and resource developments, parental involvement, assessment of speech and language abilities and of psycho-educational functioning, and an analysis of the psycho-social implications of being hearing-impaired. The intended readers include audiologists, speech pathologists, parents, administrators, and special and regular classroom teachers involved in the mainstreaming process.

Roush, J., & Matkin, N. (1992). *Infants & toddlers with hearing loss: Family-centered assessment and intervention*. Timonium, MD: York Press, Inc.

This text explores issues pertaining to identification, assessment, and early intervention programs for young children with hearing impairments within a family-oriented framework. Practitioners and educators involved in the early intervention services make up the intended audience.

Schwartz, S. (1987). *Choices in deafness: A parents' guide.* Rockville, MD: Woodbine House.

> This text provides a clear overview of three communication methods commonly used by deaf people: cued speech, the oral approach, and total communication.

Shimon, D. A. (1991). *Coping with hearing loss and hearing aids.* San Diego, CA: Singular.

> In clear, understandable language, this text is full of practical, authoritative information and advice about types of hearing loss, where to go for professional care, what to expect, how hearing aids work, how to shop for them intelligently, and how to get them repaired. Special features include a resource chapter showing where to get additional information about hearing loss, hearing devices, and hearing help, and which companies offer products made specifically for people with hearing problems.

Stuart, L. G. (1986). *Case studies in clinical rehabilitation assessment and hearing impairment.* Silver Spring, MD: The National Association for the Deaf.

Stuart, L. G. (1986). *Clinical rehabilitation assessment and hearing impairment: A guide to quality assurance.* Silver Spring, MD: The National Association for the Deaf.

> These handbooks, designed for rehabilitation, education, and other service providers, provide information related to assessment procedures, techniques, and issues in the psychological, psychiatric, neuropsychological, vocational, and related areas of education of hearing-impaired persons. Chapters deal with subjects such as psychological assessment, psychiatric assessment, and vocational assessment. Case studies evaluate such assessments.

Multimedia

Hearing and Speech Video Series. Princeton, NJ: Films for the Humanities, Inc.

> This is a series of five videos that explores the difficulties encountered by the hearing impaired and how individuals can be helped through technological advances and being taught how to sign. Tiles of videos include: **"An introduc-**

tory course in ASL"; "Hearing;" and "Crossing the silence barrier."

Periodicals

American Annals of the Deaf, published by the Conference of Educational Administrators Serving the Deaf and the Convention of American Instructors of the Deaf, typically contains research, integrative reviews, and theoretical articles pertaining to the education and delivery of services to deaf and hearing impaired students. **Write:** American Annals of the Deaf, 814 Thayer Ave., Silver Spring, MD 20910.

Journal of American Deafness and Rehabilitation Association (Formerly Journal of the Rehabilitation of the Deaf), emphasizes research, innovations, and service delivery patterns related to the needs of deaf adults. **Write:** Journal of American Deafness and Rehabilitation Association, P.O. Box 251554, Little Rock, AR 72225.

Journal of Speech and Hearing Disorders, published quarterly by the American Speech-Language-Hearing Association (ASHA), contains articles dealing with the nature, assessment, and treatment of the variety of communication disorders. **Write:** ASHA, 10801 Rockville Pike, Rockville, MD 20852.

Perspectives in Education and Deafness, published bi-monthly throughout the school year, offers practical information on successful teaching strategies, current issues in deafness, and creative ideas for family and community activities. Most articles are written by educators who deliver services to individuals with hearing impairments. **Write:** Perspectives, Gallaudet University, 800 Florida Ave., N.E., Washington, DC, 20078–0603.

Sign Language Studies, published quarterly, contains
both research studies and applied articles on topics
involving manual communication. **Write:** Sign Language Studies, Linstok Press, 9306 Mintwood Street,
Silver Spring, MD 20901.

Volta Review, published nine times a year by the Alexander Graham Bell Association for the Deaf, advocates an oral approach to the education of deaf
students and contains articles on teaching speech,
speech reading, and the use of residual hearing.
Write: Alexander Graham Bell Institute for the Deaf,
3417 Volta Place, N.W., Washington, DC 20007.

Organizations

The **Alexander Graham Bell Association for the Deaf**
encourages the use of residual hearing and the teaching of speech and speechreading. The Association's
programs and services touch every facet of hearing
impairment. Current activities include:

—Hearing Alert! (A public education program to encourage early identification of hearing loss, particularly in in-
fants, and to promote the need for prompt remedial
action)
—Parent/Infant Preschool Services Financial Aid Program
—Free First-Year Parent Membership Awards
—Children's Rights: Focusing primarily on the 1– to 16–
year-old group
—Arts and Sciences Award
—Scholarships
—Financial Aid Awards
—Publications including textbooks, the Association's professional journal,**The Volta Review,** the topical newsletter, **Newsounds,** and **Our Kids Magazine**
—Chapters: Seventeen state and provincial Association
chapters

—Regional Educational Conferences and Workshops
—Biennial International Convention
—Research Library

Write: Alexander Graham Bell Association for the Deaf, 3417 Volta Place, N.W., Washington, DC 20007–2778 or **Phone:** (202) 337–5220 (TDD and Voice).

The **American Deafness and Rehabilitation Association (ADARA)** is a network of professionals and community persons who serve people who are deaf or hard of hearing. The organization sponsors forums, conferences, and workshops, as well as publishing a journal and a newsletter. A publication list is available, as is a referral service on careers, university programs, and job opportunities. **Write:** ADARA, P.O. Box 25154, Little Rock, AR 72225 or **Phone:** (501)663–7074.

The **American Society for Deaf Children (ASDC)** offers advocacy, information, and support to families and professionals of deaf and hard-of-hearing children. It provides networking and referral services, publications and resources, and promotes signed communication for complete participation in all aspects of daily communication and life. Services include ASDC's newsletter, **The Endeavor,** position papers on critical issues in deafness, a speakers bureau, referral services, a biennial national convention, and parent-to-parent networks. **Write:** ASDC, 814 Thayer Avenue, Silver Spring, MD 20910 or **Phone:** (800) 942–ASDC.

American Speech-Language-Hearing Association (ASHA), the major organization concerned with speech and language, provides a wealth of information speech/language/hearing disorders and services available for treatment. In addition to certifying professionals, ASHA publishes professional journals, a comprehensive guide to professional services, and numerous brochures of interest to parents, educators, and therapists. **Write:** ASHA, 10801 Rockville Pike, Rockville, MD 20852.

The **Gallaudet University Bookstore** has one of the most complete collections of professional and popular literature about hearing impairments and communication disorders as well as a large selection of children's sign language books. The bookstore provides free catalogs of their holdings. **Write:** Gallaudet University Bookstore, 800 Florida Ave., N.E., Washington, DC, 20002.

The **International Hearing Society (IHS),** formerly the National Hearing Aid Society, is the professional association of hearing instrument specialists. The organization publishes and markets a number of brochures, texts, and videos pertaining to the hearing and hearing aids. **Write:** IHS, 20361 Middlebelt Road, Livonia, MI 48152 or **Phone:** (313) 478–2610.

The **National Association of the Deaf (NAD)** is committed to assuring that a comprehensive, coordinated system of services is accessible to all persons with hearing impairments enabling them to achieve their maximum potential through increased independence, productivity, and integration into the community. The organization publishes a number of books, monographs, and periodicals including **The Deaf American. Write:** NAD, 814 Thayer Avenue, Silver Spring, MD 20910–4500 or **Phone:** (301) 587–1788; (301) 587–1791 (TDD).

The **National Information Center on Deafness (NICD),** located on the Gallaudet University campus, is a centralized source of accurate, up-to-date, objective information on topics dealing with deafness and hearing loss. NICD responds to questions from the general public and hearing impaired people, their families, friends, and professionals who work with them. NICD collects, develops, and disseminates information on all aspects of hearing loss and programs and services offered to deaf and hard-of-hearing persons across the nation. **Write:** NICD, Gallaudet University, 800 Florida Ave., N.E., Washington, DC 20002–3695 or **Phone:** (202) 651–5051; (202)651–5052 (TDD).

DEAF-BLINDNESS

Deaf-blindness is concomitant hearing and visual impairments, the combination of which causes severe communication and other developmental and educational problems that cannot be accommodated in special education programs solely for children with deafness or children with blindness.

AVAILABLE RESOURCES:
Deaf-Blindness
Generic Text

Sauerburger, D. *Independence without sight or sound*. New York, NY: American Foundation for the Blind.

Resource Book

Jones, C. (1988). *Evaluation and educational programming of deaf-blind/severely multihandicapped students: Sensorimotor stage*. Springfield, IL: Charles C. Thomas.
> Included in this text are the evaluation and programming of hearing, vision, secondary senses, motor development, cognition, receptive/expressive language, and social/emotional development. A bibliography is also included.

Organizations

The **American Association of the Deaf-Blind (AADB)** is a national consumer advocacy organization for people who have combined hearing and vision impairments. It holds an annual convention and has chapters around the country. The organization also provides technical assistance to deaf-blind persons, families, educators, and service providers. **Write:** AADB, 814 Thayer Ave., Silver Spring, MD 20910, or **Phone:** (301) 588–6545.

The **National Coalition on Deaf-Blindness,** and its sponsoring organizations, is committed to the continuation of services and to advocacy of on-going federal responsibility for individuals with deaf-blindness. Membership is comprised of deaf-blind consumers, family members, professionals in the field of education and rehabilitation, and other concerned citizens. Coalition activities are primarily concerned with advocacy on the federal level and include information letters, individual testimony to congressional committees dealing with the issues on the handicapped, and direct contact with members of congress. **Write:** National Coalition on Deaf-Blindness, 175 North Beacon Street, Watertown, MA 02172 or **Phone:** (617) 924–3434, ext. 502.

Communication Disorders

Communication disorders are quite common in children and youths. In fact, children with communication problems account for approximately 23 percent of all students who receive special education services—the second largest category (students with LD comprise the largest group, accounting for 48 percent). In general, a distinction is made between speech disorders and language disorders: **speech disorders** are primarily problems in producing sounds accurately while **language disorders** involve problems in understanding and/or expressing the symbols people use to communicate with each other.

There are three major categories of speech disorders: articulation disorders, voice disorders, and fluency disorders. Articulation problems are identified when speech sounds are either omitted or produced in an abnormal fashion. Voice disorders are the absence of voice or the abnormal production of vocal quality, pitch, loudness, resonance, and/or duration. Finally, fluency disorders occur when there is an abnormal flow of verbal expression, such as in the case of stuttering.

A language disorder is the impairment or delayed development in one or more of the many systems involved in the comprehension or use of spoken or written language. The disorder may involve the form of language (phonologic, morphologic, and syntactic systems), the content of language (semantic system), and/or the function of language in communication (pragmatic system). When considering problems concerning the **form of language, phonology** refers to the linguisitic rules that govern sound combinations, **morphology** refers to the rule system that governs the structure of words and the construction of word forms, and **syntax** refers to the rule system that governs the order and combination of words to form sentences, and the relationships among elements within a sentence. When considering problems involving the **content of language, semantics** refers to attaching meaning to what is received or expressed. Finally, when considering problems related to the **function of language, pragmatics** refers to the social aspects of language designed to get things accomplished.

As there is no clear relationship between types of language problems and possible causes, most professionals rely on descriptions of language skills and competence when planning interventions.

AVAILABLE RESOURCES:
Communication Disorders
Generic Textbooks

Berko Gleason, J. (1993). *The development of language.* New York, NY: Merrill/Macmillan.

Bernstein, D., Tiegerman, E., & Radziewicz, C. (1993). *Language and communication disorders in children.* New York, NY: Merrill/Macmillan.

Brookshire, R. H. (1993). *An introduction to neurogenic communication disorders.* St. Louis: Mosby.

Camarata, S. M. (1993). *The diagnosis and treatment of phonological disorders in children.* St. Louis: Mosby.

Chapman, R. (1992). *Processes in language acquisition and disorders.* St. Louis: Mosby.

Creaghead, N. A., Newman, P. W., & Secord, W. (1989). *Assesment and remediation of articulatory and phological disorders.* Columbus, OH: Merrill.

Lass, N., McReynolds, L., Northern, J., & Yoder, D. (1988). *Handbook of speech-language pathology and audiology.* St. Louis: Mosby.

Love, R. (1992). *Childhood motor speech disability.* New York, NY: Merrill/Macmillan.

McCormick, L., & Schiefelbusch, R. (1990). *Early language intervention: An introduction.* New York, NY: Merrill/Macmillan.

Ohde, R., & Sharf, D. J. (1992). *Phonetic analysis of normal and abnormal speech.* New York, NY: Merrill/Macmillan.

Owens, R. E. *Language development: An introduction.* New York, NY: Merrill/Macmillan.

Shames, G. H., & Wiig, E. (1990). *Human communication disorders: An introduction.* New York, NY: Merrill/Macmillan.

Stemple, J. C. (1992). *Voice therapy: Clinical studies.* St. Louis: Mosby.

Taylor, J. (1992). *Speech-language pathology services in the schools.* Boston: Allyn & Bacon.

Resource Books

Beukelman, D., & Mirenda, P. *Augmentative and alternative communication: Management of severe communication disorders in children and adults.* (1992). Baltimore: Paul H. Brookes.
> This text presents strategies for preparing those involved in implementing augmentative and alternative communication and describes intervention techniques appropriate for children and adults with congenital or acquired communication disorders.

Cipani, E. (1991). *A guide to developing language competence in preschool children with severe and moderate handicaps.* Springfield, IL: Charles C. Thomas.
> Professionals and parents can use this guide as they serve young children with severe and moderate handicaps. The book suggests program planning and individual treatment planning techniques and procedures for language development.

Fletcher, P. (1992). *Specific speech and language disorders in children*. San Diego, CA: Singular.

> Text contains the latest information available on the biological, genetic, and physical bases of language disorders; brain injury, cognition, and language impairment; cross-cultural perspectives of language impairment; and the intervention and curriculum concerns in the schools.

Kagan, A., & Saling, M. (1992). *An introduction to Luria's aphasiology: Theory and application*. Baltimore, MD: Paul H. Brookes.

> The authors present a comprehensive overview of Luria's theoretical principles underlying the neuropsychological approach and the classifications of aphasia, its assessment, therapy, and clinical applications. The intended readers include speech-language pathologists, neurologists, and clinicians working with persons with aphasia or other communication disorders.

Kumin, L. (1993). *Communication skills in children with Down syndrome: A guide for parents*. Rockville, MD: Woodbine House.

> This guide to speech, communication, and language skills in children with Down syndrome spans infancy through the early teenage years. It contains information on problems that often contribute to communication delays, as well as activities that are designed to help maximize communication potential. Discussion includes speech and language therapy and evaluation, school and community performance, and intelligibility issues.

Moller, K., Starr, & Johnson, S. (1990). *A parent's guide to cleft lip & palate*. Minneapolis: University of Minnesota Press.

> The many diagrams and photographs in this book help to clarify the nature and treatment of cleft lip and palate. Also included are sections on feeding, ear problems, dental problems, speech problems, and social and psychological development.

Moore, C., Yorkston, K., & Beukelman, D. (1991). *Dysarthria and apraxia of speech*. Baltimore, MD: Paul H. Brookes.

> For educators, researchers, and practicing clinicians in the field of motor speech disorders, this text presents research from the Fifth Biennial Clinical Dysarthria Conference and includes work of speech-language pathologists, speech physiologists, physiatrists, and neurologists.

Oyer, H., Crowe, B., & Haas, W. (1987). *Speech language and hearing disorders: A guide for the teacher*. Boston: Allyn & Bacon.

> The authors provide a readable and practical overview of speech, language, and hearing conditions which affect school-aged children and what the classroom teacher can do about them.

Perkins, W.H. (1991). *Stuttering prevented*. San Diego, CA: Singular.

> Text contains information on what causes stuttering, how to prevent it, and how to stop it. The section on stutterer prevention strategies defines ways that are helpful in all circumstances.

Reichle, J., York, J., & Sigafoos, J. (1991). *Implementing augmentative and alternative communication: Strategies for learners with severe disabilities*. Baltimore, MD: Paul H. Brookes.

> This reference describes how appropriate intervention can help learners overcome severe communication barriers. It presents strategies for initiating and developing successful augmentative communication programs for people with severe communication impairments that are implemented throughout the learner's day.

Rice, M., & Schiefelbusch, R. (1989). *The teachability of language*. Baltimore, MD: Paul H. Brookes.

> This text explores the theoretical aspects of language acquisition and provides a synthesis of the teachability of language and the parameters of language, language content, learner characteristics, teaching and learning strategies, and intervention techniques.

Multimedia

Hearing and Speech Video Series. Princeton, NJ: Films for the Humanities, Inc.

> This is a series of three videos which explores various aspects of speech and language disorders. Titles include: **"Stuttering and other speech disorders"; "Speech";** and **"Figures of speech."**

Periodicals

Journal of Speech and Hearing Disorders, published quarterly by the American Speech-Language-Hearing Association (ASHA), contains articles dealing with the nature, assessment, and treatment of a variety of communication disorders. **Write:** ASHA, 10801 Rockville Pike, Rockville, MD 20852.

Language, Speech, and Hearing Services in the Schools, published quarterly by ASHA, focuses on the practical application of speech and language interventions. Numerous activities for teachers and therapists are typically provided. **Write:** ASHA, 10801 Rockville Pike, Rockville, MD 20852.

Organizations

American Speech-Language-Hearing Association (ASHA), the major organization concerned with speech and language, provides a wealth of information on speech/language/hearing disorders and services available for treatment. In addition to certifying professionals, ASHA publishes professional journals, a comprehensive guide to professional services, and numerous brochures of interest to parents, educators, and therapists. **Write:** ASHA, 10801 Rockville Pike, Rockville, MD 20852.

Cleft Palate Foundation is a non-profit organization dedicated to assisting patients with birth defects of the head and neck and their families. CPF helps patients and their families understand these birth defects through its publications, which include informational brochures and fact sheets, and the **Parents & Patients Newsletter.** Through CLEFTLINE, a toll-free informational service, CPF refers interested parties to groups of professionals in their area who are skilled in the management of cleft lip, cleft palate, and other craniofacial deformities. **Write:** Cleft Palate Foundation, 1218 Grandview Avenue, Pittsburgh, PA 15211 or **Phone:** (412) 481–1376.

Closing the Gap is an internationally recognized source of information on the use of microcomputer-related technology by and for exceptional individuals. Closing the Gap is committed to providing up-to-date information on commercially available hardware and software products that can enable individuals with communication disorders to enhance their ability to communicate. Services include conferences, information dissemination, and the publication of a bimonthly newspaper and a comprehensive resource guide directory which contains a comprehensive listing of commercially available hardware and software appropriate for special education and rehabilitation. **Write:** Closing the Gap, P.O. Box 68, Henderson, MN 56044 or **Phone:** (612) 248–3294.

Division for Children with Communication Disorders (DCCD) is dedicated to improving the education and welfare of children with hearing, speech, and language disorders. The organization publishes the **Journal of Childhood Communication Disorders** and **The DCCD Newsletter** twice yearly. **Write:** DCCD, CEC, 1920 Association Drive, Reston, VA 22091 or **Phone:** (703) 620–3660.

Stuttering Foundation of America, a nonprofit organization dedicated to the prevention and treatment of stuttering, provides a wide range of services and produces a number of helpful publications. The organization maintains a toll-free hotline (800–992–9392) to answer questions, provides a nation-wide resource list of professionals, organizes conferences, and publishes books and brochures. Of use to teachers is the brochure entitled **The Child Who Stutters at School: Notes to the Teacher. Write:** Stuttering Foundation of America, P.O. Box 11749, Memphis, TN 38111–0749.

Physical Disabilities

According to Best (1992), the area of **physical disability** is the most diverse of all the various types of exceptionality. This is due, in part, to the large number of terms and descriptors that have been used, both appropriately and inappropriately, in discussions of the disability. IDEA refers to students with physical impairments as having **orthopedic impairments**. Orthopedic disabilities are muscular, skeletal, or neurological impairments so severe that they affect a child's educational performance. The term includes impairments caused by congenital anomaly, disease, and other causes such as amputations, fractures, and burns. The three major types of orthopedic disabilities in children are **cerebral palsy (CP)**, **muscular dystrophy,** and **spina bifida.**

AVAILABLE RESOURCES:
Physical Disabilities
Generic Textbook

> Bigge, J. (1991). *Teaching individuals with physical and multiple disabilities.* New York, NY: Merrill/Macmillan.

Resource Books

> Beck, E., & Nagel, D. (1982). *Physically handicapped children: A medical atlas for teachers.* Des Moines, IA: Longwood.
> > Fundamental medical facts relevant to students with physical handicaps are presented and are accompanied by practical suggestions for teachers. A nice feature of this atlas is that it describes the disabling conditions with thoroughness and in everyday language.

> Bloom, B., & Seljeskog, E. (1988). *A parent's guide to spina bifida.* Minneapolis: University of Minnesota Press.
> > While mainly concerned with types of spina bifida, this brief book also touches on other neural tube defects such as anencephaly and encephalocele. The book discusses causes and treatment, associated problems such as hydrocephalus,

orthopedic problems, and bladder and bowel control problems, and daily care issues.

Burnett, P.S. *Independent living: Functioning with the use of
one hand in a two-handed world*. Thorofare, NJ: Slack.
This "how-to" book for individuals with only one hand includes tips on bathing, personal grooming, getting dressed,
kitchen routines, shopping for food, general housework,
caring for children, reading and writing, recreation, and
travel.

Finnie, N. (1975). *Handling the young cerebral palsied child
at home*. New York: Dutton/New American Library.
Originally published in Great Britain, this illustrated classic
describes abnormal movements and postures associated
with cerebral palsy, and explores issues related to daily
management and development.

Geralis, E. (1991). *Children with cerebral palsy: A parents'
guide*. Rockville, MD: Woodbine House.
This edited guide explains what cerebral palsy is, discusses
its diagnosis and treatment, and provides information
about daily care, positioning and handling, early intervention, therapies, educational options, and family life.

Kriegsman, K., Zaslow, E., & D'Zmura-Rechsteiner, J.
(1992). *Taking charge: Teenagers talk about life and physical disabilities*. Rockville, MD: Woodbine House.
Written for teens in grades 7 12, this book explores the
wide range of issues that teenagers with cerebral palsy,
spina bifida, muscular dystrophy, osteogenesis imperfecta,
and other physical disabilities face as they approach adulthood. The authors suggest ways for the teenagers to handle
remarks, stares, and unwanted attention; to help family,
friends, and strangers recognize the teen's individuality
first and disability second; and to emphasize personal
strengths and overcome limitations. It is a book of solutions.

Mayall, J., & Desharnais, G. (1990). *Positioning in a wheelchair: A guide for professional care givers of the disabled adult*. Thorofare, NJ: Slack.

> The purpose of the manual is to provide care givers with the knowledge of various techniques and appliances that optimize seating comfort and positioning of the older adult with mild to moderate positioning problems. Although primarily intended for adults in long-term care settings, the information will be of use for all care givers who deliver services to those in wheelchairs.

Perske, R. (1986). *Don't stop the music*. Nashville, TN: Abingdon Press.

> The author provides an action-packed adventure showing how persons with handicaps can contribute positively to the community. Joe and Jessica, two teens with cerebral palsy, become key elements in cracking an auto-theft ring.

Rowley-Kelly, F., & Reigel, D. (1992). *Teaching the student with spina bifida*. Baltimore: Paul H. Brookes.

> Designed for teachers and parents, this book offers insight into many of the commonly asked questions regarding the assessment and education of students with spina bifida.

Whinston, J.L. (1989). *I'm Joshua & "yes I can."* New York, NY: Vantage Press, Inc.

> This book is written by a parent of a child who has cerebral palsy. It focuses on the first day of first grade for Joshua, revealing both the parents' and the child's fears and anxieties. Through the support of the people around him, Joshua eventually learns that he is capable of doing many things. As a result, he can then dream, hope, and set goals as his non-handicapped peers do.

Williamson, G. *Children with spina bifida: Early intervention and preschool programming*. (1987). Baltimore: Paul H. Brookes.

> This guide for parents and educators covers assessment and intervention procedures for infants and young children with spina bifida. Topics addressed include postural control and mobility, perceptual-motor skills, speech and language, and activities of daily living.

Multimedia

"Teaching the student with spina bifida videotape," marketed by Paul H. Brookes, is a companion to the book by the same name. The 31–minute videotape provides information on the health, cognitive, and so-cial-personal needs of students with spina bifida.

Periodicals

ACCENT on Living, published quarterly, provides practical information written by and about individuals with physical and health impairments. Topics include independent living, employment, architectural barriers, and family concerns. **Write:** ACCENT on Living, P.O. Box 700, Bloomington, IL 61701.

Disability Rag is a bimonthly publication that offers an honest, sometimes spicy and irreverent look at disability issues. It is frequently a forum for opinion and debate with articles on telethons, legal issues, and media portrayals of individuals with disabilities. **Write:** The Disability Rag, P.O. Box 145, Louisville, KY 40201.

New Mobility is an informational periodical for people with spinal injury, disease, and other mobility-related disabilities including multiple sclerosis, post-polio syndrome, spina bifida, and ALS. **Write:** Spinal Network's **New Mobility** Publisher, Sam Maddox, 1911 11th Street, Suite 301, Boulder, CO 80302 or **Phone:** (303) 449–5412.

Organizations

The **Association of Birth Defect Children** is a national organization that provides technical information for

parents and professionals. The organization has a
number of useful videotapes, fact packs, and practical newsletters. **Write:** Association of Birth Defect
Children, 5400 Diplomat Circle, Suite 270, Orlando,
FL 32810 or **Phone:** (407) 629–1466.

The **Division for Physical and Health Disabilities
(DPHD)** promotes quality programs for physically
disabled and/or health impaired individuals. The or-
ganization publishes a journal, **Physical Disabilities-
Education and Related Services,** each year and the
DPH Newsletter quarterly. **Write:** DPHD, CEC, 1920
Association Drive, Reston, VA 22091 or **Phone:** (703)
620–3660.

The **Muscular Dystrophy Association's (MDA)** prime
objective is the support of scientific investigators
seeking the causes of and effective treatments for
muscular dystrophy and related neuromuscular disorders (over 40 neuromuscular diseases). In addition,
MDA provides a broad range of patient and community services including 191 MDA field offices, a network of 235 hospital-affiliated clinics which provide
diagnostic services and therapeutic and rehabilitative
follow-up care, summer camping activities geared to
the special needs of those with neuromuscular diseases (for ages 6–21), and professional and public
health education services including publications, conferences, educational materials, and postresidency
training at MDA clinics. **Write:** MDA, National Headquarters, 3561 East Sunrise Drive, Tucson, AZ 84718
or **Phone:** (602) 529–2000.

The **National Multiple Sclerosis Society** serves persons
with MS, their families, health professionals, and the
public. The Society provides funding for research,
public and professional education, advocacy, and the
design of rehabilitative and psychosocial programs.
Direct services to people with MS are provided

through 140 local chapters. Information services include publications, and client information includes pamphlets on family coping, mental and emotional health, and **Inside MS,** a membership's periodical. Professionals may request publications on treatment, nursing care, group counseling, and reprints of journal articles. Referrals, information on technical aids and equipment, and order lists for free publications can be obtained from chapters. The National Information Resource Center and Library can be reached by calling 1–800–LEARN-MS. **Write:** National Multiple Sclerosis Society, 733 Third Avenue, New York, NY 10017–3288 or **Phone:** (212) 986–3240.

The **National Spinal Cord Injury Association (NSCIA)** provides information about spinal cord injury and related subjects to individuals, families, health care professionals, and other agencies. There are 35 local chapters in a number of states across the country. Services provided include a support system for children and their families, entitled "In Town with Kids," and a referral network. **Write:** NSCIA, 600 W. Cummings Park, Suite 2000, Woburn, MA 01801 or **Phone:** (800) 962–9629.

The **National Wheelchair Athletic Association** is a multi-sport organization for disabled athletes. Through the Association, disabled athletes compete annually in regional, national, and international competitions. The NWAA acts as the coordinating body for 11 regional sports organizations which sponsor sanctioned events at the local and regional level, leading to the National Wheelchair Games. Sports include the American Wheelchair Archers; American Wheelchair Table Tennis Association; National Wheelchair Shooting Federation; U.S. Wheelchair Swimming; U.S. Wheelchair Weightlifting Federation; and Wheelchair Athletics of the U.S.A. Adult and Junior division sports opportunities are available. **Write:** National Wheelchair Athletic Association, 3595 E. Fountain Blvd., Suite L-1, Colorado Springs, CO 80910 or **Phone:** (719) 574–1150.

The **Phoenix Society for Burn Survivors** works to overcome burn trauma and to ease the return to regular, productive lives through a number of activities. The society helps educators understand the physical and emotional changes associated with this injury and how they can assist children in returning to the mainstream of life. **Write:** The Phoenix Society, 11 Rust Hill Road, Levittown, PA 19056 or **Phone:** (800) 888–BURN.

The **Spina Bifida Association of America (SBAA)** is an association of parents, adults with this birth defect, and professionals. The organization provides support and information through local chapters throughout the country. Activities include the monitoring of legislation, conferences, and workshops, as well as social and educational programs. The organization has considerable print and audio-visual materials available and publishes a newsletter, **INSIGHTS. Write:** SBAA, 1700 Rockville Pike, Suite 540, Rockville, MD 20852 or **Phone:** (800) 621–3141.

United Cerebral Palsy Associations, Inc. (UCP) is a nationwide network of approximately 180 state and local voluntary agencies which provide services, conduct public and professional education programs, and support research in cerebral palsy. Services and programs offered by the United Cerebral Palsy Association are directed to children and adults with cerebral palsy and their families. The national organization distributes a newsletter and other publications. **Write:** UCP, Governmental Activities Office, 1522 K. Street N.W., Suite 1112, Washington, DC 20005 or **Phone:** (800) USA-2UCP.

Traumatic Brain Injury and Health Impairments

Traumatic Brain Injury (TBI) is one of the newest categories of disability in IDEA. It refers to an acquired injury to the brain caused by an external force, resulting in total or partial functional disability and/or psychosocial impairment which adversely affects a child's educational performance. TBI applies to open and closed head injuries resulting in impairments in one or more of the following areas: cognition, language memory, attention, reasoning, abstract thinking, judgment, problem-solving, sensory, perceptual, and motor abilities, psychosocial behavior, information processing, and speech. TBI does not apply to congenital or degenerative brain injuries, or those caused by birth trauma.

As used in IDEA, the catchall label **"other health impairments"** refers to a wide range of acute health problems (e.g., heart problems, tuberculosis, rheumatic fever, asthma, leukemia, diabetes, etc.) that adversely affect educational performance. Also included are children who are **chronically ill** and **medically fragile** and children whose disability (e.g., Tourette syndrome or epilepsy) does not fit any of the other categories in IDEA. These problems may be the result of some specific condition or of a child's need for life support mechanisms (e.g., ventilator or oxygen dependent).

AVAILABLE RESOURCES: Health Impairments/TBI
Resource Books

Begali, V. (1993). *Head injury in children and adolescents*. Brandon, VT: CPPC.

> This resource for school and allied professionals addresses the physiological, cognitive, social, behavioral management, psychological consequences, and prognosis of traumatic head injury.

Durgin, C. D., Schmidt, N. D., & Fryer, L. J. (1993). *Staff development and clinical intervention in brain injury rehabilitation*. Gaithersburg, MD: Aspen.

> This is an edited text that features practical methods and materials for designing inservice models that assist care

providers to be more responsive to client, family, and staff needs.

Freeman, J., Vining, P., & Pillas, D. (1990). *Seizures and epilepsy in childhood: A guide for parents.* Baltimore: Johns Hopkins University Press.

>   This overview of the nature, diagnosis, and treatment of seizures emphasizes the potential of many children with epilepsy to lead relatively "normal" lives. Includes a short chapter on learning and behavior.

Fussey, I., & Giles, G. M. (1988). *Rehabilitation of the severely brain injured adult: A practical approach.* Baltimore: Paul H. Brookes.

Kreutzer, J., & Wehman, P. (1991). *Cognitive rehabilitation for persons with traumatic brain injury: A functional approach.* Baltimore: Paul H. Brookes.

>   These are two edited texts that present the most recent research and practices in the rehabilitation of individuals with brain injury. In each, specific cognitive deficiencies (e.g., memory, perception, reasoning, etc.) are described and strategies for rehabilitation program design are highlighted.

Gerring, J. P., & Carney, J. M. (1993). *Head trauma: Strategies for educational reintegration.* San Diego, CA: Singular.

>   The authors present a thorough description of the acute and post-acute care received by children with traumatic brain injury as a basis for understanding the problems these children face when they reenter schools.

Gumnit, R. J. (1990). *Living well with epilepsy.* New York, NY: Demos.

>   This is an edited text that provides up-to-date information about epilepsy and how individuals with epilepsy can take charge and live normal and productive lives. Specific chapters are provided on (a) seizures in newborns and infants, (b) treating childhood seizures, (c) epilepsy in the teen years, and (d) the protection of legal rights.

Haerle, T. (1992). *Children with Tourette syndrome: A parents' guide*. Rockville, MD: Woodbine House.
> Although primarily targeted at parents of children with Tourette syndrome, this book also includes a useful chapter on effective teaching methods and classroom adaptations. Other chapters explain symptoms, causes, medications, and other disorders such as obsessive-compulsive disorder and attention deficits which are commonly linked with Tourette syndrome, as well as development, family life, advocacy, and legal rights.

Larsen, G. (1988). *Managing the school age child with a chronic health condition.* Minnetonka, MN: Chronimed Publishing (formerly DCI).
> This edited guide covers procedures for handling medical needs such as catheterization, stoma care, etc.

Reisner, H. (1988). *Children with epilepsy: A parents' guide*. Rockville, MD: Woodbine House.
> This guide can help parents, teachers, medical professionals, and educational administrators better understand and support the child with epilepsy, first by educating them about the disorder, and then by helping them cope with its effects on the child and the family. It covers types of seizures, medications, what to do when a child has a seizure, legal and educational issues, other problems often associated with epilepsy, self-esteem, and family life.

Shapiro, B., & Heussner, R. (1991). *A parent's guide to cystic fibrosis.* Minneapolis: University of Minnesota Press.
> This succinct guide covers the genetic basis of cystic fibrosis; its effects on respiratory, digestive, and other body systems; daily care issues; and ongoing research into prevention and treatment.

Sullivan, M. W. (1981). *Living with epilepsy*. Walnut Creek, CA: Bubba Press.
> The author provides a practical and straightforward guide for people with epilepsy and their families. Specific topics in the book include emergency care, medical tests, employment, and strategies for coping.

Williams, J. M., & Kay, T. (1991). *Head injury: A family matter*. Baltimore: Paul H. Brookes.

> Text examines the issues encountered by families of persons with TBI and provides resources for intervention and family support.

Multimedia

"Just like you and me: Understanding epilepsy," marketed by Educational Productions, is a 22–minute video that provides the basic facts of epilepsy, reviews types of seizures, and explains first aid and management techniques. A facilitator's guide accompanies the video.

"School Age and Youth with Special Health Needs Video Series," marketed by Learner Managed Designs, Inc., has videotapes on the care of children with **Asthma** and **Diabetes** in child care and school settings as well as a video entitled **"Rolling along,"** which provides information on assisting children with wheelchairs.

Periodical

Headlines, published by the New Medico Neurologic System, provides in-depth reports on advances in neuroscience, medical breakthroughs, and innovation in the rehabilitation of those with neurologic injuries and conditions. **Write:** Headlines, 14 Central Avenue, Lynn, MA 01901–9925 or **Phone:** (800) 676–6000.

Organizations

The **American Diabetes Association (ADA)** is a voluntary health organization concerned with finding a prevention and cure for diabetes. ADA provides information and support for millions with the disease and educates health care professionals and the general public about diabetes. ADA carries out this mission through thousands of volunteers working through affiliates and chapters. Services include (a) camps for children with diabetes, (b) support groups, (c) education opportunities, and (d) books about diabetes for children, adolescents, parents, and health care professionals. **Write:** ADA, 1600 Duke Street, Alexandria, VA 22314.

The **American Narcolepsy Association** provides outreach to educators in the form of information packets, an information line, and a quarterly newsletter entitled **The Eye Opener. Write:** American Narcolepsy Association, Inc., 425 California Street, Suite 201, San Francisco, CA 94104 or **Phone:** (415) 788–4793.

The **Cystic Fibrosis Foundation** assures the development of the means to control and prevent cystic fibrosis, and to improve the quality of life for people with the disease. The organization supports research; develops materials to help patients, families, and the public to understand cystic fibrosis; and seeks to affect public policy. **Write:** Cystic Fibrosis Foundation, 6931 Arlington Rd., Bethesda, MD 20814 or **Phone:** (800) 344–4823.

The **Division for Physical and Health Disabilities (DPHD)** promotes quality programs for physically disabled and/or health impaired individuals. The organization publishes a journal, **Physical Disabilities-Education and Related Services,** each year and the **DPH Newsletter** quarterly. **Write:** DPHD, CEC, 1920 Association Drive, Reston, VA 22091 or **Phone:** (703) 620–3660.

The **Epilepsy Foundation of America (EFA)** helps people with epilepsy and their families learn more about the condition and how to avoid some of the negative social consequences that ignorance and prejudice can produce. For educators, EFA provides a number of resources that can assist in the handling of seizures with minimal disruption and the greatest degree of emotional support. A National Epilepsy Library and Resource Center provides authoritative information to professionals, and local program affiliates are active in improving the school environment. A number of useful brochures, pamphlets, videos, and books designed especially for teachers, schools, and recreation personnel are available from the organization. **Write:** EFA, 4351 Garden City Drive, Landover, MD 20785.

The **Juvenile Diabetes Foundation International (JDF),** a foundation dedicated to research, offers a series of informational brochures related to juvenile diabetes and its effect on a child's health and special needs. Brochures available include: A Child with Diabetes Is in Your Care; Monitoring Blood Sugar; What You Should Know about Diabetes; Your Child Has Diabetes; Information about Insulin. The JDF also publishes the periodical **Countdown,** which addresses the aspects of living as a diabetic and presents the latest developments in the field of juvenile diabetes. **Write:** The Diabetes Research Foundation, 432 Park Avenue South, New York, NY 10016 or **Phone:** (212) 889–7575.

The **National Foundation for Ectodermal Dysplasias (NFED)** is dedicated to providing support and information to ectodermal dysplasia patients and their families, assisting the medical community in the treatment of ectodermal dysplasia disorders, providing information for early diagnosis, locating treatment facilities and referral services, providing sources for genetic counseling, conducting educational meetings for families, printing educational materials, assisting with research projects, and distributing financial assistance to families for dental care. **Write:** NFED, 219 E. Main Street, Box 114, Mascoutah, IL 62258 or **Phone:** (618) 566–2020.

The **National Head Injury Foundation (NHIF)** is an advocacy group composed of families, medical, and social service professionals concerned with the physical and emotional well-being of people who have head injuries. The foundation serves as a clearinghouse for information and resources and publishes a quarterly newsletter and national directory of Head Injury Rehabilitation Services. **Write:** NHIF, 1140 Connecticut Ave., N.W., Suite 812, Washington, D.C. 20036 or **Phone:** (800) 444–6443.

The **National Organization for Rare Disorders (NORD)** is a nonprofit voluntary agency composed of national health organizations, researchers, physicians, and individuals dedicated to the interests of people concerned about rare debilitating disorders. NORD has an information and referral service and a networking program to put individuals in touch with others suffering from the same or similar illnesses. The organization publishes **Orphan Disease Update** on a quarterly schedule and produces a Rare Disease Database available on CompuServe. **Write:** NORD, P.O. Box 8923, New Fairfield, CT 06812–1783 or **Phone:** (203) 746–6518.

The **National Reye's Syndrome Foundation (NRSF)** provides a variety of information relating to Reye's Syndrome, including treatment centers, research funding, support groups, and listings of medications thought to be connected with the development of the disease. Children surviving the disease often maintain varying degrees of neurological impairment. Information on services for these children under P.L.

94–142 is also available. **Write:** NRSF, P.O. Box 829, Bryan, OH 43506 or **Phone:** (800) 233–7393.

The **Tourette Syndrome Association** distributes pamphlets, films, and videotapes about Tourette syndrome. It supports research, organizes workshops and symposiums, and organizes and assists local chapters and support groups. **Write:** TSA, 42–40 Bell Blvd., Bayside, NY 11361 or **Phone:** (800) 237–0717.

Multiple Disabilities

Students who are identified as having multiple disabilities typically exhibit significant cognitive impairments and also require special services due to accompanying motor impediments, communication, visual, and hearing impairments, and medical conditions (Heward & Orlansky, 1992). According to IDEA, **Multiple Disabilities** refers to concomitant impairments, the combination of which causes such severe educational problems that they cannot be accommodated in special education programs designed solely for students with one of the impairments.

Although we have grouped multiple disabilities under a single heading, it is important to note that individuals considered to have severe and multiple disorders are not all alike. It is generally agreed, however, that the following behavioral characteristics are typically seen: (a) severe deficits in language and communication skills, (b) deficits in many basic self-care and self-help skills, (c) social behavior that is frequently inappropriate, and (d) body malformations and limited physical mobility/prowess. Other resources helpful in working with students with multiple disabilities may be found in the sections on Mental Retardation, Physical Disabilities, and Sensory Disabilities.

AVAILABLE RESOURCES: Multiple Disabilities

Resource Books

Irons-Reavis, D. (1992). *Educational intervention for the student with multiple disabilities*. Springfield, IL: Charles C. Thomas.

> This text assists those professionals who teach students who have severe multiple disabilities by providing information on general principles of intervention and classroom organization; management; adaptive equipment; teaching eating, toileting, dressing, and hygiene skills; teaching cognition, communication, and socialization skills. The reader is reminded that teaching students with severe multiple disabilities involves the simultaneous use of many skills and the overlapping of traditional curricular areas.

Nisbet, J. (1992). *Natural supports in school, at work, and in the community for people with severe disabilities.* Baltimore: Paul H. Brookes.

> This book acknowledges that assistance for people with severe disabilities must be shaped by individual need rather than by the requirement of service systems. The noted contributors of this book combine research and first-person accounts to present the foundations of natural supports in school, at work, and in the community.

Orelove, F. P., & Sobsey, D. (1991). *Educating children with multiple disabilities: A transdisciplinary approach.* Baltimore: Paul H. Brookes.

> This text is a practical guide to curriculum planning and implementation for children with severe and profound retardation who have motor and/or sensory impairments. Chapters include information on how to enhance functional abilities, integrate health care and educational programs, and effectively deal with family issues.

Rainforth, B., York, J., & Macdonald, C. (1992). *Collaborative teams for students with severe disabilities: Integrating therapy and educational services.* Baltimore, MD: Paul H. Brookes.

> This text defines the role of a collaborative team—including educators, parents, therapists—in the successful educational experience for students with severe disabilities. As a practical guide, it suggests intervention methods to include team member selection, definition of responsibilities, and the creation of IEPs.

Sternberg, L., Ritchey, H., Pegnatore, L., Wills, L., & Hill, K. (1986). *A curriculum for profoundly handicapped students: The Broward County model program.* Austin, TX: PRO-ED.

> With this step-by-step text, teachers are provided with a sensible approach to teach and measure the progress of their students with profound handicaps, establish reasonable instructional goals, select skills—gross motor, fine motor, cognitive, receptive communication, expressive communication, social/affective—that can be taught in small groups, and determine how to set up a classroom.

Periodical

Journal of the Association for Persons with Severe Handicaps (JASH), published quarterly by The Association for Persons with Severe Handicaps, presents data-based articles, commentary, and book reviews that focus on the full range of knowledge necessary to serve individuals with severe handicaps. **Write:** JASH, 7010 Roosevelt Way, N.E., Seattle, WA 98115 or **Phone:** (206) 523–8446.

Organization

The Association for Persons with Severe Handicaps (TASH) is an organization of a diverse group of individuals (teachers, parents, therapists, etc.) concerned with all aspects of severe disabilities. The organization has long advocated for the inclusion of individuals with severe handicaps and disseminates much needed information on policies and intervention techniques. **Write:** TASH, 29 W. Susquehanna Ave., Ste. 210, Baltimore, MD 21204 or **Phone:** (410) 828–8274.

Autism

Autism, as defined by IDEA, is a developmental disability significantly affecting verbal and nonverbal communication and social interaction, generally evident before age 3. Although there is great diversity among those considered "autistic," it is generally recognized that there are three cardinal characteristics that are universal and specific to autism. These are: (1) profound failure to develop social relationships (e.g., not bonding with parents or primary caregivers; avoidance of direct eye contact); (2) failure to develop communicative language (e.g., not using speech for social communication; not using syntactically sophisticated language); and (3) ritualistic and compulsive behavior (e.g., self-stimulatory rocking and arm-flapping; repetitive play patterns). These patterns of behavior are present in nearly all children with autism and are relatively infrequent in children who do not have autism. Some secondary characteristics typically associated with autism include resistance to environmental changes, unusual responses to sensory experiences, and self-injurious behavior. Consequently, intervention efforts typically focus on the development of language, the promotion of social competence, and the management of self-stimulatory and self-injurious behaviors.

Due to the inconsistency by which autism has been defined and identified, it is difficult to estimate the prevalence of autism. It is generally believed, however, that autism appears in about 2 to 4 out of 10,000 children. The disorder appears to occur 3 to 4 times more often in males than in females, although girls with autism tend to be more significantly affected. Autism is a chronic disorder, and, unfortunately, only a few children with autism achieve complete social independence (Rosenberg et al., 1992)

AVAILABLE RESOURCES: AUTISM
Resource Books

Aarons, M., & Gittens, T. (1991). *The handbook of autism.* New York, NY: Routledge.
> Designed for both parents and professionals, this text explores autism as a developmental disorder of social understanding and communication. The authors make use of case studies to illustrate their approach.

Biklen, D. (1993). *Communication unbound: How facilitated communication is challenging traditional views of autism*

and ability/disability. New York, NY: Teachers College Press.
> The controversial intervention, facilitated communication, believed by many to break through the language barriers of those with autism and other severe disabilities, is explored through a number of compelling individual accounts.

Christopher, W., & Christopher, B. (1989). *Mixed blessings*. Nashville: Abingdon Press.
> William Christopher, "Father Mulcahy" of the television series *M*A*S*H*, and his wife share their story and struggles as parents of son with autism. They cover their son's early years and the signs that he was not developing normally through the first twenty years of his life and the variety of educational, therapy, and medical programs they utilized in their endeavors to help their son. The Chrisptophers also recount how their other son was affected by having a brother with autism.

Goodman, J., & Hoban, S. *Day by day: Raising the child with Autism/PDD*. New York, NY: Guilford.
> The challenges, struggles, and triumphs of families of children with autism/pervasive developmental disorders are addressed in this video, and coping skills and practical strategies are provided to parents of this population.

Grandin, T., & Scariano, M. (1986). *Emergence labeled autistic*. Novato, CA: Arena Press.
> This book is the life story of Temple Grandin, a recovered "autistic." Through the study of autism as a psychology student, she discovered the work of Dr. Bernard Rimland. Together they created this extraordinary account of life through the eyes of an individual with autism who became a capable college student. The story is offered to parents, educators, and individuals with autism as an example of hope and optimism.

Lovaas, O. I. *Teaching developmentally disabled children: The me book*. Austin, TX: PRO-ED.
> This is a book for parents and teachers that describes a set of programs developed and tested by Lovaas in his 30 years of working with autistic and "developmentally delayed" children at UCLA. The behavioral intervention programs

are designed to help such children lead "more meaningful lives." The book is set up as a working guide with early programs described in step-by-step detail and later programs relying on the teachers' familiarity with the steps used in earlier chapters. The book can be supplemented by videotapes which show examples of many of the programs illustrated.

Powers, M. (1989). *Children with autism: A parents' guide.* Rockville, MD: Woodbine House.

Besides offering parents straightforward guidance on raising a child with autism, this book covers information useful for special education professionals. Chapters of special interest include those on development, daily care/behavior management, and characteristics of an appropriate educational program for children with autism.

Schulze, C. (1993). *When snow turns to rain: One family's struggle to solve the riddle of autism.* Rockville, MD: Woodbine House.

This book chronicles one family's experience with autism. The author's son was diagnosed as having late-onset autism soon after his second birthday. Increasingly dissatisfied with the special education programs available through the public school system, the family tried a variety of unorthodox methods of helping their son, including enrolling him in a residential school in Japan, experimenting with megavitamin therapy and facilitated communication, and using a team of volunteer teachers to work with him around the clock.

Seifert, C. (1990). *Case studies in autism: A young child and two adults.* Lanham, MD: University Press of America.

One of a series of books written by the author (another is *Theories of Autism*) in which ideographic case histories are used to describe the symptoms and signs of autism.

Simons, J., & Oishi, S. (1987). *The hidden child: The Linwood method for reaching the autistic child.* Rockville, MD: Woodbine House.

This text provides information concerning autism and a step-by-step discussion of the treatment program developed by Jeanne Simons at the Linwood School for children with autism in Ellicott City, Maryland. It includes methods of establishing relationships, patterning good behavior, overcoming compulsions, developing skills, and fostering social and emotional development.

Smith, M. (1990). *Autism and life in the community*. Baltimore: Paul H. Brookes.

Addressing adult issues in autism, this book provides practical, nonaversive guidelines for meeting the training and management needs of people of all ages with autism. Based upon nine years of data, it examines social and vocational skills development, describes self-management training and behavior modification, and suggests way to deliver enhanced services to individuals with autism who are preparing for community integration.

Multimedia

Autism Video Series. Princeton, NJ: Films for the Humanities, Inc.

Films for the Humanities markets four videos that offer insight into autism. **"A is for autism," "Autism," "Autism: Breaking through,"** and **"Autism: Childhood and beyond"** are brief programs which explore critical concepts though compelling case studies. The company also has videos on Fetal Alcohol Syndrome and Down syndrome.

Periodicals

Focus on Autistic Behavior, published by PRO-ED, is designed for professionals who work with individuals with autism and developmental disabilities. Articles highlight practical management, instruction, treatment, and planning strategies. **Write:** PRO-ED, 8700 Shoal Creek Blvd., Austin, TX 78758–6897 or **Phone:** (512) 451–3246.

Journal of Autism and Developmental Disabilities, published quarterly by Plenum, provides research reports, integrative literature reviews, and successful program descriptions relating to individuals with autism and other developmental disabilities. **Write:** Plenum Publishing Corp., 233 Spring St., New York, NY 10013.

Organizations

The **Autism Research Institute** (formerly the Institute for Child Behavior Research) is a non-profit institute devoted to conducting research and disseminating results on methods of preventing, diagnosing, and treating autism and other severe behavioral disorders of childhood. Information is available by mail or phone. **Write:** ARI, 4182 Adams Ave., San Diego, CA 92116 or **Phone:** (619) 281–7165.

The **Autism Society of America** works through a network of over 185 state and local chapters across the country to provide information and referral to individuals with autism, their families, and professionals to increase public awareness of the disability, and to advocate for, and monitor legislation affecting, individuals with autism. The Society publishes a quarterly newsletter, **The Advocate,** which presents the latest developments in the field and also hosts an annual national conference. The Society lists and sells a series of books dealing with the autistic population. **Write**: Autism Society of America, 7910 Woodmont Ave., Suite 650, Bethesda, MD 20814 or **Phone:** (301) 657–0881; (800) 3–AUTISM.

References

Best, G. A. (1992). Physical and health impairments: In L. Bullock (Ed.), *Exceptionalities in children and youth* (pp. 392–419). Boston: Allyn & Bacon.

Blankenship, C., & Lilly, M. S. (1981). *Mainstreaming students with learning and behavior problems.* New York, NY: Holt, Rinehart, & Winston.

Heward, W. L., & Orlansky, M. D. (1992). *Exceptional children.* New York, NY: Merrill/Macmillan.

Kozma, C., & Stock, J. S. (1993). What is mental retardation? In R. Smith (ED.), *Children with mental retardation: A parent's guide.* Rockville, MD: Woodbine House.

Rosenberg, M. S., O'Shea, L., & O'Shea, D. J. (1991). *Student teacher to master teacher.* New York, NY: Macmillan.

Rosenberg, M. S., Wilson, R. J., Maheady, L., & Sindelar, P. T. (1992). *Educating students with behavior disorders.* Boston: Allyn & Bacon.

Wodrich, D. L. (1994). *Attention deficit hyperactivity disorder.* Baltimore, MD: Paul H. Brookes.

section IV : *Early Child-hood Special Education and Emerging Academic Competence*

Although many school districts and localities have provided early intervention services to infants, toddlers, and preschoolers for some time, it took much needed federal legislation to *ensure* that all of those needing such services would receive them. Currently, early intervention services are available to children from birth to two years of age who have developmental delays, have conditions that typically result in developmental delays, or are at-risk for a developmental delay. Also, P.L. 99–457 extended all of the provisions of P.L. 94–142 (now IDEA) to children three to five years of age. Clearly, this is an inspiring time for early childhood special educators: society has finally realized that young children with special needs can be identified and helped (J. Lerner, C. M. Mardell-Czudnowski, & D. Goldenberg, 1987).

According to Smith and Strain (1992), there are three primary reasons for intervening early with children who are exceptional. The first reason is to enhance the child's development. Rate of learning and development is most rapid during the preschool years and postponing intervention is simply wasteful. Second, early intervention allows for needed support and assistance to families. Early intervention can result in improved attitudes among family members and can set the occasion for instructing family members in how to best provide for their special infant, toddler, or preschooler. Finally, the child's increased developmental and educational gains can result in decreased dependence on specialized institutions and interventions in later years.

When we speak of emerging academic competence we are referring to the large number of interrelated readiness skills from every area of development necessary for success in school, home, and the community. These skills fall into a number of domains including gross motor, fine motor, visual and visual perception, auditory and auditory perception, attention span, imitation and modeling, and concept/language formulation. Although these domains are often discussed separately, it is generally believed that all preacademic skills are intertwined with each other and with all other areas of development (Allen, 1992).

In this section we provide a listing and description of the vast scope of resources pertaining to the structure, delivery, and coordination of effective early childhood special education services. We will also highlight resources available for developing preacademic competence. Types of resources available include (a) resource books, (b) curriculum guides, programs, and kits, (c) instructional materials/toys, (d) periodicals, and (e) multimedia.

AVAILABLE RESOURCES:
Early Childhood Special Education
Generic Textbooks

There are a number of early childhood special education textbooks which provide an overview of the many issues involved in the delivery of services to infants, toddlers, and young children with special needs. These books typically have chapters on normal and exceptional development, legal issues involved with early intervention, specific disabilities found in young children with special needs, and collaborative strategies for dealing with the disabilities. Some of the more popular texts are:

Allen, K. A. (1992). *The exceptional child: Mainstreaming in early childhood education*. Albany, NY: Delmar.

Bailey, D. B., & Wolery, M. (1992). *Teaching infants and preschoolers with disabilities*. New York, NY: Merrill/Macmillan.

Caputo, A. J., & Accardo, P. (1991). *Developmental disabilities in infancy and childhood*. Baltimore: Paul H. Brookes.

Cook, R. E., Tessier, A., & Klein, M. D. (1992). *Adapting early childhood curricula for children with special needs*. New York, NY: Merrill/Macmillan.

Lerner, J., Mardell-Czudnowski, C. M., & Goldenberg, D. (1987). *Special education for the early childhood years*. Boston: Allyn & Bacon.

Neisworth, J., & Bagnato, S. (1987). *The young exceptional child: Early development and education*. New York, NY: Merrill/Macmillan.

Raver, S. (1991). *Strategies for teaching at-risk and handicapped infants and toddlers: A transdisciplinary approach*. New York, NY: Merrill/Macmillan.

Thurman, S. K., & Widerstorm, A. H. (1990). *Infants and children with special needs: A developmental and ecological approach*. Baltimore: Paul H. Brookes.

Widerstrom, A. H., Mowder, B., & Sandall, S. (1991). *At-risk and handicapped newborns and infants: Development, assessment, and intervention*. Boston: Allyn & Bacon.

Resource Books

Adler, S., & King, D. (1986). *A multidisciplinary treatment program for the preschool-aged exceptional child*. Springfield, IL: Charles C. Thomas.

> This text, with its overview of exceptionalities, covers such multidisciplinary topics as health care; speech and language; functional language; teaching strategies; hearing loss; auditory processing and aural language; prehandwriting and writing skills; music, art, and dramatic play therapies; the development of optimum learning facility, and its interior design.

Anastasiow, N., & Harel, S. (1992). *At-risk infants: Interventions, families, and research*. Baltimore: Paul H. Brookes.

> This text examines the concerns and special needs of infants who are at-risk and focuses on the family as a powerful early intervention tool.

Barnett, D., & Carey, K. (1992). *Designing interventions for preschool learning and behavior problems*. San Francisco: Jossey-Bass.

Greenspan, S. I. (1992). *Infancy and early childhood: The practice of clinical assessment and intervention with emotional and developmental challenges*. Madison, CT: International Universities Press.

Hauser-Cram, P., Pierson, D., Walker, D., & Tivnan, T. (1991). *Early education in the public schools: Lessons from a comprehensive birth to kindergarten program*. San Francisco: Jossey-Bass.

> In these three related resources, Barnett and Carey present specific home and school interventions with practical strategies to stop learning and behavior problems before they increase in severity. Greenspan, through the use of practical case studies, describes the hands-on assessment of a wide range of infant and early childhood problems and a variety of psychotherapeutic interventions. Hauser-Cram et al. provide guidelines for planning, administering, and evaluating comprehensive early education programs in the public schools.

Bender, M., & Baglin, C. A. (1992). *Infants and toddlers: A resource guide for practitioners. San Diego, CA: Singular.*
> The authors provide an information resource guide for practitioners, school systems, university instructors, and local and state Infant-Toddler programs charged with implementing an interagency approach to services in the spirit of P.L. 99–457, Part H.

Bricker, D., & Cripe, J. (1992). *An activity-based approach to early intervention.* Baltimore, MD: Paul H. Brookes.
> This resource presents a strategies model in early intervention in which natural and relevant events are used to effectively and efficiently teach infants and young children of all abilities. The activity-based intervention is responsive to the need to individualize goals and objectives for children's IEPs and IFSPs.

Brown, W., Thurman, S. K., & Pearl, L. (1993). *Family-centered early intervention with infants and toddlers: Innovative cross-disciplinary approaches.* Baltimore: Paul Brookes.
> The purpose of this edited text is to promote the development of coordinated and collaborative services across agencies and disciplines. Specific early intervention practices are described and the provisions of Part H of IDEA are explained.

Coleman, J. (1993). *The early intervention dictionary: A multidisciplinary guide to terminology.* Rockville, MD: Woodbine House.
> This dictionary defines and clarifies terms used by the many different medical, therapeutic, and educational professionals who provide early intervention services. Many abbreviations, acronyms, and trade names are included.

Cripe, J., Slentz, K., & Bricker, D. (1992). *AEPS curriculum for birth to three years.* Baltimore, MD: Paul H. Brookes.
> The AEPS Curriculum, utilizing the IEP/IFSP goals developed for a child from the AEPS Test measure, provides a complete set of learning activities to facilitate children's acquisition of functional skills. Encouraging the generaliza-

tion of learned skills through the integration of teaching into daily activities is the goal of the curriculum, and teaching strategies, instructional sequences, and recommendations for environmental arrangements accompany the curriculum activities.

Ensher, G. L., & Clark, D.A. (1987). *Newborns at risk: Medical care and psychoeducational intervention.* Gaithersburg, MD: Aspen.

> The authors discuss medical and developmental problems, and methods for planning more effective interventions to give each child the chance to reach full potential.

Gibbs, E., & Teti, D. (1990). *Interdisciplinary assessment of infants: A guide for early intervention professionals.* Baltimore, MD: Paul H. Brookes.

> Infant assessment methods and information on interdisciplinary infant assessment are addressed from disciplines including psychology, physical and occupational therapy, social work, speech-language pathology, and education. Contained is information on assessing neuromotor integrity, cognitive language, and general developmental progress, infant social behavior, and social environment characteristics.

Hayes, L. G. (1991). *A fountain of language development for early childhood education and the special child, too.* New York, NY: Vantage Press, Inc.

> This book contains material for six basic areas in the education of preschool children. Each of the six areas—stories, finger plays, poems, choral speaking, number readiness, and singing activities—can enrich the child's vocabulary and stimulate language skills. Many of the activities include "finger plays" which involve the child's kinesthetic channel in learning language.

King-DeBaun, P. (1991). *Storytime: Stories, symbols, and emergent literacy activities for young special needs children.* Park City, UT: Creative Communicating.

> *Storytime* provides ten stories designed for students with special needs. The stories include simple graphics and picture symbols, plus a 36–location picture communication

symbol overlay (for students using augmentative communication methods). Also included are suggested activities for art, cooking, writing, and related stories.

Lynch, E. W., & Hanson, M. J. (1992). *Developing cross-cultural competence: A guide for working with young children and their families*. Baltimore: Paul H. Brookes.
> This edited volume is designed for professionals and paraprofessionals who work with culturally diverse families who may have or be at-risk for disability or chronic illness. Eight specific cultural case studies (e.g., Native American, African American, Asian, Latino, etc.) are presented.

Odom, S., & Karnes, M. (1988). *Early intervention for infants and children with handicaps: An empirical base*. Baltimore, MD: Paul H. Brookes.
> The authors examine research related to issues in early childhood special education. Research questions are addressed and issues in interaction, development, and adaptation of families are discussed, as are service delivery options.

Odom, S., McConnell, S., & McEvoy, M. (1992). *Social competence of young children with disabilities: Issues and strategies for intervention*. Baltimore, MD: Paul H. Brookes.
> This text addresses the social competence of young children with developmental disabilities. Graduate students, researchers, and professional practitioners, the target readers, can review current knowledge and are provided intervention practices to promote peer-related social competence of young children with developmental disabilities, and can review specific issues concerning children with speech-language, vision, and hearing impairments.

Rogovin, A. (1990). *Let me do it!* Nashville: Abingdon Press.
> This is an activity book to be used by parents, teachers, and primary care givers with preschool and young primary-aged children. More then 300 projects allow children to learn at their own rates. Therefore, these projects are practical and useful for all children, including those with learn-

ing disabilities, autism, mental retardation, or other handicapping conditions. Using materials found around the house or classroom, the activities help children to develop interests, independence, confidence, and have fun at the same time.

Safford, P. (1989). *Integrated teaching in early childhood: Starting in the mainstream.* White Plains, NY: Longman.

This text emphasizes the benefits of inclusive education for young children with and without disabilities. Included are specific strategies for integrating children with different disabilities, including visual impairments, hearing impairments, motor impairments, and developmental delays or behavioral problems. Other chapters focus on considerations in individualized and group instruction.

Schwartz, S., & Miller, J. (1988). *The language of toys: Teaching communication skills to special-needs children.* Rockville, MD: Woodbine House.

This guide for parents and teachers offers strategies for improving the communication skills of children with disabilities through the use of everyday toys and books, both commercial and homemade. Activities are appropriate for children with developmental ages up to 60 months.

Segal, M. (1988). *In time and with love: Caring for the special needs baby.* New York, NY: Newmarket Press.

In an illustrated format, this book provides advice on play and care for the preterm and handicapped child and covers such issues as anger and favoritism; nursing, feeding, dressing; interacting with siblings; coping with advice from doctors; discipline; social skill development; tough decision making. It also includes an entire section on games and activities designed to promote emotional development, and encourage motor and language skills.

Urbano, M. T. (1992). *Preschool children with special health care needs.* San Diego, CA: Singular.

Designed for early childhood and special educators, nurses, physical and occupational therapists, psychologists, speech-language pathologists, audiologists, and nutritionists working in early intervention settings, this text contains practical advice about the health needs shared by all children. It also covers in-depth the more complex medical problems of children with special needs.

Multimedia

Learner Managed Designs markets a number of videos that focus on infants and young children with special needs. Titles and topics include: **"Nutrition for infants and toddlers with special needs," "Home tracheostomy care for infants and young children," "Instruction," "Communication,"** and **"Inclusion."** Full descriptions of these videos (and others) are contained in an attractive catalog.

"Oh say what they see: An introduction to indirect language stimulation techniques." Portland, OR: Educational Productions.
> This 30–minute video demonstrates easy-to-learn techniques designed to promote the acquisition of language by language-delayed young children. Viewers are provided with demonstrations as to how children acquire language and how parents and teachers can assist in the development of expressive and receptive language.

Variety Preschoolers' Workshop Videos. Syosset, NY: Variety Preschoolers' Workshop.
> This series of five video programs for parents and professionals focuses on preschool children with special needs. One program, for example, features procedures for teaching children self-control while another highlights a prescriptive language development program for two children with autism.

Periodicals

Infants and Young Children, published quarterly by Aspen, is an interdisciplinary journal devoted to clinical management of infants and young children and their families with or at-risk for developmental disabilities. Articles provide up-to-date information regarding health care, education, and therapeutic practices. **Write:** Aspen Publishers, Inc., 200 Orchard Ridge Drive, Gaithersburg, MD 20878 or **Phone:** (800) 638–8437.

Journal of Early Intervention, published quarterly by the Division of Early Childhood of CEC, highlights research, program descriptions, and integrative reviews relevant to those who provide early intervention services to infants and toddlers with special needs. **Write:** Division for Early Childhood, CEC, 1920 Association Drive, Reston, VA 22091–1589 or **Phone:** (703) 620–3660.

Topics in Early Childhood Special Education, published quarterly by PRO-ED, is designed for professionals who serve young children with special needs. Articles focus on topics such as social policies initiatives, assessment, intervention alternatives, and strategies for collaboration. **Write:** PRO-ED Journals, 8700 Shoal Creek Blvd., Austin, TX 78758–6897 or **Phone:** (512) 451–3246.

Organizations

The **Division for Early Childhood (DEC)** promotes services, including special education, for young children with special needs and their families. DEC sponsors an annual international conference and publishes the **Journal of Early Intervention** and the **DEC Communicator** newsletter, each quarterly. **Write:** DEC, CEC, 1920 Association Drive, Reston, VA 22091 or **Phone:** (703) 620–3660.

The **National Association for the Education of Young Children (NAEYC)** is the nation's largest membership organization of early childhood professionals and offers a wide range of services to assist early childhood professionals, parents, policy makers, and others to learn more about child development and early education and to improve available services through the NAEYC annual conference, the National Academy of Early Childhood Programs, **Young Children,** a bimonthly journal, public affairs, affiliate groups, and information service. Its early childhood resources catalog offers titles in accreditation, curriculum, developmentally appropriate practice, discipline, early childhood profession, parents, infants and toddlers, language arts, multicultural education, physical environment, play, programs and schools, quality, compensation, affordability, and teachers and caregivers. Contact NAEYC for the most recent catalog. **Write:** NAEYC, 1834 Connecticut Avenue, N.W., Washington, DC 20009 or **Phone:** (800) 424–2460.

Curriculum Guides/Kits

Communication Skill Builder's Kits. Tucson, AZ: Communication Skill Builders.

> Communication Skill Builders markets a number of early intervention curricular materials and kits designed to strengthen preacademic readiness skills. Materials and kits focus on language development/remediation (e.g., **Language Stories, Songs for Language Learning, Let's Be Social**) and motor skills development (e.g., **Three to Get Ready**).

Johnson-Martin, N., Attermeier, S., & Hacker, B. (1990). **The Carolina curriculum for preschoolers with special needs**. Baltimore, MD: Paul H. Brookes.

Johnson-Martin, N., Jens, K., Attermeier, S., & Hacker, B. (1991). **The Carolina curriculum for infants and toddlers with special needs**. Baltimore, MD: Paul H. Brookes.

Each of the texts provides a field-tested curriculum for the assessment and teaching of children, the first for children from birth to 24 months, the second from two to five, who are considered at risk for developmental delay or who exhibit special needs. Each includes detailed assessment and intervention sequences, daily routine integration strategies, and sensorimotor adaptations covering subdomains of development. A sample assessment log charting a child's individual progress is included with each curriculum.

PLDK: Peabody Language Development Kits/Peabody Early Experiences Kits. Circle Pines, MN: American Guidance Service.

A series of kits—each replete with puppets, soundbooks, cassettes, song cards, photos, story cards, and teacher manuals—designed to encourage overall language skills for preschool children, early primary children, and older children with learning difficulties. The wide range of activities is indexed by skill and subject area to assist in IEP and specific lesson planning.

ThemeWorks: An Integrated Curriculum for Young Children. Sunnyvale (1991). Sunnyvale, CA: Creative Publications.

This program offers an integrated curriculum designed for children pre-K through second grade. It consists of six thematic units: (a) Night Time, (b) Rain, (c) At the Seashore, (d) Trees, (e) Houses, and (f) Under the Ground. Each unit begins with a fun kick-off activity and ends with a culminating activity. Each theme book contains numerous multisensory activities in language, mathematics, science, art, literature, social studies, music, and dramatic play.

VORT Early Intervention Kits and Materials. Palo Alto, CA: VORT.

VORT markets a number of curriculum guides and kits designed for assessment and intervention with infants, toddlers, and young children with special needs. For example, the Hawaii Early Learning Profile (HELP) program contains checklists, charts, activity guides, and curriculum suggestions for both teachers and parents.

Instructional Materials/Toys

Communication/Therapy Skill Builders Early Intervention Materials. Tucson, AZ: Communication/Therapy Skill Builders.

> Communication/Therapy Skill Builders markets a number of materials and kits designed to intervene with preacademic problems such as feeding/oral motor skills, neonatal/infant development, hand development, language, and visual development. Send for their informative catalog.

Constructive Playthings. Grandview, MO: Constructive Playthings.

> Constructive Playthings markets preschool age learning materials and playground designs. The catalog features active play toys and structures which allow for different ability levels. Items include blocks, furniture, school supplies, and videocassettes that facilitate pretend play, infant care, manipulatives, perception, language skills, mathematics, music, science, and after school games.

Creative Publication Primary Grades Materials. Oak Lawn, IL: Creative Publications.

> Creative Publications markets a number of instructional materials designed specifically for preschool and primary classrooms. Consult their catalog for a full description of manipulatives, integrated curricula alternatives, and attractive content-specific items.

Educational Performance Associates. Ridgefield, NJ: EFA.

> EFA publishes specialized educational materials for instructional use in special education, particularly pre-school, kindergarten, and primary classroom programs. Educational materials are available for language development and speech; self-care, health, and physical education; diagnostic testing/evaluation/record keeping; independent living/occupational skills; perception; basic skills; and other materials. A wide array of computer software is also available in special education, vocational education, and special needs.

Fisher-Price Toys and Learning Resources. East Aurora, NY: Fisher Price.

> Fisher-Price, Inc. is one of the world's leading marketers of infant and preschool toys and juvenile products and equipment. Send for its extensive catalog.

Fitzhugh Program. Niles, MI: Allied Publishing Company.

> A program of nine workbooks that incorporates an individualized, self-teaching process. The programmed workbooks include activities such as: spatial organization (shape matching, shape analysis, sequencing, and shape completion), language and numbers series (alphabet and common nouns, language and numbers, addition, subtraction and multiplication, action verbs, narrative problems and division), grammar, and general knowledge.

Holcomb's Educational Materials. Cleveland, OH: Holcomb's.

> Holcomb's markets a wide range of educational materials for infants, toddlers, and young children. Their colorful and descriptive catalog illustrates specialized language, play, and social awareness materials as well as furniture, classroom supplies, and books.

Kaplan School Supply. Lewisville, NC: Kaplan.

> Kaplan School Supply Company markets classroom and teaching aids and equipment including classroom furnishings, cots, infant/toddler furnishings, play equipment, and materials relating to a wide variety of young children's curricular areas. Write for their colorful catalog.

Kimbo's Educational Records and Cassettes. Long Branch, NJ: Kimbo Educational.

> Kimbo produces a number of recorded materials that contain songs and activities that teach a number of critical skills such as sharing, socialization, community living, and self-help. Each of the kits comes with an LP or cassette and an accompanying manual.

Lakeshore Learning Materials. Carson, CA: Lakeshore.

Lakeshore markets a large supply of materials designed for preschool and primary classrooms. Their attractive catalog organizes materials into areas such as furniture, dramatic play, manipulatives, active play, and language.

Phoenix Learning Resources. St. Louis, MO: Phoenix.

Phoenix Learning Resources offers an extensive catalog of learning toys, programs, and equipment geared toward early childhood to adult education. Programs and texts are provided for preschool, primary K-3, middle school, secondary, adult basic skills, special education, and ESL levels and curriculum and include early childhood materials, reading, language arts, mathematics, preventive education, keyboarding study skills, social studies, and professional books. Call or write for the catalog.

TFH Achievement and Special Needs. Gibsonia, PA: T.F.H. Ltd.

TFH markets a number of play and instructional materials designed for sensory stimulation, soft play, and the improvement of dexterity and movement.

References

Allen, K. A. (1992). *The exceptional child: Mainstreaming in early childhood education.* Albany, NY: Delmar.

Lerner, J., Mardell-Czudnowski, C. M., & Goldenberg, D. (1987). *Special education for the early childhood years.* Englewood Cliffs, NJ: Prentice Hall.

Smith, B., & Strain, P. (1992). Early childhood special education. In L. Bullock (Ed.), *Exceptionalities in children and youth* (pp. 92–123). Boston: Allyn & Bacon.

section V : *Promoting Academic, Social, and Functional Competence*

This section highlights resources that assist with the teaching and development of specific skills typically addressed in remedial and special education settings. Following an overview of Assessment resources, we will present a number of commercially developed materials, curriculum guides, resource books, periodicals, and multimedia packages under three major categories: Academic Skills and Strategies, Social Competence, and Functional Competence. A general category concerning Technology and where to locate relevant software programs for the three major categories concludes this section.

Assessment

From an educational perspective, **assessment** can be defined as a continuous process in which information is systematically gathered regarding an individual student's characteristics, qualities, and behaviors (i.e., all relevant areas of a student's functioning) in order to assist in the delivery of instruction. According to

Evans and Evans (1992), assessment is one of the most critical components in educational programming for students identified as exceptional; without an accurate assessment, it would be almost impossible to develop, plan, implement, modify, and/or evaluate an educational program.

Clearly, assessment is linked closely with the development of individualized educational programs (IEPs). It is the process through which current levels of performance are identified and the means by which student progress is monitored and instructional approaches are evaluated. Formalized and highly structured assessment procedures are also used to identify disability conditions and to determine a student's eligibility for special education services.

In general, there are three types of assessment procedures: **case histories, formal assessment devices,** and **informal assessment procedures.** Case histories, such as student records, provide a large amount of information about the student's family history, health, and previous education performance. Formal assessment devices are generally norm-referenced or standardized tests that allow comparison of one student's performance with that of an identified sample. Informal assessment procedures can be any number of data collection techniques which sample a student's performance in an identified skill area. As is the case in **curriculum-based assessment (CBA),** these teacher-developed procedures assist in focusing attention on changes in behavior within the specific curriculum being used, therefore strengthening the bridge between testing and instruction.

Unfortunately, it is beyond the scope of this *Sourcebook* to list and describe all of the formal assessment devices available commercially. What we have done is to provide a listing of assessment resources (e.g., books, catalogs, etc.) that (a) allow for a better understanding of the assessment process and assist in the development of informal assessment procedures, and (b) provide either listings and/or reviews of commercially available formal assessment devices.

AVAILABLE RESOURCES: Assessment
General Assessment Textbooks

The following texts provide information on how to understand and use assessment procedures.

Choate, J. et al. (1992). *Curriculum-based assessment and programming*. Boston: Allyn & Bacon.

Hoy, C., & Gregg, N. (1994). *Assessment: The special educators role*. Belmont, CA: Wadsworth.

McLoughlin, J. A., & Lewis, R. B. (1990). *Assessing special students: Strategies and procedures*. Columbus, OH: Merrill/Macmillan.

Overton, T. (1992). *Assessment in special education: An applied approach*. New York, NY: Merrill/Macmillan.

Salvia, J. A., & Hughes, C. (1990). *Curriculum-based assessment: Testing what is taught*. Columbus, OH: Merrill/Macmillan.

Tindal, G. A., & Marston, D. B. (1990). *Classroom-based assessment: Evaluating instructional outcomes*. Columbus, OH: Merrill/Macmillan.

Wallace, G., Larsen, S., & Elksinin, L. (1992). *Educational assessment of learning problems: Testing for teaching*. Boston: Allyn & Bacon.

Resource Books

Browder, D. (1991). *Assessment of individuals with severe disabilities: An applied behavior approach to life skills assessment*. Baltimore, MD: Paul H. Brookes.

Teachers designing comprehensive educational assessments for individuals with severe disabilities are offered guidelines utilizing applied behavior analysis. The approach assesses critical functions and life skills with emphasis on academic, motor skills, communication, and social behavior. Personal futures planning, integration and generalization, IEPs/IHPs, routine task analysis, and assessment of adults of retirement age are included.

Cohen, L., & Spruill, J. (1990). *A practical guide to curriculum-based assessment for special educators*. Springfield, IL: Charles C. Thomas.

This book uses curriculum-based assessment as a tool to improving learning outcomes, and links assessment to instruction, particularly for practitioners and college students. An overview of CBA is provided, describing the methods of implementation and their variations.

Gable, R. A., & Hendricksen, J. M. (1990). *Assessing students with special needs: A sourcebook for analyzing and correcting errors in academics.* White Plains, NY: Longman.

> This is an edited volume that contains step-by-step guidelines for the informal, classroom-based assessment of students with special needs. A specific emphasis is placed on error analysis procedures to remediate learning problems.

Hammill, D. D., Brown, L., & Bryant, B. R. (1992). *A consumer's guide to tests in print.* Austin, TX: PRO-ED.

> Over 250 frequently used norm-referenced tests are reviewed according to accepted psychometric principles, both technical and nontechnical. The first portion of the guide contains a thorough discussion of the principles used to construct the rating system and the remainder is devoted to the reviews which are presented in tabular form. Types of tests reviewed include Achievement, Aptitude/Developmental Abilities, Affect, and General Intelligence.

Assessment Instrumentation Vendors

Academic Therapy Publications. Novato, CA.

> Academic Therapy markets a number of achievement, basic skills, speech/language, and process (e.g., memory, perceptual motor) tests. Materials relating to test interpretation are also described in their comprehensive catalog of materials.

T. M. Achenbach. Burlington, VT.

> This is a small, nonprofit corporation which markets a select number of rating forms and profiles (e.g., The Child Behavior Checklist-CBCL) that assess student behavior.

American Guidance Services. Circle Pines, MN.

> AGS has a large number of educational tests and accessories that are typically used in remedial and special education settings. Well over 55 pages of the most recent AGS catalog is devoted to assessment instrumentation in areas such as early development (e.g., AGS Early Screening Pro-

files); educational achievement/diagnosis (e.g., PIAT); general ability and development (e.g., K-ABC; Vineland); language development (e.g., Khan-Lewis Phonological Analysis); and social skills development (e.g., Social Skills Rating System).

Communication Skill Builders. Tucson, AZ.

Communication Skill Builders market a wide range of assessment instrumentation focusing on all aspects of receptive and expressive language. Write for a catalog.

CPPC. Brandon, VT.

CPPC markets a number of psychological and educational tests as well as software that can be used to assist in the analyses of available data. A catalog describes over a dozen new and existing holdings.

DLM. Allen, TX.

Among its many educational materials, DLM markets a number of popular assessment devices used by educators (e.g., Woodcock-Johnson Psycho-Educational Battery, Behavior Dimensions Rating Scale, etc.). The specific Assessment catalog organizes holdings into specific areas such as behavior, speech and language, and early childhood.

Hawthorne Educational Services, Inc. Columbia, MO.

Hawthorne markets easily administered screening and identification instruments for the identification of children's school and home-based problems. Different screening and diagnostic scales are available for the evaluation of Attention Deficit Disorder, Learning Disabilities, and Behavior Disorders of preschool and school-aged children. Technical manuals provide data on standardization, reliability, and validity. Intervention manuals, referenced by item to the teacher and parent checklists, provide lists of strategies to address each identified student problem. These manuals are very easy to understand and use and may be of particular interest to regular educators and other professionals responsible for service delivery. Many other materials are distributed by Hawthorne, covering topics such as transition/vocational needs of students and teacher supervision/evaluation.

PRO-ED. Austin, TX.

PRO-ED markets a large number of assessment devices (e.g., Detroit Test of Learning Aptitude, Test of Written Language, etc.) that are frequently used in remedial and special education settings. In fact, 56 pages of its most recent catalog is devoted to assessment instrumentation in areas such as intelligence, achievement, speech and language, hearing impairment, reading, writing, spelling, mathematics, adaptive behavior, social competence, and vocational skills.

Psychological Assessment Resources, Inc. Odessa, FL.

PAR markets a wide range of psychological and educational assessment devices and materials. Their extensive 100+ page catalog includes a helpful resource finder that divides the contents into easily referenced categories (e.g., behavior problems, achievement, attention disorders, etc.).

Psychological Corporation of Harcourt Brace Jovanovich, Inc. San Antonio, TX.

Psychological Corporation markets a number of assessment devices in the areas of early childhood, speech and language, academic achievement, and social functioning. Write for their specific catalog offerings.

Riverside Clinical and Special Needs. Chicago, IL.

Riverside publishes and markets a wide range of assessment instrumentation, resource books, and accessories. As a result of their recent acquisition of DLM, the company now is the publisher of the Woodcock-Johnson Psycho-Educational Battery and the Battelle Developmental Inventory.

Slosson Educational Publication, Inc. East Aurora, NY.

Slosson markets a number of assessment devices and scales to identify and diagnose special learning and behavioral problems. Their catalog provides descriptions under the specific headings of (a) Intelligence, Aptitude, Achievement, (b) Speech/Language, (c) Motor/Behavior/Vocational, and (d) Reading, Writing, Math, and Spelling. Computer report software and some learning aids are also available.

Western Psychological Services. Los Angeles, CA.
Western's catalog contains over 270 pages of tests, books, and software related to psychological and educational assessment. Special sections are devoted to special education, speech and language, and academic achievement.

Periodicals

Diagnostique, published quarterly by the Council for Educational Diagnostic Services (CEDS) of CEC, publishes research and integrative reviews pertaining to the educational diagnostic services of all individuals with disabilities. **Write:** CEDS, CEC, 1920 Association Drive, Reston, VA 22091–1589 or **Phone:** (703) 620–3660.

Journal of Psychoeducational Assessment is a quarterly journal designed to keep school psychologists and diagnosticians up-to-date with current psychological and educational assessment practices, legal mandates, and new instrumentation. **Write:** CPPC, 4 Conant Square, Brandon, VT 05733.

Organization

The **Council for Educational Diagnostic Services (CEDS),** a division of CEC, promotes high quality appraisal and diagnostic services for children and youth. The division publishes a journal, **Diagnostique,** and a newsletter, **CEDS Communique,** each quarterly. **Write:** CEDS, CEC, 1920 Association Drive, Reston, VA 22091–1589 or **Phone:** (703) 620–3660.

Academic Skills and Strategies

A large majority of students with disabilities have specific academic skill and/or strategy deficiencies that signal the need for special or remedial education efforts. In this section we present instructional resources that assist in promoting academic competence. (By academic competence, we mean the myriad of content area skills and learning strategies that are associated with achievement in school and success in postschool environments.) Resources that approach academic skill and strategy performance in a **generic** (i.e., cross-content) fashion are presented first. Many of these resources involve teaching "thinking skills" or strategies (e.g., self-instruction strategy instruction, self-monitoring, etc.) that can be used to solve problems in a number of curricular areas. Others provide information on generic teaching methodologies (direct instruction, cooperative learning, etc.) that can be applied to diverse content areas. These "general approach" resources are followed by sections containing resources devoted to these specific content areas: **Reading, Spoken and Written Language, Mathematics,** and **Science/Social Studies.**

Academic Skills and Strategies

GENERAL APPROACHES

There are a number of general texts that focus on generic methods for teaching academic skills and strategies for students with learning problems. Typically, chapters in these texts provide "tried and true" methods concerning the organization of classrooms, principles of instructional design, and specific approaches for teaching academic content areas such as reading, math, spoken and written language, social studies, and science. Some of the more popular texts are listed below.

Textbooks

Bos, C., & Vaughn, S. (1991). *Strategies for teaching students with learning and behavior disorders*. Boston: Allyn & Bacon.

Hammill, D., & Bartel, N. (1990). *Teaching students with learning and behavior problems*. Boston: Allyn & Bacon.

Kameenui, E., & Simmons, D. (1990). *Designing instructional strategies: The prevention of academic learning problems*. New York, NY: Merrill/Macmillan.

Langone, J. (1990). *Teaching students with mild and moderate learning problems*. Boston: Allyn & Bacon.

Polloway, E. A., & Patton, J. R. (1993). *Strategies for teaching learners with special needs*. New York, NY: Merrill/Macmillan.

Schloss, P., Schloss, C., & Smith, M. (1990). *Instructional methods for adolescents with learning and behavior problems*. Boston: Allyn & Bacon.

Smith, D. D. (1989). *Teaching students with learning and behavior problems*. Boston: Allyn & Bacon.

Waldron, K. (1992). *Teaching students with learning disabilities: Strategies for success*. San Diego: Singular.

Wolery, M., Bailey, D., & Sugai, G. (1988). *Effective teaching: Principles and procedures of applied behavior analysis with exceptional children*. Boston: Allyn & Bacon.

Resource Books

Bailey, S. (1993). *Wings to fly: Bringing theatre arts to students with special needs*. Rockville, MD: Woodbine House.

Based on the author's experiences in developing drama programs for students with disabilities such as mental retardation, learning disabilities, cerebral palsy, and hearing
impairment, this text explains how to help children with
disabilities reap educational, therapeutic, and recreational
benefits as students through involvement in the arts. Topics
addressed include improvisational acting, puppetry, using
drama as a teaching tool in the classroom, performing plays
with children with special needs, and using drama in mainstreamed settings. The strategies outlined in the book can
be used by educators, drama professionals, and parents.

Banas, N., & Wills, I. H. (1982). *WISC-R Prescriptions:
How to work with individual learning styles.* Novato,
CA: Academic Therapy Publications.

This book is designed to help teachers, parents, and students learn to analyze the results of the WISC-R IQ test. The
authors describe each subtest in terms of testing procedures, scoring guidelines, skills required for success on the
task, and prescriptions for teaching to students' individual
learning styles (with notable highs or lows in a given subtest).

Book Lab (1982). *Guidelines for teaching children with learning problems.* North Bergen, NJ: Author.

This is a comprehensive handbook for teachers and parents
that addresses various types of problems faced by students
with learning problems of all ages. It provides background
on developmental patterns, information on needs assessments, and possible solutions to problems related to language development, reading, behavior disorders, and
many other academic disabilities. The book, written in a direct practical manner, is useful to parents as well as educators.

Edmondson, H. P. (1991). *Self-directed education: The secret to educational success in ten easy steps for teenage students.* New York, NY: Vantage.

The author suggests that the school performance of teenage
students can improve dramatically if a ten-step process is
followed. The process includes utilizing the power of educational strategies, goal definition, listening, habit formation,

personality, faith, happiness, desire, emotion, and employment strategies.

Harwell, J. M. (1993). *Ready to use learning disabilities activities kit*. Boston: Allyn & Bacon.

> This is a resource book which contains over 200 reproducible activities designed to assist students learn and retain basic reading, writing, listening, and math skills.

Hoover, J. (1991). *Classroom applications of cognitive learning styles*. Boulder, CO: Hamilton Publications.

> This book provides practical and current information about seven critical cognitive learning styles and six learning strategies essential for student success in the classroom.

Hoover, J. (1988). *Curriculum adaptation for students with learning and behavior problems: Principles and practices*. Boulder, CO: Hamilton Publications.

> This book explains how to adapt curriculum for students with learning and behavior problems. The topics discussed in this practical book include the Curriculum Adaption Model and best practices for adapting curriculum in special and mainstreamed classes.

Mann, P., Suiter, P., & McClung, R. (1987). *Handbook in diagnostic-prescriptive teaching*. Des Moines, IA: Longwood.

> This handbook is a comprehensive and detailed practical approach to assessment and program planning. This manual contains masters for easy reproduction of assessment tools and content area instructional interventions.

Mastropieri, M. A., & Scruggs, T. E. (1991). *Teaching students ways to remember: Strategies for learning mnemonically*. Cambridge, MA: Brookline.

> The authors provide a practical translation of mnemonic research into practice. Mnemonic techniques that help students acquire basic skills, concepts, facts, and systems of facts are highlighted. Specific content area applications presented include reading, math, social studies, and science.

Means, B., Chelmer, C., & Knapp, M. (1991). *Teaching advanced academic skills to at-risk students: Views from research and practice*. San Francisco: Jossey-Bass.
    Instructional models that have been successful in teaching advanced skills such as reading comprehension, written composition, and mathematical reasoning are presented. Specific "how-to" suggestions are provided for improvement in instruction.

Nelson-Burford, A. (1985). *How to focus the distractible child*. Saratoga, CA: R & E Publishers.
    Geared toward the distractible child, teachers, and parents, the author provides holistic coping strategies and activities that allow the child to control senses and responses and focus on specific tasks by utilizing imagery, relaxation techniques, and yoga.

Pehrsson, R. S., & Denner, P. R. (1989). *Semantic organizers: A study strategy for special needs learners*. Gaithersburg, MD: Aspen.
    Text provides step-by-step instructions for teaching students to organize and use information, improve study strategies, achieve better grades by efficient learning, and overcome the fear of failure.

Peterson, P. (1989). *The know it all resource book for kids*. Tucson, AZ: Zephyr Press.
    This book contains definitions and "how to" examples about many school-related subjects and topics. The book is organized like an encyclopedia and topics relate to mathematics, geometry, geography, grammar, time, science, vocabulary, punctuation, measurement, writing, history, and money.

Pressley, M., and Associates (1990). *Cognitive strategy instruction that **really** improves children's academic performance*. Cambridge, MA: Brookline.
    The authors summarize validated cognitive strategies for teaching academic content to children in the elementary and middle grades. The focus is on **how** to teach strategies in the areas of decoding, reading comprehension, vocabulary, spelling, writing, and mathematics.

Rief, S. (1993). *How to reach and teach ADD/ADHD children: Practical techniques, strategies, and interventions for helping children with attention problems and hyperactivity.* West Nyack, NY: Center for Applied Research in Education.

> The author provides a holistic and team approach to teaching children with attention deficits. Included in the text are ways to identify ADD/ADHD; school-tested management strategies aimed at the prevention of behavioral problems; home-school intervention plans; parent participation programs; multisensory activities for teaching language arts, math, and writing to ADD/ADHD students; modifications of assignments and tests to accommodate these students; and methods for building a support team of administrators, teachers, tutors, and volunteers. Different sections of the text address the special challenges of kindergarten, middle school, and junior high.

Rosner, J. (1979). *Helping children overcome learning difficulties.* New York, NY: Walker & Co.

> Designed for parents and teachers, this handbook includes (a) methods for evaluating a child's perceptual skills, (b) activities to teach perceptual skills, (c) aids to help a child with academic subjects, and (d) suggestions for obtaining a learning environment suited to your child's needs. It is a comprehensive step-by-step parent guide intended to answer questions in many areas of concern for parents of children with special needs.

Schulz, L. (1989). *Creative play activities for children with disabilities.* Champaign, IL: Human Kinetics Publishers.

> This is a resource book that contains 250 games and activities designed to help infants to 8–year olds with all types of physical and mental disabilities grow through play. Detailed directions, necessary equipment, the activity's benefits, and, where possible, adaptations for different disabilities are listed for each activity.

Scruggs, T. E., & Mastropieri, M. A. (1992). *Teaching test-taking skills: Helping students show what they know.* Cambridge, MA: Brookline.

> This is a practical resource that informs teachers and parents how they can help their children become better test-takers. The text highlights issues related to test format and other conditions of testing that can assist learners to demonstrate the skills that they really do know.

Sheinker, J. & Sheinker, A. (1989). *Metacognitive approach to study strategies.* Gaithersburg, MD: Aspen.

> This text is a step-by-step guide to teaching essential skills in grades 4–12. It contains ready-to-use lesson plans to help students learn to skim materials quickly; write summaries of texts, films, lectures; take notes in social studies, English, and other subjects; develop outlines of content area information; and master study skills that can be applied to all subjects.

Strichart, S., & Mangrum, C. (1993). *Teaching study strategies to students with learning disabilities.* Des Moines, IA: Longwood.

> Ten specific study skills needed by middle and high school students are presented in this practical worktext with reproducibles. Specific skills presented include remembering information, taking notes, using the library, taking tests, and managing time.

Wallace, G., DeWolfe, J., & Herman, S. *BOLD-2: Behavioral objectives for learning disabilities.* Austin, TX: PRO-ED.

> The authors provide a curriculum guide to help plan for students with learning or behavioral problems in preschool through high school. Behavioral objectives are listed in careful developmental sequence, and numerous teaching-learning activities are suggested for each objective, along with appropriate materials and various classroom-tested evaluative procedures. Skill areas include sensory motor/readiness, conceptual, spoken language, reading, writing, math, science/social studies, study/organizational, and social skills.

Curriculum Guides/Comprehensive Programs/Kits

AIMS: An Instructional Manipulative Series. Elizabethtown, PA: Continental Press.

> Available for math, reading, and language arts, these motivating manipulative activities reinforce essential skills for students in elementary and special education settings. In all, 15 programs are available for prereading, basic reading, phonics, comprehension, language, computation, and applied math skills. Each program folder comes with teacher guides that provide directions, instructional strategies, suggestions for related activities, and reproducible evaluation charts.

EBSCO Curriculum Materials. Birmingham, AL: EBSCO Industries.

> EBSCO publishes a number of print, software, and multimedia kits as well as instructional materials designed to assist students to master basic and advanced skills in diverse curricular areas. Their well-organized catalog illustrates and describes their large product line.

Kiducation–Music and movement in the classroom. (1989). By S. Traugh. Cypress, CA: Creative Teaching Press.

> Kiducation is a combination of materials and teaching techniques designed to channel students' natural enthusiasm for music and movement into productive learning experiences. Kiducation provides one 20–25–minute lesson per week, ranging from kindergarten through sixth grade. The program supports the basic curriculum, relates rhythm and math, motivates students, bridges the gap between academics and fun, helps teachers think about different ways to teach, and provides a forum for students to share their learning through performance.

Learning to Study. Providence, RI: Jamestown Publishers.

> This series of books uses a step-by-step approach to help students develop skills in location—using dictionaries, almanacs and other references; organization—outlining, class-

ifying, summarizing, sequencing, and researching; interpretation—graphs, maps, fact, and opinion; retention—learning to concentrate; test-taking; skimming, scanning; and study strategies. Teacher's editions provide background information, teaching tips, enrichment activities, and their answers.

Picture Thoughts: Critical Thinking Through Visual Arts. (1989). By Dorothy Hamilton. Latham, NY: Hamilton Associates/Starry Night Distributors.

This is a systematic, organized, and flexible program that uses the visual arts to focus on critical thinking skills across the curriculum. The program is appropriate for all students, yet has been especially useful with students who are not working up to their potential (e.g., those with LD). It comes with a detailed manual describing the program, 12 museum quality reproductions, and a guidebook with study guides for each of the reproductions. Inservice training on the program is also available.

Reading, Writing, and Studying Strategies: An Integrated Curriculum. (1991). By P. L. Seidenberg. Gaithersburg, MD: Aspen.

This integrated curriculum is designed for secondary and college students who have not acquired (or are at-risk for not acquiring) the reading and writing skills needed to (a) understand textbook reading materials or (b) complete expository writing tasks typical of secondary and postsecondary settings. In this comprehensive curriculum, students are taught to organize information for expository reading and writing through overlapping activities. The program is made up of two major strands (Reading/ Writing and Reading/Studying) and a culminating unit on "Writing Well Organized Essays." Each of the 15 comprehensive units includes (1) a lesson script that provides a recommended instructional procedure for presentation of the strategy of skill; (2) reproducible handout materials; (3) reproducible controlled practice exercises; and (4) reproducible answer keys. Pre- and post-test materials are provided as well as forms for program management.

Instructional Materials/Toys

Ann Arbor Program Materials. Novato, CA: Academic Therapy Publications.

> Ann Arbor materials are used for the diagnosis and remediation of perceptual skills believed to underlie all academic learning. Many of the materials employ a reusable marking system or are available in reproducible form. Titles in the series include: Sentence Tracking, Cues and Signals in Math, ABC Mazes, and Programmed Spelling.

Carolrhoda Books. Minneapolis, MN: Carolrhoda.

> Carolrhoda publishes an array of children's books that cover different academic skills and age levels. Titles include books about ecology, biographies, crafts and activities, science, beginning readers, fiction, social studies, and picture books. Contact the publisher for its most recent catalog.

Chelsea Curriculum Publications. Yeadon, PA: Chelsea House Publishers.

> Chelsea publishes a number of high interest multicultural, language arts, social studies, science, and reading materials. The Junior World Biographies Curriculum Sets (e.g., African Americans in History, Women in History, etc.) are particularly appropriate for students with special needs as well as those who may be in ESL or bilingual settings.

Creative Teaching Press Materials. Cypress, CA: Creative Teaching Press, Inc.

> Creative Teaching Press markets a number of charts, activity books, displays, and content area materials designed for students with special education needs. Their comprehensive catalog describes their holdings and details discounts for large orders.

Curriculum Associates Materials. N. Billerica, MA: Curriculum Associates, Inc.

> Curriculum Associates markets textbooks, curriculum guides, videos, and other preacademic and academic programs including early childhood screening, parents as partners in education, whole language, language arts/reading, study skills, social studies/geography/science, drug educa-

tion/self-esteem, problem solving/math, and ESL/bilingual education. Write for the comprehensive listing of their well-organized catalog of holdings.

DLM (Developmental Learning Materials) Instructional Materials. Allen, TX: DLM.

DLM markets a number of instructional materials for a variety of content areas. Their catalog organizes the holdings into the following areas: Reading, Language Arts, Language Development and Speech, Practical Life Skills, Social Studies, Mathematics, and Early Childhood.

Edmark Learning Materials. Redmond, VA: Edmark.

Edmark offers an extensive catalog of products developed specifically to help meet the needs of special education students. Of special note is the Edmark Reading Program that is available in print or software and which provides a beginning reading program that teaches recognition and comprehension of 350 commonly used words. Also available is the Reading Milestones Program, other reading programs and books, and early learning materials. Additional titles and programs cover deaf education, mathematics, writing, teacher and parent resources, social and behavior skills, independent daily living skills, transitional vocational skills, tests and assessments, TouchWindow, Bartholomew's Book House, Millicent's Math House, and software that covers early concepts, reading, mathematics, art, writing, teacher tools, and hardware.

Golden Books and Games. Golden Press. Racine, WI: Western Publishing.

Golden publishes a large number of attractive, high interest books, videos, and games that can be adapted for any number of reading, math, social studies, and science lessons. In particular, the Little Golden Book Classics and the various special libraries (Sesame Street, Disney, Garfield, etc.) are attractive and motivating.

Macmillan's Books for Children and Young Adults. New York, NY: Macmillan Children's Book Group.

Under a number of imprints including Aladdin Books, Collier Books, Bradbury Press, Four Winds Press, and Margaret McElderry Books, Macmillan offers a large number of high interest books for children and youth. Consult their catalogs for a full, descriptive listing of the titles.

Perma-Bound. Jackson, IL: Perma-Bound Books.

Perma-Bound markets a large number of durable reading books and series for classroom use. Their lengthy catalog contains suggested titles for remedial settings and materials which integrate audiocassette activities.

Society For Visual Education (SVE) Materials. Chicago, IL: SVE.

SVE markets an extensive number of audiovisual programs for virtually all curriculum areas. A well-organized catalog describes CD-ROM software, filmstrips, laserdiscs, software, and videocassettes for social studies, science, health and safety, mathematics, reading, language arts, literature, and the arts.

Success by Design Materials. Hoffman Estates, IL: Success by Design, Inc.

Success by Design promotes a complete line of organizational materials. These products are easy to use and should help students use their time more effectively while improving study skills. They include a number of variations for assignment notebooks and time planners as well as a customized option.

Periodicals

The **ADHD Report,** published six times per year by National Professional Resources, is a newsletter written for practitioners, educators, and researchers who require up-to- date information on clinical practices involving individuals with ADHD. **Write:** National Professional Resources, 25 S. Regent St., Port Chester, NY 10573 or **Phone:** (800) 453–7641.

Educational Leadership, published monthly (September-May) by the Association for Supervision and Curriculum Development (ASCD), is a journal intended primarily for leaders in elementary, middle, and secondary education but is also for anyone interested in curriculum, instruction, supervision, and leadership in schools. ASCD also publishes guidebooks to assist in the teaching process. Examples include: *Making Connections: Teaching and the Human Brain; A Different Kind of Classroom: Teaching with Dimensions of Learning; and Tools for Learning: A Guide to Teaching Study Skills.* **Write:** ASCD, 1250 N. Pitt Street, Alexandria, VA 22314–1403.

Education and Treatment of Children, published quarterly by PRO-ED, is a behaviorally oriented journal that focuses on material of direct value to teachers and other childcare professionals who are interested in improving their teaching and clinical effectiveness. **Write:** PRO-ED Journals, 8700 Shoal Creek Blvd., Austin, TX 78758–6897 or **Phone:** (512) 451–3246.

Intervention in School and Clinic (formerly **Academic Therapy**), published five times a year by PRO-ED, is a hands-on, how-to resource for teachers and clinicians who require practical information for immediate implementation of educational research. **Write:** PRO-ED Journals, 8700 Shoal Creek Blvd., Austin, TX 78758–6897 or **Phone:** (512) 451–3246.

Remedial and Special Education, published quarterly by PRO-ED, is designed to bridge the gap between theory and practice and highlights applied research and integrative reviews of the literature. **Write:** PRO-ED Journals, 8700 Shoal Creek Blvd., Austin, TX 78758–6897 or **Phone:** (512) 451–3246.

Teaching Exceptional Children, published four times per year by CEC, is a practical classroom-oriented magazine that explores instructional methods, materials, and techniques for working with children who have disabilities. Articles reflect the need to blend theory, research, and practice. **Write:** CEC, 1920 Association Drive, Reston, VA 22091–1589 or **Phone:** (703) 620–3660.

Multimedia/Hardware

"ADHD: What do we know?" and **"ADHD: What can we do?"** New York, NY: Guilford.

These are two video programs which explore the causes of ADHD and the range of management techniques that can be used at home and in the classroom. Each tape comes with a facilitator's manual.

BFA Low Cost Videos. St. Louis: BFA Educational Media.

BFA markets a number of low cost videos (all priced below $49.95) in the areas of language arts, social studies, science, guidance, and fine arts. Their catalog describes each video within a well-organized framework.

Disabilities and Special Education Film and Video Rental Service. Bloomington, IN: Indiana University Audio Visual Center.

A large and diverse collection of films and videos are available to all recognized schools, institutions, and organizations throughout the United States. Approximately 200 holdings on *all* facets of teaching individuals with special education needs are available. Write for their descriptive catalog of holdings.

Educational Activities Video, Multimedia, and Software. Baldwin, NY: Educational Activities, Inc.

Educational activities markets a large number of video, filmstrips, audio, and computer-based materials designed to teach a diverse number of content and process areas including reading, language, math, and science. Materials are available for early childhood populations through adulthood. Write for the collection of descriptive and colorful catalogs.

NPR Videos. Port Chester, NY: National Professional Resources.

> NPR markets a number of useful videos pertaining to ADD and "thinking skills." **"Educating inattentive children,"** for example, is a two-hour video designed for inservice use. Write for their descriptive catalog.

Strategies for Training Regular Educators to Teach Children with Handicaps (STRETCH). Northbrook, IL: Hubbard.

> STRETCH materials fall into three categories: concepts, strategies, and subject matter. The concept strand includes videotapes and pamphlets to help regular education teachers understand basic issues in special education such as identifying behavior, grouping for instruction, learning styles, peer tutoring, assessment, and mainstreaming. The strategies section includes information on learning centers, individualized instruction, classroom management, behavior modification, questioning skills, and parent counseling. The third strand provides information on special students in content areas such as spelling, art, career education, language experience, mathematics, and reading.

"Teaching mildly handicapped students: Video training in effective instruction." Reston, VA: CEC.

> This is a package of two 20–minute videos in which teachers demonstrate effective teaching. Components demonstrated include gaining attention, reviewing past learning, modeling skills to be learned, prompting, and checking for understanding. Teacher guides are provided for each tape.

Organizations

The **Division for Culturally and Linguistically Diverse Exceptional Learners (DDEL)** is dedicated to advancing and improving educational opportunities for culturally and linguistically diverse exceptional children, their families, and the professionals who serve them. Key areas of focus include advocacy, collaboration, research, training, and leadership development. The division publishes a yearly monograph and the **DDEL Newsletter** three times per year. **Write:** DDEL, CEC, 1920 Association Drive, Reston, VA 22091–1589 or **Phone:** (703) 620–3660.

The **Division for Research (DR)** of CEC promotes research and the utilization of knowledge to enhance the education of exceptional children. The division publishes the journal **Exceptionality** quarterly and **Focus on Research,** a newsletter, three times per year. **Write:** DR, CEC, 1920 Association Drive, Reston, VA 22091–1589 or **Phone:** (703) 620–3660.

READING

Generic Textbooks

There are a number of generic textbooks that focus on the diagnosis and remediation of specific reading difficulties typical of students with special education needs. In general, these texts provide individual sections or chapters on various facets of reading and reading instruction including (a) the diagnosis of reading difficulties, (b) phonics instruction, and (c) methods for promoting comprehension. Some of the more popular texts are listed below.

Bond, G., Tinker, M., Wasson, B., & Wasson, B. (1989). *Reading difficulties: Their diagnosis and correction.* Boston: Allyn & Bacon.

Carnine, D., Silbert, J., & Kameenui, E. J. (1990). *Direct instruction reading.* New York, NY: Merrill/Macmillan.

Choate, J., & Rakes, T. A. (1989). *Reading: Detecting and correcting special needs.* Boston: Allyn & Bacon.

Ekwall, E. E., & Shanker, J. L. (1993). *Locating and correcting reading difficulties.* New York, NY: Merrill/Macmillan.

Rubin, D. (1991). *Diagnosis & correction in reading instruction*. Boston: Allyn & Bacon.

Swaby, B. (1989). *Diagnosis and correction of reading difficulties*. Boston: Allyn & Bacon.

Resource Books

Aaron, P., & Baker, C. (1991). *Reading disabilities in college and high school: Diagnosis and management*. Timonium, MD: York Press, Inc.

> The authors concentrate on the academic problems faced by students as they encounter more independent work and focus on improving reading, writing, listening, note taking, and test taking skills of students in secondary and postsecondary institutions. The text reviews specific procedures including the psychological process that underlies reading, types of reading disabilities, targeted instruction, diagnostic assessment, components-based assessment, management of problems, teaching strategies and support, and a model reading disabilities program.

Book Lab (1975). *Guidelines to teaching remedial reading*. North Bergen, NJ: Author.

> This is a manual for tutors teaching remedial reading to children, adolescents, or adults that provides basic information about problems students with reading problems encounter. Background information on skills needed for reading is also given. Assessment techniques for determining strengths and weaknesses and reading levels are presented. Finally, a practical program of instruction is detailed and suggestions for economical materials is included to aid tutorial programs with limited funds.

Cutting, B. (1989). *Getting started in whole language*. Bothell, WA: The Wright Group.

> This is a good introduction to the concept of "emergent literacy" and whole language learning. Unfortunately, special education teachers do not always receive training in these strategies, although these models are excellent for students with special needs.

Damico, J. (1992). *Whole language for special needs children.* Educom Associates; distributed by United Educational Services.

> This guide provides an introduction to teaching reading to children with disabilities using a whole language approach.

Fry, E., Kress, J., & Fountoukidis, D. (1993). *The reading teacher's book of lists.* Englewood Cliffs, NJ: Prentice Hall.

> The authors provide a large collection of ready-to-use, reproducible word lists to assist in reading instruction. Over a dozen sections contain lists of foundation words, word groups, word origins, comprehension aids, study skills, signs and symbols, and books.

International Reading Association. *Invitation to read: More children's literature in the reading program.* Newark, DE: Author.

> This resource book is divided into three major sections: an examination of the different genres available for teaching reading (books for emergent readers, acting it out, realistic fiction, informational books); thematic issues (enrichment through the arts, author studies, magic, multicultural understanding, international selections); and decisions regarding choosing a literature-based instructional program (reading workshop, exploring books, literature with students at risk, resources, and censorship). The book argues in favor of a literature-based instructional program and describes how to implement such programs.

Libretto, E. V. (1990). *High/low handbook: Encouraging literacy in the 1990s* (3rd edition). New York, NY: R.R. Bowker.

> This handbook is intended for teachers, librarians, and other individuals or institutions who provide easy reading material for disabled or reluctant teenage readers. It cites materials with a wide range of reading and interest levels for the student with poor reading skills. There is also support material to assist and inspire the professional who is looking for reading material to use with teenagers who have reading problems.

Rose, L. (1992). *Folktales: Teaching reading through visualization and drawing*.

> With this book, children visualize and draw the events of each story as the teacher reads aloud. Students can translate the words of the story into vivid and personal images. Each tale presents a story from a particular culture, deals with important issues, encourages discussion of ethics and values, and offers literature enrichment to the classroom.

Curriculum Guides/Comprehensive Programs/Kits

Barnell-Loft Multiple Skills Series. Baldwin, NY: Barnell-Loft.

> This is a series of books, which may be particularly helpful for children with hyperlexia or for children who are already reading but who may have problems with literal or interpretive comprehension skills. The series consists of books of short stories followed by multiple-choice questions.

Breaking the Code. (1975). Peru, IL: Open Court Publishing.

> This comprehensive, well-organized phonics-based remedial reading program is for students in Grades 4 and up. The program begins with basic sound-symbol relationships and progresses to where students build words into sentences and sentences into paragraphs. A detailed teacher's guide provides structured lesson plans and supplemental activities.

Chall-Popp Phonics Program. Elizabethtown, PA: Continental Press.

> This is a four level (K-3) integrated phonics and language arts program which makes use of literature and poetry. Comprehensive teacher editions provide lesson plans, assessment devices, and parent components as well as strategies for the use of the program's Students Books and manipulatives. There is also a **Chall-Popp Reading Books Program** which is designed to strengthen reading comprehension and thinking skills through literature.

Home Run Reading. (1992). Palo Alto, CA: Good Morning Teacher Publishing Co.

The Home Run Reading program is an interactive program for new and beginning readers that combines phonics and whole language approaches. The audio tape/workbook format centers around a baseball theme. The program includes four workbook levels: (a) first base, (b) second base, (c) third base, (d) home plate, and thirteen audio tapes as well as a guide. Critical thinking skills are encouraged throughout the program. Self-pacing and self-correction aspects of the program require the student's active participation. The multisensory activities format makes this a successful tool for use with all children.

Hooked on Phonics. Orange, CA: Gateway Educational Products.

This heavily advertised program is a series of 12 audio tapes, 380 flashcards, and 7 workbooks which teach all the basic phonetic sounds of the English language and is geared for ages 2 to adult. The SRA Reading Library Kit is used in conjunction with Hooked on Phonics to work on comprehension.

Jamestown Heritage Readers: An integrated reading/literature/language arts program for grades K-6. Providence, RI: Jamestown Publishers.

The Readers are big books filled with beautifully illustrated children's classics. Kindergartners and first graders read stories about Goldilocks, the Gingerbread Man, and the Little Red Hen, together with Mother Goose nursery rhymes that provide beginner readers with rhyme, rhythm, repetition, predictable sentence patterns, and matched illustrations. Complete lesson and activity guides are included in each big book. Readers in grades 1 to 6 have stories, folktales, fables, poems, nonfiction, myths, paintings, watercolors, drawings, and illustrations by such writers and artists as Beatrix Potter, Robert McCloskey, Virginia Hamilton, and James Thurber. The teacher's editions include before reading and after reading activities, linked experiences, writing connection, additional readings, and art lessons.

Jamestown's Timed Readings. Providence, RI: Jamestown Publishers.

> This series is based on practice to improve reading speed while retaining and improving comprehension. The reading selections are nonfiction and topics include travel, psychology, safety, sports, history, the human body, and inventions. The series can be used with one student or an entire class, are uniform in word length that can be easily timed, include drills for practice, are presented at ten reading levels for precise placement, and include questions to reinforce comprehension. Reading levels include 4–college. Jamestown also has a program for vocabulary, **Vocabulary Drills,** and **The Single Skills Series,** a program designed to strengthen specific reading skills.

Learning to Read & Think. Providence, RI: Jamestown Publishers.

> This six-book series provides students with lessons and re-inforcement activities they need to become critical readers and thinkers. Skills are introduced at the appropriate levels and reinforced and developed at subsequent levels. Skills include distinguishing between facts and opinions; identifying words that describe, judge, and persuade; identifying slanted writing; identifying author's purpose; drawing logical conclusions; detecting facts from unrelated facts; and judging sources. Teachers' guides are also included.

Living Phonics—The Scaredy Cat Reading System (1991). By J. Herzog. Cornerstones, Inc.

> A program designed by a teacher of students with LD that teaches concepts through simple stories with letters, **Scaredy Cat Reading** is a flexible approach that incorporates phonics, linguistics, and whole language approaches. The basic program is contained in two easy-to-use binders: (a) **The PreReading Kit** which provides methods and materials for teaching beginning sounds and blends and (b) **The Complete Reading Manual** which begins with blending and continues through prefixes, suffixes, and the importance of foreign words in our English language.

Open Court Reading and Writing (1989). Peru, IL: Open Court Publishing.

This innovative, integrated K-6 language arts program is designed to build strategies to develop students' thinking, reading, and writing abilities. This comprehensive program makes use of authentic literature and easy-to-follow teacher guides demonstrate how lessons can be tailored to meet students' specific needs and the variety of ways specific strategies can be modeled during reading lessons. Each lesson in the program includes strategies to help students make effective use of the writing process. The program is appropriate for all students yet is especially useful for students with reading problems due to the emphasis on the direct modeling of specific language arts strategies. Program materials for each of the grade levels include student reader anthologies; comprehensive teacher resource books containing tests, transparencies, record sheets, and enrichment exercises; teacher guides; and student work materials. A variety of useful support materials (i.e., games, journals, practice books, log books, etc.) are also available. Of particular interest is the **Catching On Comprehension and Thinking Skills** workbooks that translate recent cognitive process research into entertaining activities for students.

Phillip Roy Survival Skills Reading Program. (1992). Indian Rocks Beach, FL: Phillip Roy.

Designed to prepare students for the transition into the work environment, this program is divided into four areas: (a) the Work Series which is all about the process of getting and keeping a job; (b) the Personal Consumerism Series which addresses shopping, consumer laws, understanding ads, and buying a car; (c) the Contemporary Living Series which provides information on decision making and map reading skills; and (d) the Personal Finance Series which covers topics such as insurance, establishing credit, and handling money. A third and fifth grade reading level version is provided in each of these programs. The program's emphasis is on comprehension and critical thinking skills. The information in the computer program is integrated with worktexts and audiocassettes. The program's multisensory approach is designed for students with a variety of disabilities.

Phoenix Reading Curriculum. St. Louis, MO: Phoenix Learning Resources.

This is a comprehensive step-by-step reading program for all levels that utilizes high interest materials. Programmed format allows for flexible pacing, and the teacher's guides have duplicating masters and instructional suggestions. Phoenix also markets a language arts and spelling curriculum.

Phono-Visual Reading Program. Gaithersburg, MD: Phonovisual Products, Inc.

A reading program that does not teach reading in and of itself, but once mastered, this initial step in decoding enables students to acquire comprehension, encoding, and additional decoding skills and to apply these skills to their reading, spelling, and writing. Materials include such products as the *Phonovisual Consonant Flipsticks*, *Phonovisual Consonant Picture-Pack*, *Textbook for Teachers*, *The Phonovisual Road to Power and Confidence*, *The Phonovisual Readiness Workbook*, *The Phonovisual Transition Workbook*, *The Phonovisual Consonant Workbook*, *The Phonovisual Vowel Workbook*, and *The Phonovisual Mastery Workbook*. The program is designed to promote security and confidence in reading, spelling, and writing for all students.

Primary Phonics. Cambridge, MA: Educators Publishing Service.

Workbooks and phonetic storybooks for grades K-4. These workbooks focus on word families and are particularly easy to adapt into games in order to make reading more "hands on" for students with special needs.

The Reading Connection. (1984). Peru, IL: Open Court Publishing.

This resource is a comprehensive, research-based remedial reading program designed for use in grades 7–12 with students who are LD or who are reading below grade level. The program is based on the premise that older students who are poor readers have certain unique reading problems in common. The program's three strands—reading comprehension, vocabulary, and writing—help make explicit the connection between cognitive skills and the application of those skills to reading while using adult reading formats. Specific lesson formats are provided in the easy-to-use teacher's guides.

Reading in the Content Areas. (1990). Syracuse: New Readers Press.

Reading in the Content Areas: Literature, Social Studies, and Science is a comprehensive reading comprehension program. The fifth grade and up reading level makes this program suitable for adults and young adults who have mastered decoding skills but have difficulty with comprehension. Each content area contains two anthologies, teaching guides, and photocopy masters. The teaching guide for each reading selection is organized into learning objectives, background information, prereading activities, teaching suggestions, and post-reading activities. Critical thinking skills, cooperative learning activities, and integrative learning tasks involving listening, speaking, and writing skills are emphasized. New Readers Press also publishes *Challenger,* an eight reading levels (1.0–8.5) book, high interest series designed for older teens and adults with reading deficiencies. Skills emphasized in the worktexts include phonics, word analysis, vocabulary, comprehension, writing, and study skills.

ReadingLinks: The Phonics-Literature Connection. (1992). Austin, TX: Steck-Vaughn Company.

This is a comprehensive program for primary phonics instruction that combines high quality literature, phonics instruction, and a variety of interactive practice and assessment activities. A teacher resource box provides convenient color-coded organization to the large number of activity masters, games, and extension activities. Activities included involve five important features: quality literature, comprehension development, activity-based instruction, review and assessment options, and home-school connections.

Reading Mastery Series. (1988). Chicago: SRA.

The Reading Mastery is a complete, direct instruction reading program intended for students in the first through sixth grades. Although it is not specifically designed for students with disabilities, a number of prominent research studies have shown that these materials produce significant academic gains across a range of disability conditions. A few principles have guided the program since its inception in the 1960s. First and foremost, the program, along with the teacher, accepts responsibility for teaching **every** student to read. Second, lessons are direct with tasks and activities specified in detail. Finally, students receive consistent daily practice, and assessment is continuous, with errors corrected the instant they occur. At each level (1–6), materials are provided including (a) presentation books, (b) teacher guides, (c) skills profile folders, and (d) student books and workbooks. Teacher-directed and independent student activities focus on decoding and comprehension, thinking skills and strategies, as well as literature and language.

Reading the Content Fields. Providence, RI: Jamestown Publishers.

This series of books and cassettes teaches students how to read and comprehend the specialized vocabulary and subject matter of five major study areas: science, social studies, mathematics, English, and practical arts. Each of the series is available on both middle and advanced levels for placement at optimum instructional levels.

Remedial Reading Drills. (1982). Ann Arbor, MI: George Wahr Publishing.

This is a set of drills for students with reading difficulties designed by Samuel Kirk, a pioneer in the field of LD. Drill sheets are preceded by detailed directions for use.

Say the Word. (1991). Syracuse, NY: New Readers Press.

This diagnostic remedial reading program is intended for young adult and adult readers at or below eighth grade reading levels. Say the Word is a phonics-based approach aimed at improving fluency and word recognition skills. The program contains screening tests, diagnostic tests, and a student handbook sectioned to allow independent work on problem areas pinpointed by the tests. The program also includes "test yourself" pages to encourage student participation in self-assessment and monitoring. The program format lends itself to use without direct instruction.

Steck-Vaughn Comprehension Skills. (1992). Austin, TX: Steck-Vaughn.

This resource is a flexible reading supplement that provides focused instruction and practice in critical comprehension skills including inference, main idea, context, facts, sequence, and conclusions. Materials are available for grade levels six to twelve, yet presented at reading levels two to six.

Steck-Vaughn Reading Comprehension Series. (1993). Austin, TX: Steck-Vaughn.

This series is a self-paced comprehension program comprised of short, high-interest worktexts. Designed for students in grades one to six, these eight titles build comprehension skills through the use of a controlled vocabulary. A separate teacher's guide is available for each title in the series.

Sunshine. Bothell, WA: The Wright Group.

Sunshine is a whole-language reading program that immerses children in print and cooperative learning from the first day of school. Learning to read is viewed as more than just learning to decode print; other successful strategies are employed. Activities using all three reading cue systems (semantic, graphophonic, and syntactic) are programmed in a system which encourages experimentation, mutual support, and individualization. As it is the philosophy of the program that children learn by reading, the program includes a variety of exciting reading material. For the teacher, the program has a comprehensive, well-sequenced teacher's guide that (a) explains the theoretical underpinnings of the program, (b) illustrates how to create themes and set up the program, (c) shows how to evaluate the program, and (d) contains reproducibles. A full chapter is devoted to strategies for adapting the program for students with special needs.

The Wright Group also publishes a quarterly newsletter entitled **The Whole Idea** that is intended as an open forum for excellence in education with an emphasis on Whole Language philosophy.

Instructional Materials/Toys

Henry Holt Reading Materials. New York, NY: Henry Holt.

Henry Holt and Company offers an extensive list of award-winning, beautifully written, beautifully illustrated children's books. The catalog lists each holding according to reading level and subject area. Subject areas include activity, play and imagination, adventure, alphabet and counting, animals, anthologies, art, biographies and autobiographies, board books, classics, contemporary issues, dance, disabilities, ethics, family, fantasy, health and fitness, fairy and folk tales, friendship, geography, government and politics, grief, history, multiculturalism and individual cultural groups, music, nature and the environment, pop-up books, reference books, religion, science and math, sex education, social studies, sports, and many more. Special education titles include *Knots on a counting rope, My buddy, Someone special, just like you, Certain small shepherd, And don't bring Jeremy, Secret garden, Thin air, Wish on a unicorn,* and *Probably still Nick Swansen.*

High Noon Books. Novato, CA: Academic Therapy Publications.

A wide variety (about 150) of short, engaging novels for students ages nine through the teen years. The novels are written at the first through fourth grade reading levels and are designed to strengthen sight vocabulary, thinking skills, and reading comprehension. A full catalog of the books is available.

Know Your World Extra. Middletown, CT: Weekly Reader.

Know Your World Extra is a biweekly periodical written specifically for special education students in the middle and senior high grades with high-interest/low reading levels. Each issue contains a news feature, science articles, language arts and social studies, life skill activities, a teacher's guide, and skills extenders.

Lerner Books for Children and Young Adults. Minneapolis: Lerner Publications Co.

Lerner Publications offers a variety of new titles for children and young adults. The books focus on topics ranging from capital punishment to vegetarian cooking. Many of the books can be categorized into series. The **"Pro/Con"** series promotes thinking skills by addressing a variety of issues such as capital punishment and abortion. The **"People's History"** series provides a social history of the U.S. The **"Creative Minds Biographies"** series gives the biographies of several men and women and their contributions to society. The **"Then and Now"** series is devoted to the changing republics of the former Soviet Union. The **"Easy Menu Ethnic Cookbooks"** give a variety of recipes from many nations. These series represent a few of the titles available from Lerner Publishing and many are suitable for children with special needs.

Pacemaker Classics Reading Materials. Belmont, CA: Fearon/Janus/Quercus.

High interest classic literature has been adapted for students with reading levels as low as 3.0. There are over 30 titles, including *Moby Dick*, *A Tale of Two Cities*, and *The Call of the Wild*. Study guides and books on tape are also available. Fearon/Janus/Quercus also markets a number of other high interest/low reading programs including **"World Myths and Legends," "Our Century Magazines,"** and **"Hopes and Dreams."** A number of short, fastpaced reading series are also available in the **"Fastbacks"** collection. A well-organized catalog describes the many reading series available.

Poetry Alive Publications. Ashville, NC: Poetry Alive.

Poetry Alive offers books and tapes with repeatable lines for emergent readers. They are especially useful for students with low reading skills because content is easy to follow, lines are predictable, and the tapes provide opportunities for independent "reading."

Rigby Reading Materials. Crystal Lake, IL: Rigby.

Rigby markets a number of reading series and titles that are appropriate for individuals with special needs. The **"Liter-**

acy 2000" series is a collection of books divided into eight stages that provide guided and independent reading, writing, and thinking activities across the curriculum. A colorful catalog also highlights a number of resources for emergent, early, and fluent readers.

Steck-Vaughn High Interest, Low Reading Level Reading Activity Books. Austin, TX: Steck-Vaughn.

Steck-Vaughn has a large number of high interest, low level reading activity books available as reading program supplements. Series titles include: (a) **"Spotlight,"** for fourth to eighth graders (reading level two to four), which focuses on sports and entertainment figures, (b) **"On Stage,"** for grades four to ten (reading level two to six), a series of high interest playbooks, and (c) **"The Great Series,"** for grades six to twelve (reading level two to four) which highlights fast-paced adventure topics in magazine style. In each of the books of the series, illustrated stories are followed by high interest reading activities.

Troll Read Alongs. Mahwah, NJ: Troll Associates.

Troll Read Alongs focus on the fun in reading. There is a wide range of books and reading centers designed to appeal to even the most reluctant of readers. Tapes accompany high interest reading materials from K-Grade 8. A colorful and descriptive catalog describes the wide variety of topical reading material available.

Turman High Interest, Easy Reading Materials. Seattle, WA: Turman Publishing.

Turman has several collections of easy-to-read paperbacks and reproducible workbooks that are designed to encourage readers with difficulties (reading levels 2.5–6). Short, fast-action paperbacks and magazine-like workbooks (six new issues each year) focus on celebrities (e.g., Bruce Springsteen, Tom Cruise, etc.), mystery stories, animal stories, and multicultural studies.

Vowels and Stories. North Bergen, NJ: Book-Lab.

This resource features a remedial reading approach focusing on vowel sounds and basic reading skills. The volume can be used with readers above the first grade in a variety of instructional settings. Each lesson contains a short reading selection focusing on a particular vowel sound. The selection presents that sound in a variety of words. Proficiency with consonant sounds is necessary for success with this program. Each lesson is followed by a student worksheet which addresses comprehension skills and other skills related to reading proficiency.

Organization

The **International Reading Association** is an incorporated, non-profit organization dedicated to reading, reading education, reading teacher training, and publishing materials on how to teach reading. The IRA has a journal, **The Reading Teacher,** and holds numerous conferences. **Write:** International Reading Association, 800 Barksdale Road, P.O. Box 8139, Newark, DE 19714–8139 or **Phone:** (302) 731–1600.

SPOKEN AND WRITTEN LANGUAGE

Generic Textbooks

Generic textbooks of language development typically include coverage of general language development, disabilities in language functioning, and means for teaching spoken and written language skills to students with special needs. Some of the more popular texts are listed below.

Choate, J. S. (1989). *Language arts: Detecting and correcting special needs*. Boston: Allyn & Bacon.

Crawford, L. W. (1993). *Language and literacy learning in multicultural classrooms*. Boston: Allyn & Bacon.

Polloway, E. A., & Smith, T. E. C. (1992). *Language instruction for students with disabilities*. Denver: Love.

Rowell, C. G. (1993). *Assessment and correction in the elementary language arts.* Boston: Allyn & Bacon.

Thomas, P. J., & Carmack, F. (1990). *Speech and language: Detecting and correcting special needs.* Boston: Allyn & Bacon.

Resource Books

Brinton, B., & Fujiki, M. (1989). *Conversational management with language-impaired children: Pragmatic assessment and intervention.* Gaithersburg, MD: Aspen.

> This comprehensive hands-on review is a guide for successful intervention with children who are language-impaired. It offers sound, state-of-the-art information for speech-language clinicians.

Cole, M. L., & Cole, J. T. (1989). *Effective intervention with the language impaired child.* Gaithersburg, MD: Aspen.

> This text provides practical information and materials such as telltale signs of language delay, assessment instruments, a seven-step model for language training, sample goals and activities for prespeech intervention, specific activities for 24 language problems, enrichment activities, and criteria for evaluating language programs and software.

Harris, K. R., & Graham, S. (1992). *Helping young writers master the craft: Strategy instruction & self-regulation in the writing process.* Cambridge, MA: Brookline.

> This is a practical guide designed for teachers to assist young writers develop the "know-how" of good writing. This "know-how" includes helping students (a) develop strategies for planning, generating, organizing, and revising their writing, and (b) strategies for directing and regulating their efforts. The book also contains chapters on how to evaluate writing strategy programs and tips for beginning and maintaining such programs.

Norris, J., & Hoffman, P. (1993). *Whole language intervention for the school-aged child*. San Diego, CA: Singular.
The authors advocate and set forth intervention plans and strategies to integrate the treatment of oral and written aspects of language using the child's classroom language. This approach can be easily adapted to different curricula to enhance children's abilities to talk and write about the activities of the classroom. Specific strategies focus on language development, use, and higher-level comprehension through reading, writing, and oral discussion.

Ross-Swain, D. (1992). *Cognitive-linguistic improvement program (CLIP): A program for speech-language pathologists treating neuropathologies of speech and language and learning disabilities*. San Diego, CA: Singular.
This text explores the diverse tasks needed to (a) improve memory skills and orientation and organizational abilities and (b) strengthen and improve skills of abstraction, judgment, reasoning, and processing. It is designed expressly for special educators, speech-language pathologists, psychologists, and occupational therapists involved in the treatment of communication deficits following traumatic brain injury. The book's main sections cover tasks for immediate memory, recent memory, temporal orientation, conceptual relationships and associations, organization and categorization, problem solving and abstract reasoning, and activities for independence.

Worthley, W. J. *Sourcebook of language learning activities: Instructional strategies and methods*. Austin, TX: PRO-ED.
This sourcebook details the essentials in language therapy, describes how to set up teaching programs, and explores how to select among a number of language activity sets. One hundred sets are provided and coded to indicate their levels of complexity, and can be used as day-to-day language learning experiences. These activities, along with the teaching, evaluation, and assessment techniques provided in this text, provide practical information on all aspects of work with the language impaired.

Curriculum Guides/Comprehensive Programs/Kits

Articulation Modification Programs. Austin, TX: PRO-ED.

> Each of the six programs included in this series is geared toward the kindergarten through grade four aged child and the older child with speech-disorders and includes stimulus pictures, "producing sentences" steps, rate drills, pre- and posttests, a terminal objective that establishes target phonemes in conversational speech, exercises at the single word, phrase, and sentence levels, and a carry-over program. Together, the six programs teach nine target phonemes in a programmed format with a constantly shifting stimulus.

The **Boone Voice Program for Children.** Austin, TX: PRO-ED.

> This program provides a cognitive approach to voice therapy and is designed to give useful step-by-step guidelines and materials for diagnosis and remediation of voice disorders in children. Teachers of the targeted group of kindergarten through grade eight aged children are provided a complete program including components such as screening, evaluation and referral manual, voice screening forms, voice evaluation forms, remediation manual, and voice improvement recording forms.

Communication Skill Builder's Kits. Tucson, AZ: Communication Skill Builders.

> Communication Skill Builders markets a number of language remediation/development kits for school-aged children. These kits range from comprehensive programs for developing expressive language to more specific programs that focus on vocabulary building and thinking skills. A colorful well-organized catalog describes each of the programs by highlighting specific purposes and benefits.

DISTAR Language. (1987). By S. Engelmann, & J. Osborn. Chicago: SRA.

> DISTAR provides a complete, direct instruction program intended for primary and remedial students that teaches stu-

dents to (a) understand the language of the classroom, (b) reason logically, and (c) express themselves clearly. In each of the three levels, 160 scripted 1/2 hour lessons are provided. Each of the three kits include (a) presentation books, (b) a teacher guide, (c) group progress indicators, and (d) student take-home workbooks.

Exploring English. Elizabethtown, PA: Continental Press.

This comprehensive six-book integrated language series (grades one to six) has been designed for students reading at or below grade. High interest activities in speaking, reading, listening, and writing are provided. Program components include student books and teacher editions which contain unit presentations and lesson plans.

Expressive Writing 1 & 2. (1983). Chicago: SRA.

Designed for middle and high school students with special needs, these two structured programs focus on the development of sentence, paragraph, and editing skills. Program 1 consists of 50 lessons and program 2 contains 45 lessons. It is estimated that each lesson takes 45 minutes to complete. Each program includes a teacher presentation book and a consumable student workbook.

Horizons Series. By S. Tilkin. Tulsa, OK: Educational Development Corp.

This is a series of reading and writing workbooks designed for children in the primary and secondary grades. Topics in the workbooks include nouns and pronouns; prepositions and conjunctions; verbs; paragraph writing and topic sentences; predicting outcomes; recognizing cause and effect; following directions; distinguishing between fact and opinion; and recognizing plot, character, and mood.

Listening Kit. East Moline, IL: LinguiSystems.

This kit is a comprehensive program for students ages five to eleven designed to improve the listening skills of students. The package includes games, audio tapes, and activity books.

PALS: Pragmatic Activities in Language and Speech. Austin, TX: PRO-ED.

> PALS is a teacher's source book that provides 180 communication lessons for introducing the total spectrum of communication skills. Each lesson contains vocabulary study and allows the students to participate actively in everyday, two-way communications situations. Children receive practice in non-verbal communication, active listening, remembering, speaking and reading formally and informally, language study, and writing.

PLUSS: Putting Language to Use in Social Situations. By T. Zirkelbach. Austin, TX: PRO-ED.

> This program is designed to teach language-delayed students in grades three through eight pragmatic language skills while reinforcing and stabilizing semantic and syntactic skills. Through a variety of games, home activities, and classroom presentations, students learn to request, inform, inquire, express feelings, introduce, and participate in class discussions. Using the PLUSS program, teachers provide guidance, set guidelines, make suggestions, correct errors, and reinforce appropriate communicative behavior while the students practice communicating in a variety of real-life situations.

Stevenson Language Skills Program. Attleboro, MA: Stevenson Learning Skills, Inc.

> This program presents an alternative approach for teaching reading and writing that uses familiar techniques in new ways to create a structured curriculum of comprehensive language skills. The program uses images which are anchored in the student's concrete experiences to teach abstract concepts. The program applies this approach to an extensive set of language units, each sequenced to create a solid foundation for mastering English.

Systematic Fluency Training for Young Children. Austin TX: PRO-ED.

> This is a step-by-step training program designed to provide comprehensive training procedures, assessment, and models for the direct management of the young stutterer, aged three through nine. Fluency is gained through a progressive series of exercises that children perform with the help

of clinicians and household members. An important component of the program involves parent counseling, home programming, and environmental transfer procedures.

Vocabulary Victory. East Moline, IL: LinguiSystems.

This is a vocabulary program for middle and high school students who continue to do poorly with vocabulary. Written by Albert Brigance, the program consists of a four-book set, ranging from the third to sixth grade reading level.

Windows on Language Through Literature. (1989). Sunnyvale, CA: Creative Publications.

Windows is a program containing six resource books organized around selected themes including (a) The Family, (b) Home and Neighborhood, (c) Friendship, (d) Fears and Fantasies, (e) Animal Adventures, and (f) Once Upon A Time. The program, for use with young children, requires use of 48 popular children's storybooks. A variety of multisensory interactive activities are designed for each of the storybooks used in the thematic resourcebooks. The program focuses on language development and communication skills.

Instructional Materials

Annick Whole Language Materials. Willowdale, Ontario.

Annick markets whole language materials designed to be used in regular and special education classrooms. Materials include Annick's "Books About You", teacher's guides, and activity cards. Special interest books include titles such as the following: *Draw-And-Tell: Reading, Writing, Listening, Speaking, Viewing, Shaping*, and *You Won't Believe Your Eyes*.

Fearon/Janus/Quercus Language Arts Materials. Belmont, CA: Fearon/Janus/Quercus.

Fearon markets a number of high interest language arts materials designed to motivate reluctant learners. Some titles include *Vocabulary: Meaning and Message, Practical English*, and the *Pacemaker Practical English Series*.

Imaginart Communication Products. Bisbee, AZ: Imaginart.

> Imaginart markets a number of speech/language instructional materials for addressing problems due to cleft palate, stuttering, articulation disorders, and disorganized thinking. Write for a descriptive catalog.

LinguiSystems Listening and Language Materials. East Moline, IL: LinguiSystems.

> LinguiSystems markets a large number of instructional materials and programs designed to promote spoken and written language competence. A colorful catalog highlights a large number of materials focusing on listening, vocabulary, articulation, and language.

Steck-Vaughn Language Exercises (1990). Austin, TX: Steck-Vaughn.

> For grade levels one to eight, this drill and practice program provides focused practice in traditional problem areas of writing including composition, grammar, vocabulary, and sentence structure. Work texts are supplemented by teacher guides which contain scope and sequence charts, suggestions for effective teaching, and tests.

Structures in Spelling. (1992). Syracuse: New Readers Press.

> Structures in Spelling uses auditory, visual, and kinesthetic techniques to teach spelling to adults and young adults. The program provides a structural approach to spelling and is intended for more advanced learners. It is grounded in research centering on the cognitive processes used in spelling. The program has two components: (a) a student workbook and (b) a teaching guide. The program focuses on prefixes, suffixes, root words, and the combining of word parts to produce a predictable pattern for spelling much of the English language. The success of multimodality approaches in teaching makes this a promising spelling program for students with disabilities.

Target Spelling. (1991). Austin, TX: Steck-Vaughn.

> Target offers a controlled pace, easy-to-read (reading level one to six) six-volume spelling program for students in grades two to ten. Activities in the worktext include cloze

paragraphs and cursive writing exercises. Teacher's edition contains suggestions for instruction, scope and sequence charts, and placement tests.

The 'Write' Way to Spell. North Bergen: BOOK-LAB. Two-volume program which teaches basic sight words compiled from Started Word lists. Each workbook contains 36 lessons which teach spelling through writing. The writing activities build on the words from previous lessons and encourage creative writing, sentence structure, listening, and comprehension skills. The program is intended for use with ESL and special needs students, but can be used with any student who has mastered primer vocabulary.

MATHEMATICS

Generic Textbooks

There are several textbooks that focus on the diagnosis and remediation of specific math difficulties typical of students with special education needs. In general, these texts provide individual sections or chapters on the specific characteristics of students experiencing difficulties in mathematics, various approaches for diagnosing math difficulties, and alternative methods for teaching basic computation and advanced problem-solving skills. Some of the more popular texts are listed below.

Cawley, J. F. (1984). *Developmental teaching of mathematics for the learning disabled.* Austin, TX: PRO-ED.

Cawley, J. F., Fitzmaurice-Hayes, A. M., & Shaw, R. A. (1988). *Mathematics for the mildly handicapped: A guide for curriculum and instruction.* Boston: Allyn & Bacon.

Enright, B. (1989). *Basic mathematics: Detecting and correcting special needs.* Boston: Allyn & Bacon.

Silbert, J., Carnine, D., & Stein, M. (1990). *Direct instruction mathematics.* Columbus, OH: Merrill.

Spikell, M. (1993). *Teaching mathematics with manipulatives: A resource of activities for the K-12 teacher*. Boston: Allyn & Bacon.

Resource Books

Miles, T. R., & Miles, E. (1991). *Dyslexia and mathematics*. New York, NY: Routledge.
> Strategies and approaches for presenting mathematics to students with dyslexia are presented in this edited volume. The authors make use of case studies to illustrate their recommendations.

Nolting, P. D. (1991). *Math and the learning disabled student: A practical guide for accommodations*. Pompano Beach, FL: Academic Success Press.
> This is a practical guidebook geared toward counselors, teachers, and administrators to assist in the definition of the specific learning disabilities, including their effects on mathematics achievement and the accommodations that can be made for students with LD.

Nolting, P. D. (1991). *Successful math study skills*. Pompano Beach, FL: Academic Success Press.
Nolting, P. D. (1991). *Winning at math: Your guide to learning mathematics through successful study habits*. Pompano Beach, FL: Academic Success Press.
> In these two resources, tips and procedures to help students improve their grades in math are provided. Suggestions are especially geared toward students who have previously failed mathematics and/or students who are visually impaired or learning disabled.

Curriculum Guides/Comprehensive Programs/Kits

Basic Mathematics: The Pacemaker Curriculum. Belmont, CA: Fearon/Janus/Quercus.
> This high interest/low reading level math program contains short, clear, and single concept lessons. Fearon also

markets other high interest/low reading level math programs including *Practical Mathematics* and the worktexts *Working Makes Sense*, *Using Dollars and Sense*, *Money Makes Sense*, and *Career Math Makes Sense*.

Connecting Math Concepts A, B, C, & D. (1992). By S. Engelmann, D. Carnine, & O. Engelmann. Chicago: SRA.

Designed for general education primary and at-risk students, this basal math program provides scripted step-by-step lessons that ensure that students understand the connections (a) among related concepts in mathematics, (b) across daily instructional activities involving mathematics, and (c) between mathematics and the world around us. Each level contains 120 lessons that take approximately 30–55 minutes. The program is organized by tracks (an ongoing development of a particular topic) and students work on three to five different tracks within each lesson. Each program includes teacher presentation books, a teacher's guide, consumable student workbooks, and a textbook for Level C.

Learner Activity Program for Developmental Mathematics. By J. Cawley et al. Austin, TX: PRO-ED.

This program is an interactive approach to teaching math—number concepts, whole numbers, fractions—for grades K-9. The program's flexibility benefits all students, including those who experience difficulty in math. The teacher is shown how to assess her students' divergent learning styles and needs and design instruction plans that build on their strengths. A complete program is offered to be used with individuals, small groups, and classes.

LML Math Kits. Baltimore, MD: LML, Inc.

LML offers mathematical education kits for preschool-aged children through adults. Special populations benefit in particular using manipulation, dexterity, sequencing, and visual discrimination skills. Kit offerings include: *Chameleon*, *Funny Money*, and *Alfa*. Teacher's guides are included.

Mastering Math. (1988). Austin, TX: Steck-Vaughn.

A developmental math program for grades one to six that is presented in workbook form at a low reading level. The six-book program is carefully sequenced with easy to use scope and sequence charts. Additional practice activities are available in specially designed practice books.

Math for the Real World. (1990). Syracuse: New Readers Press.

Math for the Real World is a remedial math program for older students. The program places emphasis on functional math skills and provides realistic practical math problems. Word problems and critical thinking exercises utilize everyday situations to make this program more relevant for the adult learner. The program has two workbooks, one for whole number operations and one for fractions, decimals, and percents. The teaching guide contains pre- and post-tests for math objectives, teaching suggestions, and a section on common errors made for each unit objective.

Math Teachers Press Math Program. (1990). Minneapolis: Math Teachers Press.

The Math Teachers Press program is divided into four levels (K-2), (3–4), (5–6), and (7–8). Each level contains three instructional components: (a) math capsules, (b) student workbook, and (c) skill builders activity masters. Math capsules is the diagnostic prescriptive portion which includes reproducible diagnostic tests, daily reviews, a list of math objectives, and a student record sheet. The list of math objectives is intended to aid in the formation of IEPs. Math objectives are addressed in the student workbooks and skill builders activity masters. The entire system is integrated with manipulative and cooperative learning games and activities. This system uses multimodality approaches to promote optimum success for students with disabilities.

Real Math. (1991). By S. Willoughby, C. Bereiter, P. Hilton, & J. Rubinstein. Peru, IL: Open Court Publishers.

This is a comprehensive **process** oriented program that is based on the idea of making mathematics real for students. Using empirically tested principles, this complete K-8 basal program helps children see that math is useful and important in their everyday lives. Thinking skills, problem-solving strategies, and geometry are emphasized at all levels. A well-organized, easy-to-use teacher's guide—viewed as the "heart of the program"—provides a variety of teaching activities. A number of other core, support, and ancillary materials make this a comprehensive method for all children, particularly those experiencing difficulties with math.

Recipe for Math. (1985). North Bergen, NJ: Author.

This diagnostic-prescriptive program is designed for students with disabilities, remedial students, and ESL students. The program contains an instructor's manual, manipulative kit, four workbooks, and a diagnostic placement test. Math concepts in addition, subtraction, multiplication, division, fractions, decimals, and percentage are the focus of the program. A variety of learning methods, multisensory activities, and skills presented at small sequential increments makes the program a successful experience for learners with special needs.

Saxon Math Program. Norman, OK: Saxon Publishers.

This is a comprehensive and sequential math program based on the philosophy that concepts are best taught through doing: gentle repetition, extended over considerable time. Saxon has materials that extend from K-3 instructional activities all the way to algebra and calculus. The earlier programs emphasize a hands-on approach with the use of manipulatives. A catalog explains the philosophy of the program and illustrates the materials.

Semple Math. Attleboro, MA: Stevenson Leadership Skills, Inc.

Semple Math is a basic skills mathematics program for beginning, high-risk, and/or remedial students of all ages. It is designed to accommodate the many needs of the beginning and math-disabled learner. The program teaches students how to learn the basic math materials through a strategies approach. The pupil is taught how to store new and abstract information in memory so that retrieval is accurate and more efficient.

Stern Structural Arithmetic. Cambridge, MA: Educators Publishing Service.

This is a program for preschoolers to third graders that teaches the fundamentals of mathematics in a logical, concrete way. Using strong color blocks, it teaches addition, subtraction, multiplication, and division by reasoning and doing rather than by rote. After completing an initial set of games and experiments, children learn all 50 addition and subtraction facts and are ready to move on to multiplication and division.

Windows on Mathematics. (1987). Sunnyvale: Creative Publications.

> Windows is a comprehensive math program for young children pre-K through second grade that is divided into 12 developmental math topics. The multisensory activities involve students in manipulative activities, movement, songs, plays, and many other concrete experiences. The books can be used as supplemental activities to basal programs, as an informal program, or as a primary math lab. A teaching guide is provided which contains assessment forms, math objective lists for each topic, and reproducible lesson aids.

Instructional Materials/Toys

Building Math Skills: Step by Step. Elizabethtown, PA: Continental Press.

> Continental offers two high interest series designed to enhance the math skills for students in the primary and intermediate grades. These practice activities are supplemented by well-organized teacher's guides. Also available is the **Special Needs Curriculum** which offers specially designed activities for students to master fundamental math concepts (e.g., time, number operations, money, measurement, etc).

Cuisenaire. White Plains, NY: Cuisenaire Co. of America.

> Cuisenaire produces a large number of materials (yes, lots of manipulatives) to assist in the teaching of mathematics. In addition to a number of attractive and motivating sorting, counting, and classification materials, Cuisenaire also produces measurement materials, problem solving resources, and an extensive line of teacher resource manuals and videos. Consult their catalog.

Mathematics Skills for Consumers. (1992). Circle Pines, MN: American Guidance Services.

This is a text that addresses math skills through practical situations. Chapter topics include buying food, shopping for clothes, traveling, budgeting money, paying taxes, and banking and investing. It is intended for use with students grade eight and up. The text is easy to read, and each problem is presented with clear step-by-step solutions and many practice exercises. Computer and calculator skills have also been added to each chapter. A student workbook and teaching guide with blacklines and two alternate forms of chapter tests complete the set.

Mathematics Their Way. Menlo Park, CA: Addison-Wesley.

This is a book of activities designed to develop understanding and insight of the patterns of mathematics through the use of concrete materials. The activities, which are to be used with preschoolers to second graders, are designed to help young children see relationships, interconnections in mathematics, and to enable them to deal flexibly with mathematical ideas and concepts.

Math Stories. (1992). Syracuse, NY: New Readers Press.

Math Stories contains a teaching guide and three consumable workbooks which are designed to aid in the development of math skills and general reading comprehension. The series progresses from whole number operations to fractions, decimals, and percents. The workbooks provide students with set-up prompts and work space near the word problem. These prompts are phased out as the student progresses through each workbook. An answer key is provided in the back of each workbook to encourage self-checking. These books are flexibly designed to be used in the classroom, in one-to-one tutorial sessions, or by individual students. The three to four reading level makes them readily accessible to a variety of student populations.

Unifix Structural Mathematics. Peabody, MA: Didax.

Instructional manipulative interlocking cubes are designed to assist in teaching counting, matching, and numerical relationships. Didax also markets association puzzles and pattern recognition materials.

SCIENCE/SOCIAL STUDIES

General Text/Resource Books

Rakes, T. A., & Choate, J. (1989). *Science and health: Detecting and correcting special needs*. Boston: Allyn & Bacon.

Smith, L., & Smith, D. (1989). *Social studies: Detecting and correcting special needs*. Boston: Allyn & Bacon.

Curriculum Guides/Comprehensive Programs/Kits

Controlled Language Science Series. Austin, TX: PRO-ED.

> The controlled language readers and workbooks in the series provide students with better comprehension of complex concepts. They develop an interest in and a positive attitude toward science while relating science vocabulary to everyday life. The series is especially geared toward students who are not capable of handling traditional texts. *Introduction to Insect Life* and *Introduction to Reptiles* are included in the series, as are teachers' guides.

The History of the United States. (1989). North Bergen: BOOK-LAB.

> This two-volume social studies program is intended for use with English Second Language (ESL) students, special education students, and those students working toward a GED. The texts are designed to be high interest, low readability texts. The reading level in the texts is third to fourth grade. The content covers economic, political, and social issues relevant to U.S. development from early exploration to the election of George Bush to the Presidency. Each chapter contains introductory vocabulary, concise paragraphs, context clues and main ideas displayed in section headings and subheadings, and comprehension questions. The text set includes a teaching guide, and corresponding student workbooks are also available.

Windows on Beginning Science. (1988). Sunnyvale, CA: Creative Publications.

This resource is a comprehensive, high interest collection of six resource books on topics of nature and science processes designed for young children. Each book contains lessons on everyday things of interest to young children such as water, light, bugs, seeds, and rocks. The hands-on activities emphasize thinking skills. Each activity consists of step-by-step instructions, list of everyday materials necessary, and preparation hints.

Instructional Materials/Toys

Cuisenaire. White Plains, NY: Cuisenaire Co. of America.

Cuisenaire produces a large number of physical and life science materials that assist in the instruction of science. A vast number of valuable teacher resource materials are also available. Consult their catalog for a full listing of holdings.

Fearon/Janus/Quercus Social Studies and Science Materials. Belmont, CA: Fearon/Janus/Quercus.

Fearon markets a number of high interest, low reading level social studies and science materials designed to motivate reluctant learners. Most come with teacher's guides and supplemental materials. Some titles include *American government: The pacemaker curriculum*, *Our government in action*, *Economics*, *African Americans in U.S. history*, *World history*, *General science*, and *Biology*.

Getting to Know the United States: Our Constitution, Our Government. (1985). North Bergen: BOOK-LAB.

This workbook is intended to teach students about our government through the study of the Constitution. The reading level is fourth grade, but the concepts are aimed at middle school through secondary school students. Each lesson introduces new vocabulary and is divided into manageable paragraphs. Section and subsection headings provide main ideas and content clues. The lessons end with exercises in reading comprehension and expressive writing activities.

Our Nation's History. (1992). Circle Pines, MN: American Guidance Services.

> This text is designed to meet the needs of the special education student and is presented in an easy-to-read format. The chapters are divided into short sections which conclude with comprehension questions and vocabulary for that section. The chapter review addresses the main information presented in each section through summary, vocabulary activities, critical thinking skills, and writing activities. The history of the U.S. is presented from colonization to the Persian Gulf War. The appendix includes both Spanish and English versions of the Constitution, the Declaration of Independence, and the Bill of Rights. The set includes the text, student workbook, teaching guide, blackline masters, and a teacher resource center.

Steck-Vaughn Social Studies Series, Secondary Social Studies Series, and Science Today Series. (1987). Austin, TX: Steck-Vaughn.

> For all grade levels, these high interest, low reading level (reading level one to five) core science and social studies worktext series include interesting reading selections which parallel standard science and social studies curriculum. Teacher editions provide suggested teaching strategies, vocabulary lists, and evaluation alternatives. Social studies topics include world geography, American government, map skills, families, and neighborhoods. Science topics include life science, earth science, and physical science.

United States Government. Circle Pines, MN: American Guidance Services.

> The United States Government text is intended for use with students reading below level and for ESL students. Material is presented in a high interest, low readability format and covers all areas of U.S. government. The chapters are divided into short sections and each section ends with activities focused on comprehension, critical thinking skills, and writing skills. An accompanying workbook, teaching guide, blackline masters, and resource binder are also available.

Usborne Books. Tulsa, OK: EDC Publishing.

EDC markets a wide variety of high interest books for social studies and science. Although not designed specifically for learners with deficiencies, this wide variety of attractive books may be adapted for appropriate use.

Social Competence and Self-Esteem

When we speak of social competence, we are referring to the wide range of behaviors that enable an individual to interact effectively with others and to reasonably conform to the demands of a specific situation. Unfortunately, a large number of children, particularly those with special educational needs, do not develop the social skills (e.g., dealing with frustration, cooperation, assertion, self-control) necessary for social competence. Consequently, these students tend to develop negative relationships with teachers, parents, and peers. To promote social competence and self-esteem, teachers typically (a) develop classroom management systems designed to prevent and reduce problem behaviors and (b) develop instructional programs to directly teach those social skills and problem-solving processes thought to be lacking in the behavioral repertoires of the students.

Consistent with this process, we have organized the wide array of available resources into two major sections: **Classroom Management** and **Teaching Social Competence and Self-Esteem.**

CLASSROOM MANAGEMENT
Generic Textbooks

Alberto, P., & Troutman, A. (1990). *Applied behavior analysis for teachers: Influencing student performance.* New York, NY: Merrill/Macmillan.

Bauer, A. M., & Sapona, R. H. (1991). *Managing classrooms to facilitate learning.* Englewood Cliffs, NJ: Prentice Hall.

Charles, C. M. (1989). *Building classroom discipline: From models to practice.* New York, NY: Longman.

Clarizio, H. (1986). *Toward positive classroom discipline.* New York, NY: Macmillan.

Evans, W., Evans, S., & Schmid, R. (1989). *Behavior and instructional management: An ecological approach*. Boston: Allyn & Bacon.

Kauffman, J. M., Hallahan, D., Mostert, M., Trent, S., & Nuttycombe, D. (1993). *Managing classroom behavior: A reflective case-based approach*. Boston: Allyn & Bacon.

Rusch, F., Rose, T., & Greenwood, C. (1988). *Introduction to behavior analysis in special education*. Boston: Allyn & Bacon.

Sparzo, F. J., & Poteet, J. A. (1989). *Classroom behavior: Detecting and correcting special problems*. Boston: Allyn & Bacon.

Walker, J. & Shea, T. (1991). *Behavior management: A practical approach for educators*. New York, NY: Merrill/Macmillan.

Wolfgang, C. H., & Glickman, C. D. (1986). *Solving discipline problems: Strategies for classroom teachers*. Boston: Allyn & Bacon.

Zirpoli, T., & Melloy, K. (1993). *Behavior management: Applications for teachers and parents*. New York, NY: Merrill/Macmillan.

Resource Books

Algozzine, B. *Problem behavior management: Educator's resource service*. Gaithersburg, MD: Aspen.

> Teacher-tested strategies for helping students learn self-control; concrete ways to defuse a tense or dangerous situation; learning activities for students of all ages; suggestions for getting more help from parents; alternative ways to teach math to problem learners; interventions using art, music, and relaxation therapies; checklists and guidelines for substitutes; easy-to-read digests of the latest research; recommendations to help students perform to their individual

potential; and side effects of 16 therapeutic drugs students may use are all addressed in this practical resource. Automatic updates are available every year.

Burke, J. C. (1992). *Decreasing classroom behavior problems*. San Diego, CA: Singular.

This text presents basic and advanced procedures along with practical guidelines for decreasing behavior problems in the classroom. The main sections include an interdisciplinary historical overview, assessment procedures, intervention programs, and methods for increasing cooperative classroom behaviors, strategies for reducing inappropriate classroom behaviors, and suggestions for integrating behavior management into a student's Individualized Educational Program.

Cohen, J. J., & Fish, M. C. (1993). *Handbook of school-based interventions: Resolving student problems and promoting healthy educational environments*. San Francisco: Jossey-Bass.

Using the results of studies from the professional literature, this handbook describes interventions for all types of problem behaviors exhibited by students in elementary and secondary settings.

McCord, J., & Tremblay, R. (1992). *Preventing antisocial behavior: Interventions from birth through adolescence*. New York, NY: Guilford.

The edited text establishes the link between theory, measurement, and intervention programs, and presents a collection of studies that utilize experimental approaches to evaluate intervention programs for preventing deviant behavior. The book's contents are broken down into prevention experiments during infancy and early childhood; prevention experiments during the middle years; and prevention experiments during adolescence.

McIntyre, T. (1989). *The behavior management handbook: Setting up effective behavior management systems*. Des Moines, IA: Longwood.

This resource text contains a step-by-step guide for implementing effective behavior management techniques such as token economies, contracts, and assertive discipline programs.

Repp, A., & Singh, N. (1990). *Perspectives on the use of nonaversive and aversive interventions for persons with developmental disabilities*. Sycamore, IL: Sycamore Publishing.

> This edited text tackles the controversial issue of whether nonaversives alone are sufficient for challenging behavior problems. Both sides of the issue are presented across a variety of topics including ethics, interventions, functional assessment, basic and applied research, and treatment providers.

Savage, T. V. (1991). *Discipline for self-control*. Englewood Cliffs, NJ: Prentice Hall.

> The author identifies the dimensions of classroom organization and management, and illustrates those practices which make the teacher an effective manager and disciplinarian. Frequent use of case studies are found in this resource text.

Curriculum Guides/Kits

How to Teach Series. Austin, TX: PRO-ED.

> Written by leading behavioral researchers, this series, edited by Azrin et al., includes 16 booklets that provide step-by-step instructions to psychologists, parent trainers, educators, and mental health workers so that these professionals can in turn teach basic behavior management skills to other adults dealing directly with those who exhibit problem behaviors. The series focuses on specific procedures that help the user modify behaviors of classroom students, children at home, and other clients needing therapy. Each booklet in the series provides examples and exercises that help the teacher, parent, or client practice skills that allow the client to be more effective at managing behavior.

Larrivee, B. (1993). *Strategies for effective classroom management: Creating a collaborative climate*. Des Moines, IA: Longwood.

> This is a two-volume professional development package, complete with a leader's guide and teacher's handbook, de-

signed to assist individual schools or school districts provide quality training in classroom management.

Multimedia/Hardware

**"Cooperative discipline: Classroom management that
promotes self-esteem"** (Combined Services, Video
Resources Division, 1990). **"A teacher's guide to cooperative discipline: How to manage your classroom and promote self-esteem"** (Albert, 1989). Circle
Pines, Minnesota: American Guidance Service.

> The teacher's guide and videotape provide training for
> teachers in managing student misbehavior while encourag-
> ing student responsibility and parent involvement. The
> teacher's guide describes cues to correctly identifying stu-
> dent goals and needs, strategies for avoiding or defusing
> student confrontations, and methods for cooperative prob-
> lem solving. Based on Dreikurs' four goals of student mis-
> behavior, the videotape gives teachers practice at
> identifying goals of student misbehavior, selecting appro-
> priate interventions, and implementing interventions effec-
> tively and immediately. This video is intended for use by
> regular educators in workshops, inservice training, or uni-
> versity classes, but has significant application for special
> educators as well.

**"Nonviolent crisis intervention for the educator: Vol-
ume I: The disruptive child; Volume II: The disruptive adolescent; Volume III: The assaultive
student." "Breaking up fights: How to safely defuse
explosive conflicts." "The art of setting limits."
"Documentation: Your best defense."** Brookfield,
WI: National Crisis Prevention Institute.

> This video series is intended for teachers of potentially
> disruptive or assaultive students at the elementary and sec-
> ondary levels. The series demonstrates ways in which teach-
> ers can recognize and defuse potentially explosive
> situations, provide needed therapeutic support to students,
> and react in nonviolent ways to student aggression. Brief
> guides included with each videotape review the crisis de-
> velopment behaviors of students, as well as the preventa-

tive techniques and teacher attitudes necessary for defusing potentially violent situations and helping students regain and maintain self-control.

In addition to training materials (and a journal—**The Journal of Safe Management of Disruptive or Assaultive Behavior**), NCPI delivers its own training program. A number of options as to the length and intensity are available. For those who opt for the intensive four-day intervention workshop, instructor certification is available. NCPI will also customize training for specific locations.

TEACHING SOCIAL COMPETENCE AND SELF-ESTEEM

Resource Books

Arendt, R. P. (1992). *Trust building with children who hurt: A one-to-one support program for children who hurt*. West Nyack, NY: Center for Applied Research in Education.

> A practical resource for counselors and teachers that includes step-by-step strategies and worksheets for working with students who act out in self-destructive ways. Specific sessions are detailed with an easy-to-follow pattern of warmth, trust, and open discussion.

Canfield, J., & Siccone, F. (1992). *101 ways to develop student self-esteem and responsibility*. Des Moines, IA: Longwood.

> This is a two-volume series for middle and high school teachers that contains over 100 activities to assist students to improve their self-esteem. Initial chapters in the two volumes prepare the teacher to lead the variety of instructional activities designed to help students learn to be happy, successful, and responsible young adults.

Friedman, B., & Brooks, C. (1990). *On BASE*. Kansas City, MO: Westport Publishers.

> BASE—Behavioral Alternatives Through Self-Esteem—consists of short, simple, communication activities that encourage positive behavior. Exercises and activities for 15

developmental levels (birth to 18 years) address core building blocks of self-esteem: approval, trust, sense of power, acceptance, responsibility, self-respect, respect for others, flexibility, pride, and sense of importance.

Fugitt, E. (1983). *He hit me back first*. Rolling Hills, CA: Jalmar.

Principles of psychosynthesis are used as the basis of activities directed toward developing within the child an awareness of his own inner authority and ability to choose, and the resulting sense of responsibility, freedom, and self-esteem.

Goode, C. B., & Watson, J. L. (1992). *The mind fitness program for esteem and excellence: Guided stories for imagery in whole-brain learning*. Tucson, AZ: Zephyr Press.

Three guiding principles—relaxation, visualization, and affirmation—are presented in each lesson in this program. These tools are used to develop self-esteem, positive relationships with others and the environment, and creative and cognitive skills. Lessons include activities in relaxation, self-worth, self and relationships, and self-discovery.

Jalmar Press Books on Self-Esteem. Rolling Hills, CA: Jalmar Press.

The Jalmar Press has several books on promoting self-esteem and communication skills. There are books for all age levels. There is also a series of books on creating a positive environment in the classroom and encouraging whole brain thinking. Titles include: *The parent book: raising emotionally mature children (ages 3–15); Free flight: Celebrating your right brain; Squib the Owl series (ages 5–up); Stress management for educators: A guide to manage our response to stress; Feel better now; Good morning class—I love you; Project self-esteem; Unlocking doors to self-esteem; and many others.*

Kendall, P., & Braswell, L. (1993). *Cognitive-behavioral therapy for impulsive children*. New York, NY: Guilford.

The authors describe a program to help children reduce impulsivity and improve their self control. The program can be used with children with a wide range of problems including impulsive behavior both with and without ADHD, conduct disorder, and learning disabilities. Treatment strategies are provided that include the systematic involvement of parents and teachers, and include case examples and transcripts.

Parenting Press Books. Seattle, WA: Parenting Press, Inc.

Parenting Press offers a series of books to help children deal with their feelings, how feelings affect their behavior, feelings about being different, and with problem-solving strategies. Specific titles available include: *Ellie's day* (let's talk about feelings); *I can't wait* (a problem solving book); *I'm frustrated* (dealing with feelings); *I'm mad* (dealing with feelings); *I'm proud* (dealing with feelings); *It's my body* (a book to teach young children how to resist uncomfortable touch); *I want it* (a children's problem solving book); *My name is not dummy* (a children's solving book).

Salmon, L. S. (1992). *Activities for building confidence through dramatic arts.* Tucson, AZ: Zephyr Press.

The goal of this program is to encourage self-confidence through the dramatic arts. Dramatic arts can acquaint students with the rewards of non-graded activities: a sense that learning can be enjoyable, that no one has to fail, and that each is capable and talented. The activities in this book are designed for elementary school children, and reading is not necessary; so, special needs students can participate fully.

Curriculum Guides/Kits

The ACCEPTS Program: A Curriculum for Children's Effective Peer and Teacher Skills and **The ACCESS Program: Adolescent Curriculum for Communication and Effective Social Skills.** By H. Walker et al. Austin, TX: PRO-ED.

Together, the ACCEPTS and ACCESS programs make up the complete Walker Social Skills Curriculum, but each is complete in itself. ACCEPTS is a curriculum for teaching classroom and peer-to-peer social skills to handicapped and nonhandicapped children in grades K-6. Both regular and special education teachers use the curriculum to cognitively teach social skills as subject matter content in one-on-one, small groups, or large group formats. ACCESS teaches effective social skills to students at middle and high school levels in the same environments as ACCEPTS. However, ACCESS teaches peer-to-peer skills, skills for relating to adults, and self-management skills.

Aggression Replacement Training. Champaign, IL: Research Press.

This program is a coordinated, three-part training approach designed to teach adolescents to understand and replace aggression and antisocial behavior with positive alternatives. Students involved learn prosocial skills, anger control, and moral reasoning. The text provides all necessary information to implement the program.

Be Cool Video Series: Coping with Difficult People. Santa Barbara, CA: James Stanfield Company, Inc.

The video curriculum series illustrates techniques for managing many of the difficult interpersonal behaviors faced by children and adolescents. A series of videotapes illustrates effective and ineffective responses to difficult people and situations. Titles include: **"Coping with teasing"; "Coping with anger"; "Coping with criticism";** and **"Coping with bullying."** Through the demonstration of COLD (passive), HOT (aggressive), and COOL (assertive) responses, students are instructed to respond to situations in a calm and thought-out manner. A well-written teacher guide complete with detailed lessons is provided with each of the four modules.

Fearon/Janus/Quercus Coping Materials. Belmont, CA: Fearon/Janus/ Quercus.

Fearon markets a number of high interest, low reading level materials designed to help students deal with troubling issues such as living with a single parent, divorce, stepfamilies, AIDS, marriage, and dating. Several of their series titles include *The need to know library*, *Making smart choices about your future*, *Janus survival guides*, and *The values library*. Most programs have a teacher's guide.

Mind Your Manners: A Six Part Video Series on Essential Social Skills for Persons with Special Needs. (1987). Santa Barbara, CA: James Stanfield Company, Inc.

The video curriculum series illustrates for teens and young adults with special needs the social behaviors—or good manners—that will allow them to fit into everyday social situations. The objectives of the six-tape series are for students to identify proper behaviors to use at home, at the table, at school, in public, and when greeting and conversing with others. A teacher's resource guide provides specific lesson objectives, procedures for introducing and guiding the lesson, and checklists for assessing students' performance during role plays.

The Prepare Curriculum. Champaign, IL: Research Press.

The Prepare Curriculum is a comprehensive training program for adolescent students who are chronically aggressive, withdrawn, or otherwise weak in prosocial competencies. The curriculum includes ten course-length interventions that involve games, simulations, role playing, group discussions, and other activities that enhance group participation and motivation for learning. It also examines issues such as classroom management, trainee motivation, assessment and individualization, and curriculum utilization for both remedial and preventive purposes.

Skillstreaming. Champaign, IL: Research Press.

This is a training program that addresses the social skill needs of youngsters who display aggression, immaturity, withdrawal, or other problem behaviors. The various programs are designed to help kids increase self-esteem, to contribute to a positive classroom atmosphere, and to develop competence in dealing with interpersonal conflicts. The training approach utilizes modeling, role playing, performance feedback, and transfer training. Skillstreaming programs are available for early childhood, elementary age children, and for adolescents. A Skillstreaming video demonstrating the approach is available as are specific instructional materials such as skill cards and progress forms.

Think Aloud. Champaign, IL: Research Press.
> This is a program in which children can be taught to solve problems and behave in a socially appropriate manner as they are taught academic skills. Each of three volumes (grade levels one to two, three to four, and five to six) provides structured lessons that teach students how to use verbal mediation to guide their social behavior and to cope with daily problem situations. Each lesson specifies teaching strategies, prerequisites, objectives, and necessary materials.

Thinking It Through. Champaign, IL: Research Press.
> This resource is an easy-to-use training program for teaching problem solving to persons with developmental disabilities, chronic mental illness, brain injuries, or adolescents with emotional problems. The program focuses on problem areas such as emergencies and injuries, safety, dealing with authority figures, peer issues, and more.

Instructional Materials/Toys

KIDSRIGHTS Educational Materials. Mount Dora, FL: Kidsrights.
> Kidsrights markets a number of print and video materials that focus on the prevention of school and family behavior problems and the development of positive self-esteem. A comprehensive catalog highlights materials appropriate from preschool to professional.

Multimedia/Hardware

Asset. Champaign, IL: Research Press.
> This program uses behavior modeling videotapes, group discussion, role playing, and homework assignments to teach adolescents the skills they need for successful social interactions. The tapes feature modeling scenes of adolescents interacting with peers, parents, teachers, and other adults. The program is divided into eight teaching units with videotapes, program materials, and a leader's guide.

"Being with people: Social skills training for persons with special needs." Champaign, IL: Research Press.

This eight-part video series teaches the essential social skills needed to establish positive relations with friends, dates, housemates, and others. Titles available include: **"Being with friends"; "Being with a date"; "Being with housemates";** and **"Being with authority figures, acquaintances, & strangers."** The tapes illustrate the do's and don't's of social performance using videomodeling (the use of role ideals or models to demonstrate specific social behaviors with the intent of promoting emulation). A teacher resource guide lists goals and objectives as well as provides sample lesson plans.

Dealing with Anger. Champaign, IL: Research Press.
This video-based training program was developed to teach African-American youth skills that could reduce their disproportionate risk of becoming victims or perpetrators of violence. The program focuses especially on the social environment of African-American adolescents and is built around three video tapes: **"Givin' it," "Takin' it,"** and **"Workin' it out."** Students learn skills for dealing with conflicts, role playing some of the situations, and giving or receiving feedback on their role play performances. The program also includes a leader's guide and a set of skill cards.

"Feeling good about yourself." Kailua-Kona, HI: Feeling Good Associates.
This 22–minute video or film program, with accompanying manual, is designed to assist those who work with people who have disabilities to build their self-esteem and improve their assertiveness and decision making skills. Feeling Good Associates also produces a sound filmstrip entitled **"I can say no!,"** specifically designed for disabled students to say no in peer pressure situations.

"Learning to manage anger." Champaign, IL: Research Press.
This is a video training program designed to teach junior and senior high school students the seven-step RETHINK method for controlling anger and resolving conflict. It is divided into several segments allowing time for group discussion and/or role playing. The video is accompanied by a leader's guide.

Functional Competence

Functional Skills include the wide range of nonacademic skills necessary to meet the many demands of daily living. These skills, which are often difficult for students with developmental delays and severe/multiple disabilities to master, include, but are not limited to: **personal hygiene, home management, recreation and leisure, physical education, personal safety,** and the broad array of component skills necessary for **community integration and involvement.** Unfortunately, many school-based programs devote little time to formal instruction in the realities and demands of everyday life (Patton et al., 1989). Consequently, many students with disabilities exit school with significant deficiencies in: (a) using community resources, (b) planning recreational outings, (c) financial planning, (d) basic personal grooming, (e) dealing with medical emergencies, and (f) managing a home successfully. The resources that follow can assist educators in providing this much needed instruction.

AVAILABLE RESOURCES: Functional Competence
Resource Books

Baker, B.L., Brightman, A.J., Blacher, J.B., Heifetz, L.J., Hinshaw, S.P., & Murphy, D.M. (1989). Second Edition. *Steps to independence: A skills training guide for parents and teachers of children with special needs.* Baltimore: Paul H. Brookes.

> This guide offers step-by-step instructions for teaching self-help skills such as dressing, grooming, feeding, and toileting, plus play, household care, and other skills necessary for independence. It includes information on selecting appropriate goals and monitoring progress toward their achievement, as well as a section on behavior management.

Baladerian, N. (1991). *The sexual assault survivor's handbook for people with developmental disabilities and their advocates.* Saratoga, CA: R & E Publishers.

> Persons with developmental disabilities, learning disabilities, speech and hearing impairments, mobility impairments, and visual impairments are specifically addressed in

terms of surviving and dealing with the effects of sexual assaults. The author provides step-by-step guidelines for survivors and their families.

Bender, M., & Valletutti, P. *Teaching functional skills: A curriculum guide for adolescents and adults with learning problems.* Austin, TX: PRO-ED.

Special educators and counselors can use this complete curriculum guide to teach students/adults with mild disabilities the basic reading, writing, and arithmetic needed to function capably in society. A full series of flexible instructional programs is offered that promotes competence as a resident, student, worker, consumer, and leisure participant.

Brown, M. E. *Therapeutic recreation and exercise.* Thorofare, NJ: Slack.

This book presents a wide variety of activities promoting wellness and rehabilitation through range-of-motion activities. These activities are designed for therapist-directed use with individuals of all ages. Activities include adapting motion games, motion games for children, and body awareness. The book contains an extensive bibliography and musical arrangements.

Drake, M. (1992). *Crafts in therapy and rehabilitation.* Thorofare, NJ: Slack.

This text presents the history, development, and therapeutic application of crafts in occupational therapy treatment programs. It adopts a historical-anthropological approach to the development of the craft and provides therapeutic applications (including screening and evaluation) for physical dysfunction, mental health, pediatrics, and geriatrics. Extensive bibliographical information is also included.

Eichstaedt, C., & Lavay, B. (1992). *Physical activity for individuals with mental retardation.* Champaign, IL: Human Kinetics.

This text describes the characteristics and unique needs of people with mental retardation. The book also provides instructional strategies gleaned from adapted/special physical education, traditional physical education, therapeutic recreation, recreation, physical therapy, occupational therapy, kinesitherapy, and medicine.

Fine, A., & Fine, N. (1988). *Therapeutic recreation for exceptional children: Let me in, I want to play.* Springfield, IL: Charles C. Thomas.

> This text defines therapeutic recreation and the development and assessment of an effective therapeutic recreation program in a collaborative manner to best serve the exceptional child.

Gilfoyle, E. M., Grady, A. P., & Moore, J. C. (1990). *Children adapt: A theory of sensorimotor-sensory development.* Thorofare, NJ: Slack.

> This is a text which provides a description of developmental approach to pediatric rehabilitation and a theoretical framework for the evaluation and treatment of children. The specific focus of the book is on how children can be taught to adapt to changing environmental demands. A number of photographs and extensive references are contained in the text.

Horvat, M. (1990). *Physical education and sport for exceptional students.* Dubuque, IA: Wm. C. Brown.

> This text explains different disorders and disabilities and offers techniques for programming physical education activities. Topics include teaching students with learning and behavior disabilities, sensory impairments, and orthopedic and other health impairments. The text also includes a suggested physical education curriculum.

Jones, J. (1988). *Training guide to cerebral palsy sports.* Champaign, IL: Human Kinetics.

> This fully illustrated training manual gives physical therapists and others working with people with cerebral palsy practical advice on strategies, weight training, nutrition, flexibility, and wheelchair selection as well as tips for coaching.

McKee, L., & Blacklidge, V. (1986). *An easy guide for caring parents: Sexuality and socialization.* Walnut Creek, CA: Planned Parenthood Shasta-Diablo.

The authors provide parents and educators with an honest, straightforward guide about sexuality and social needs of people with mental handicaps.

Schleien, S., & Ray, M. (1988). *Community recreation and persons with disabilities*. Baltimore: Paul H. Brookes.
This "how-to" guide focuses on a "systems change" approach that moves away from segregation and toward an integrated program—one that addresses the needs of all individuals. The book is filled with concrete models designed to simplify the creation and implementation of successful integrated leisure programs for persons with disabilities.

Shepard, R. (1990). *Fitness in special populations*. Champaign, IL: Human Kinetics.
This book provides a compilation of research on fitness assessment, programming, and performance for people with various forms of physical disabilities, including spinal cord injury, amputations, blindness, deafness, cerebral palsy, muscular dystrophies, multiple sclerosis, scoliosis, and mental retardation.

Sherrill, C. (1988). *Leadership training in adapted physical education*. Champaign, IL: Human Kinetics.
The text covers such adapted physical education topics as developing and evaluating curriculums, motor behavior and learning, advocacy, legislation, writing grants, serving on professional organizations, publishing articles, conducting research, and providing in-service training.

Wehman, P., Renszaglia, A., & Bates, P. (1985). *Functional living skills for moderately and severely handicapped individuals*. Austin, TX: PRO-ED.
Domestic living, community mobility and social interaction training, leisure skills instruction, vocational training, and advocacy are the major focus areas of this text as it describes how functional and age-appropriate programs can be implemented for moderately and severely handicapped adolescents and adults. Instructional guidelines are included.

Winnick, J. (1989). *Adapted physical education and sport.*
Champaign, IL: Human Kinetics.
> The text, written for future physical educators of children
> with physical and mental disabilities, focuses on best prac-
> tices for developing basic motor skills as well as emphasiz-
> ing the importance of integrating children with disabilities
> into activities and sports within the community.

Winnick, J., & Short, F. (1985). *Physical fitness testing of
the disabled.* Champaign, IL: Human Kinetics.
> The manual offers fitness tests, activities, and programs for
> instructors of children with cerebral palsy, spinal
> neuromuscular conditions, and visual and auditory impair-
> ments. It contains the development and administration of
> the Project UNIQUE physical fitness test and offers a recom-
> mended training program for developing fitness, describ-
> ing activities, and modifying sports of various disabilities.

Curriculum Guides/Kits

Attainment Functional Skill Materials. Verona, WI: Attainment.
> Attainment offers books, programs, activities, videos, and
> software that are written, designed, and geared toward in-
> dependent living. Life skills materials include an inde-
> pendent living series; a curriculum library; a picture
> prompt system; and a series of independent living pro-
> grams—looking good, keeping house, shopping smart,
> home cooking, daily planning, etc. Talking software avail-
> able includes a survival signs sampler; grocery survival
> words; safety signs; information signs; employment signs;
> community signs; transportation signs; and medical words.
> Available work activities include computer data entry;
> work activity packages; discrimination activities; assembly
> activities; and packaging activities.

Gamco Industries Kits. Big Spring, TX: Gamco.
> Gamco produces and markets a large number of kits (e.g.,
> **Everyday Living and Related Math, New Visions: Sur-
> vival Skills, Personal Health and Conduct**) that provide
> multimedia instructional activities. These kits typically con-
> tain filmstrips, cassettes, reproducible worksheets, and a

teacher's guide. Consult the catalog for a full listing of the available kits and software.

IMPACT: A Functional Curriculum for Students with Moderate to Severe Disabilities. By R. Neel and F. Billingsly. Baltimore, MD: Paul H. Brookes.

The IMPACT program is designed to accommodate student needs, educational setting requirements, and teaching styles. Methods of integrating traditional services and activities into functional instruction formats are provided, and the accompanying materials allow for an easier classroom implementation.

LifeFacts Series: Essential Information about Life for Persons with Special Needs. Santa Barbara: James Stanfield Company, Inc.

The LifeFacts Series is a course of study for persons with special needs on topics relevant to living life more fully, safely, and healthfully. Each kit presents a diagnostic prescriptive curriculum which uses a sequence of objectives and lesson plans to guide instruction. All of the kits include large teaching pictures, assessment questions, and a variety of other useful resources when appropriate (e.g., slides, parent booklets, student worksheets, etc). Kits available include: Illness and Injury (Stangle & Stanfield, 1991); Substance Abuse (Cowardin & Stanfield, 1990); AIDS (Stangle, 1991); Sexuality (Stanfield & Cowardin, 1990); Managing Emotions (Stanfield & Stanfield, 1992); Sexual Abuse Prevention (Cowardin, Downer, & Stanfield, 1990).

Life Horizons I: The Physiological and Emotional Aspects of Being Male and Female—Sex Education for Persons with Special Needs.
Life Horizons II: The Moral, Social, and Legal Aspects of Sexuality. Both written by Winifred Kempton, Instructional Design by James Stanfield (1988). Santa Barbara: James Stanfield Company, Inc.

The two-part slide series, designed primarily for persons with mild handicaps (although the materials can be adapted for moderately and severely handicapped), presents the physiological/psychological and social aspects of sexuality and socialization. The first part emphasizes relevant factual material such as the parts of the body, human reproduction, the sexual life cycle, birth control, and sexual health. The second part highlights the social aspects of being a complete sexual person and presents material on building self-esteem and establishing relationships, male and female social sexual behavior, dating, marriage, parenting, and preventing sexual abuse. Manuals are provided demonstrating how the slides should be used as well as suggested narration. A videotape with the authors explaining the series is also provided. A recent addition, *Socialization and sex education: The Life Horizons curriculum module* (Rouse & Birch, 1991), also distributed by Stanfield contains a series of instructionally sound activities that can assist in the acquisition and maintenance of the concepts presented.

Personal Care Skills. Austin, TX: PRO-ED.

The Personal Care Skills program teaches skills such as brushing teeth, blowing the nose, washing hands, washing hair, using sanitary napkins, shaving, and eating. The mastery of these skills enables the targeted population to be more independent and fosters increased self-esteem. The program includes teaching strategies and training manuals.

Social Skills for Adults with Severe Retardation. Champaign, IL: Research Press.

This resource is a basic inventory and training program for teaching skills that are essential for living more independently. Both the inventory and the training program are comprehensive and sequentially arranged so that success in one objective leads directly into the next area. Some program objectives include: appropriate physical interactions, reaction to name, touching/manipulating objects, social smiling, and eye contact.

The Syracuse Community-Referenced Curriculum Guide For Students with Moderate and Severe Disabilities. By A. Ford et al. Baltimore, MD: Paul H. Brookes.

Professionals and parents responsible directly for preparing a student to function in the community can use this curriculum targeted for kindergarten-aged children through 21–year olds. Community living domains, functional academics, and embedded skills are examined, and practical implementation strategies are emphasized.

Taking Care of Simple Injuries. Austin, TX: PRO-ED.
Moderately and severely mentally handicapped children and adults are taught how to care for minor injuries and how to get medical attention when needed. The self-care skills taught in this program foster an increased sense of well-being and allow more self-reliance and independence. The complete program includes training manuals, filmstrips, stimulus cards, student review books, and certificates of success.

Toilet Training Persons with Developmental Disabilities. Champaign, IL: Research Press.
This resource is a rapid program for day and nighttime independent toileting. This manual provides step-by-step procedures for toilet training that have proven successful and can be readily implemented.

Multimedia/Hardware

ETR Health Videos. Santa Cruz, CA: ETR Associates.
ETR markets a large number of videos that focus on health issues concerning children and adolescents. Topics include tobacco and drug use prevention, HIV/AIDS education, and sexual abuse prevention. Write for the descriptive catalog.

Teaching People with Developmental Disabilities.
Champaign, IL: Research Press.
This is a hands-on video training program designed to help teachers, staff, volunteers, or family members master four behavioral techniques (task analysis, prompting, reinforcement, and error correction) vital to teaching functional living skills. This training program conveys a positive set of values for teaching people with developmental disabilities and stresses the importance of structuring training to each student's ability, helping students develop functional living

skills, and transferring learning from the classroom to the real world.

Organizations

The **American Alliance for Health, Physical Education, Recreation, and Dance** is a membership organization of professionals in the fields of physical education, recreation, health and safety, and dance. The organization's Adapted Physical Activity Council has a nationwide network to provide information about adapting curricula and activities to the needs of people with disabilities as well as a journal, **Able Bodies. Write:** The Alliance, 1900 Association Drive, Reston, VA 22091 or **Phone:** (703) 476–3400.

The **National Therapeutic Recreation Society** is concerned with providing recreation and leisure services to children and adults with disabilities. Recreation therapy is covered under P.L. 101–476 as a related service. NTRS offers technical assistance and consulting services on therapeutic recreation along with a vast amount of related information. **Write:** National Therapeutic Recreation Society, National Recreation and Park Association, 2775 South Quincy Street, Suite 300, Arlington, VA 22206 or **Phone:** (703) 820–4940 ext. 548.

The **Resource Center on Substance Abuse and Disability**, a new clearinghouse, provides information on programs, reference materials, and research related to drug prevention and disability. **Write:** 1331 F Street, N.W., Suite 800, Washington, DC 20004 or **Phone:** (202) 783–2900; TDD (202) 737–0645.

Technology in Special Education

The rapid growth in educational technology continues to influence the way educators deliver services to students with disabilities. As the direct result of technological innovations ranging from simple switches to complex hardware/software computer interfaces, students with disabilities are able to access resources and function with greater independence. What follows are several categories of technology resources. First, general technology resources (e.g., textbooks, resource books, organizations, databases, etc.) are provided. This is followed by a listing of assistive technology vendors. By assistive technology, we mean technological devices that can be used to enhance the independent functioning of students with disabilities. In addition to microcomputers, types of assistive devices may include augmentative communication devices, mobility devices, and adaptive access devices for microcomputers (e.g., expanded keyboards, joy-sticks, single switch mechanisms). The section concludes with lists of educational software sources. Both public domain outlets and software vendors are provided.

One cautionary note: Although this section on technology appears in isolation from other educational issues (i.e., academic skills, functional skills. etc.), it is clear that to be most effective, technology must be integrated into all appropriate aspects of the curriculum. As noted by Edyburn (1989), the goal of integrating technology into the curriculum is to include software and computer activities into the instructional sequence so they facilitate the teaching and learning of specific objectives. This **curriculum correspondence** is necessary if technology-based learning activities are to benefit students.

AVAILABLE RESOURCES: Technology
General Textbooks

> Alessi, S., & Trollip, S. (1991). *Computer-based instruction.* Englewood Cliffs, NJ: Prentice Hall.

> Behrmann, M. (1984). *Handbook of microcomputer in special education.* Boston, MA: College-Hill Press.

Behrmann, M. (1988). *Integrating computers into the curriculum: A handbook for special educators.* Boston, MA: Little, Brown and Co.

Bitter, G. G., & Camuse, R. A. (1988). *Using microcomputers in the classroom.* Englewood Cliffs, NJ: Prentice-Hall.

Budoff, M., Thorman, J., & Gras, A. (1985). *Microcomputers in special education: An introduction to instructional applications.* Cambridge, MA: Brookline.

Cain, E. J., & Taber, F. (1987). *Educating disabled people in the 21st century.* Boston, MA: Little, Brown and Co.

Church, G., & Bender, M. (1989). *Teaching with computers: A curriculum for special educators.* Boston, MA: College Hill Press.

Criswell, E. (1989). *The design of computer-based instruction.* New York, NY: Macmillan.

Davis, K. Y., & Budoff, M. (1986). *Using authoring in education.* Cambridge, MA: Brookline.

Geisert, P. G., & Furtress, M. K. (1990). *Teachers, computers and curriculum: Microcomputers in the classroom.* New York, NY: Allyn & Bacon.

Goldenburg, E. P., Russell, S. J., & Carter, C. J. (1984). *Computers, education and special needs.* Menlo Park, CA: Addison-Wesley.

Heerman, B. (1986). *Teaching and learning with computers: A guide for college faculty and school administrators.* San Francisco, CA: Jossey-Bass.

Hofmeister, A. (1984). *Microcomputer applications in the classroom.* New York, NY: CBS College Publishing.

Johnson, D. L. (1987). *Computers in the special education classroom*. New York, NY: CBS College Publishing.

Levin, J., & Scherfenberg, L. (1990). *Selection and use of simple technology in home, school, work, and community settings*. Minneapolis, MN: Ablenet.

Lillie, D. L., Hannum, W. H., & Struck, G. B. (1989). *Computer and effective instruction*. New York, NY: Longman.

Male, M. (1988). *Special magic: Computers, classroom strategies, and exceptional children*. Mountain View, CA: Mayfield.

Roberts, N., & Carter, M. (1989). *Integrating computers into your elementary and middle school*. Englewood Cliffs, NJ: Prentice-Hall.

Russell, S. J., Corwin, R., Mokros, J. R., & Kapisovsky, P. M. (1989). *Beyond drill and practice: Expanding the computer mainstream*. Reston, VA: CEC.

Wager, W., Wager, S., & Duffield, J. (1989). *Computers in the teaching: A complete training manual for teachers to use computers in their classroom*. Cambridge, MA: Brookline.

Resource Books

Adams, D., & Fuchs, M. (1986). *Educational computing: Issues, trends and a practical guide*. Springfield, IL: Charles C. Thomas.

> The guide includes information about computer-based technology, and strategies for fitting computers into educational curriculums. Also included are sections related directly to computers and children with special needs.

Berliss, J. R., Borden, P. A., Ford, K., & Vanderheiden, G. (1991–92). *Trace resource book: Assistive technologies for communication*. Madison, WI: Trace Research and Development Center.

> Comprehensive guide to communication aids, computer adaptations, and computer application software for special education and rehabilitation. The guide is 887 pages and contains numerous photos and drawings of devices.

Church, G., & Glennen, S. (1991). *The handbook of assistive technology*. San Diego, CA: Singular.

> The book covers computer access, augmentative communication seating and power mobility, adaptive play and environmental control, and integrating assistive technology into the client's home, school, and community. It responds to daily questions about how one establishes, maintains, or expands assistive technology services for individuals with developmental and acquired disabilities.

Clancy, J. *Special needs software and resources: A guide and directory*. Newton Highlands, MA: Author.

> This resource is a guide and directory to over 800 special needs software packages and resources for school personnel.

EPIE. *The educational software selector (TESS)*. Water Mill, NY: Author.

> TESS contains detailed descriptions of over 7,700 programs for all types of microcomputers and subject areas. In many cases evaluation data are included.

Grossens, C., & Crain, S. *Utilizing switch interfaces with children who are severely physically challenged*. Austin, TX: PRO-ED.

> Utilizing this clinical handbook, teachers, clinicians, and therapists can provide reliable switch access to children who are severely physically challenged. Computer access is used to unlock social, emotional, linguistic, and academic growth. This detailed, illustrated how-to text is appropriate for both the beginning and the advanced professional.

Lindsey, J. *Computers and exceptional individuals.* Austin, TX: PRO-ED.

> In this edited volume, authors—special educators and computer technologists—provide practical and state-of-the-art discussions of computer technology issues for individuals with disabilities, gifts, and talents. Designed for computer novices, experienced technologists, educators, and exceptional individuals, this text delineates specific and general technology concepts that can be used with and by exceptional individuals. Concepts include but are not limited to computer access, adaptive devices, augmentative communication, and interactive videodiscs and are provided with practical activities and pertinent resources.

Margalit, M. (1990). *Effective technology integration for disabled children: The family perspective.* New York, NY: Springer-Verlag.

> This is a research-based text in which an ecological approach to computing is explored within the context of family systems analysis.

Russell, S., Corwin, R., Mokros, J., & Kapisovsky, P. (1989). *Beyond drill and practice: Expanding the computer mainstream.* Reston, VA: CEC.

> This teacher-based resource describes how computers can be used with students who have special learning needs. Sections are provided on creative uses of LOGO and the use of problem solving software.

Periodicals and Databases

Abledata provides descriptive information on commercial products for rehabilitation and independent living. Services include on-line search services, information dissemination, and search strategy consultation. **Write:** National Rehabilitation Information Center, 8455 Colesville Rd., Suite 935, Silver Spring, MD 20910. **Phone:** (800) 227–0216 or (800) 346–2742.

Assistive Technology, published quarterly, is an interdisciplinary journal dedicated to the advancement of rehabilitation and assistive technologies that provide information on applied research, reviews, practical implementations of devices, and reports on small studies. **Write:** Assistive Technology, Demos Publications, 156 5th Ave., Suite 1018, New York, NY 10010 or **Phone:** (202) 857–1199.

Catalyst, published by the Western Center for Microcomputers in Special Education, is a newsletter that communicates research, development, and product applications of technology for special education populations. **Write:** Western Center for Microcomputers in Special Education, 1259 El Camino Real, Suite 275, Menlo Park, CA 94025 or **Phone:** (415) 326–6997.

Compuserve is a database that contains information on all aspects of technology used by individuals who are disabled. **Write:** Compuserve, 5000 Arlington Centre Blvd., P.O. Box 20212, Columbus, OH 43220 or **Phone:** (614) 457–8600.

The Computing Teacher, published eight times per year by the International Society for Technology in Education, presents articles on teaching about computers, teaching the use of computers, and the affect of computers on curricula. **Write:** The Computing Teacher, University of Oregon, 1787 Agate St., Eugene, OR 97403.

Electronic Learning presents educational applications of microcomputers and other technology-based learning aids for elementary and secondary settings in a nontechnical fashion. The magazine contains a software review section with practitioner-based critiques. **Write:** Scholastic Inc., 730 Broadway, New York, NY 10003–9538 or **Phone:** (212) 503–3000.

Hyper-Abledata-Plus, the CD-ROM version of Abledata, provides information on over 16,000 assistive technology products. The database also provides pictures and sound samples of many items as well as an access system for users who are blind or visually impaired. **Write:** Trace Center Reprint Service, 1500 Highland Ave., S-151–Waisman Ctr., Madison, WI 53706 or **Phone:** (608) 263–6966.

Journal of Special Education Technology (JSET), published by the Technology and Media Division of CEC, publishes reports of original research and integrative reviews concerning the application of technology to students with disabilities. **Write:** JSET, CEC, 1920 Association Drive, Reston, VA 22091 or **Phone:** (703) 620–3660.

Mobility LTD. is a bimonthly magazine that provides articles and news for people with mobility impairments. Features typically include reviews of new products and services as well as equipment classifieds. **Write:** Mobility LTD., 401 Linden Center Dr., Fort Collins, CO 80524 or **Phone:** (303) 484–7969.

Technology and Disability, published quarterly by Andover Medical Publishers, is a journal that deals with the application of rehabilitative and assistive technology to persons with disabilities in all major life functions including education, employment, and recreation. **Write:** Andover Medical Publishers, 80 Montvale Ave., Stoneham, MA 02180 or **Phone:** (800) 366–2665.

Technology Organizations

Ablenet, Inc. is an organization which offers products (e.g., switches and control units), publications, and services (workshops) that allow for the application of technology in educational, domestic, vocational, and community settings. Three resource books focusing on simple to use assistive devices, *Breaking barriers*

(Levin & Scherfenberg, 1990); *Selection and use of simple technology in home, school, work, and community settings* (Levin & Scherfenberg, 1990); and *Fun for everyone* (Levin & Enselein, 1990) are published by the organization. **Write:** Ablenet, 1081 Tenth Ave, S.E., Minneapolis, MN 55414–1312 or **Phone:** (800) 322–0956.

Accessibility Resource Center offers information dissemination and training services in computer applications and related technology areas. **Write:** Accessibility Resource Center, 1056 E. 19th Ave., B-410, Denver, CO 80218–1088 or **Phone:** (303) 861–6250.

The **Alliance for Technology Access** conducts research and provides information dissemination, database resources, referral services, and training related to the implementation of microcomputer technology for children and adults with disabilities. **Write:** The Alliance for Technology Access, Apple Computer, Inc., 20525 Nariani Ave., MS 43S, Cupertino, CA 95014 or **Phone:** (415) 528–0747.

The **Center for Computer Assistance to the Disabled** is a clearinghouse for user information on computer aids for disabled persons. The center also provides referral and advocacy services, training, diagnostic evaluations, and related support services in the area of computer-based assistive technology. **Write:** Center for Computer Assistance to the Disabled, 617 Seventh Ave., Fort Worth, TX 76104 or **Phone:** (817) 870–9082.

The **Clearinghouse On Computer Accommodation (COCA)** is a demonstration and technical resources center of the General Services Administration. The center demonstrates hardware and software, provides technical assistance, and conducts workshops on computer accommodation for individuals with disabilities. **Write:** COCA, KGDO, 18th and F St. N.W., Rm. 2022, Washington, DC 20405 or **Phone:** (202) 523–1906.

Closing the Gap is an internationally recognized source of information on the use of microcomputer-related technology by and for exceptional individuals. Closing the Gap is committed to providing up-to-date information on commercially available hardware and software products that can enable individuals with disabilities to access the microcomputer and the opportunities for education and independent living that it offers. Services include conferences, information dissemination, and the publication of a bi-monthly newspaper and of a comprehensive resource guide directory which contains a comprehensive listing of commercially available hardware and software appropriate for special education and rehabilitation. **Write:** Closing the Gap, P.O. Box 68, Henderson, MN 56044 or **Phone:** (612) 248–3294.

IBM National Support Center for Persons with Disabilities is a clearinghouse for information on technologies and products from computer vendors that affect the education of individuals with disabilities. A number of resource guides are published by the Center. **Write:** IBM, P.O. Box 2150, Atlanta, GA 30301–2150 or **Phone:** (800) 426–2133; TDD (800) 284–9482.

The **International Society for Augmentative and Alternative Communication (ISAAC)** is an information and referral organization whose focus is the international advancement of augmentative and alternative communication techniques and aids. **Write:** ISAAC, P.O. Box 1762, Sta. R., Toronto, Ontario M4G 4A3, Canada or **Phone:** (416) 737–9308.

The **Kennedy-Kreiger Institute Assistive Technology Center** is a nonprofit hospital that provides interdisciplinary technology information, referral, advocacy, assessment, and prescription services. Equipment modification and fabrication services are also offered. The institute provides education and training in the use of assistive technology. **Write:** Kennedy-Kreiger Institute Assistive Technology Center, 707 North Broadway, Baltimore, MD 21205 or **Phone:** (410) 550–5897.

Learning Independence Through Computers (LINC) is a resource center that offers adapted computer technology to children and adults with disabilities. Services offered include technical assistance, consultation, demonstrations, and training. **Write:** LINC, 28 E. Ostend Street, Suite 140, Baltimore, MD 21230 or **Phone:** (410) 659–LINC.

The **Pacer Computer Resource Center** is a parent-based center which provides access to assistive technology hardware and software, offering children and adults with disabilities the opportunity to try devices and evaluate their effectiveness. The center also provides information on technology and training. **Write:** Pacer Computer Resource Center, 4826 Chicago Ave., Minneapolis, MN 55417–1055 or **Phone:** (612) 827–2966.

RESNA is an interdisciplinary association devoted to the advancement of rehabilitation and assistive technology. The organization offers conferences, publications, and networking services to professionals, advocates, and consumers on practical applications of technology in vocational, educational, and independent living settings. RESNA publishes *Rehabilitation technology service delivery: A practical guide* and *The rehabilitation technology service delivery directory*. **Write:** RESNA, 1101 Connecticut Ave. N.W., Suite 700, Washington, DC 20036 or **Phone:** (202) 857–1199.

The **Technology and Media Division (TAM)** of CEC promotes research, development, training, and demonstration activities related to the application of technology with individuals with disabilities. The division publishes the **Journal of Special Education Technology,** quarterly, and the **TAM Newsletter,** five times per year. **Write:** TAM, CEC, 1920 Association Drive, Reston, VA 22091–1589 or **Phone:** (703) 620–3660.

Assistive Technology Vendors

What follows is a listing of several **Assistive Technology** vendors. This listing is a partial listing of vendors and is adapted from similar listings found in *Closing the gap* and *The handbook of assistive technology* by G. Church and S. Glennen. Each of these vendors has catalogs or brochures which detail their products. In the interest of saving space, these producers are *not* cataloged in the comprehensive listing of Resource Producers found in Appendix A.

Ability System Corp.
1422 Arnold Ave.
Roslyn, PA 19001
(215) 657–4338

Ablenet
1081 10th Ave. S.E.
Minneapolis, MN 55414
(800) 322–0956

Access Unlimited
9039 Katy Freeway, #414
Houston, TX 77024
(713) 461–0006

ACTT (Activating Children Through Technology)
Project ACTT, 27 Horrabin Hall,
W. Illinois University
Macomb, IL 61455
(308) 298–1014

Adaptive Communication Systems, Inc.
1400 Lee Dr.
Coropolis, PA 15108
(800) 227–2922

Adaptive Computers
11 Fullerton St., Ste. 110
Albany, NY 12209
(518) 434–8860

Adaptive Equipment for the Handicapped
P.O. Box 496
Ocean Park, ME 04063–0496
(207) 934–2952

Adhoc Reading Systems, Inc.
28 Brunswick Woods Dr.
E. Brunswick, NJ 08816
(201) 254–7300

American Printing House for the Blind
P.O. Box 6085
Louisville, KY 40206–0085
(502) 895–2405

American Thermoform Corp.
2311 Travers Ave.
City of Commerce, CA 90040
(213) 723–9021

Animated Voices Corp.
P.O. Box 819
San Macros, CA 92069
(800) 942–3699

Apple Computer, Inc.
20525 Mariani Ave.
Cupertino, CA 95014
(408) 974–7910

Arkenstone, Inc.
1185 Bordeaux Dr., Ste. D
Sunnyvale, CA 94089
(800) 444–4443

Arroyo & Associates, Inc.
2549 Rockville Centre Pkwy.
Oceanside, NY 11572
(516) 763–1407

Arthur Schwatrz
1801 E. 12th St., #1119
Cleveland, OH 44114
(216) 371–3820

Artic Technologies
55 Park St., Ste. 2
Troy, MI 48083
(313) 588–7370

Articulate Systems, Inc.
600 West Cummings Pk., Ste. 4500
Woburn, MA 01801
(800) 443–7077

Artificial Language Laboratory
405 Computer Ctr., Michigan State University
East Lansing, MI 48824–1042
(517) 353–5339

Asaflex Manufacturing
S.E. 525 Water St.
Pullman, WA 99163
(509) 332–2205

Assistive Device Center, School of Engineering
and Computer Science
California State University
Sacramento, CA 95819
(916) 278–6422

Automated Functions, Inc.
6424 N. 28th St.
Arlington, VA 22207
(703) 536–7741

Berkeley Systems, Inc.
2095 Rose St.
Berkeley, CA 94709
(510) 540–5535

Blazie Engineering
3600 Mill Green Rd.
Street, MD 21154
(301) 879–4944

Bloorview Children's Hospital
Communication & Assistive Technology
25 Buchan Ct.
Willowdale, ON M2J 4S9 Canada
(416) 494–2222

Bradley Murray, S.J.
5704 Roland Ave.
Baltimore, MD 21210
(301) 435–1833

Burkhart (Linda)
8503 Rhode Island Ave.
College Park, MD 20740
(301) 345–9152

ComputAbility Corp.
40000 Grand River, Ste. 109
Novi, MI 48375
(313) 477–6720

Consultants for Communication Technology
508 Bellevue Terrace
Pittsburgh, PA 15202
(412) 761–6062

R. J. Cooper and Associates
24843 DelPrado, Ste. 283
Dana Point, CA 92629
(714) 240–1912

Covox, Inc.
675 Conger St.
Eugene, OR 94702
(503) 342–1271

Creative Communicating/Playware
P.O. Box 3358
Park City, UT 84060
(801) 645 7737

Creative Switch Industries
P.O. Box 5256
Des Moines, IA 50306
(515) 287–5748

Crestwood Company
P.O. Box 04606
Milwaukee, WI 53204–0606
(414) 461–9876

Detroit Institute for Children
5447 Woodward Ave.
Detroit, MI 48202
(313) 832–1100

Don Johnson Developmental Equipment, Inc.
1000 N.Rand Rd., Bldg.115, P.O.Box 639
Wauconda, IL 60084
(800) 999–4660

DU-IT Control Systems Groups, Inc.
8765 Twp. Rd. 513
Shreve, OH 44676–9241
(216) 567–2906

Dunamis, Inc.
3620 Hwy. 317
Suwanee, GA 30174
(800) 828–2443

Easter Seal Communication Institute
250 Ferrand Dr., Ste. 200
Don Mills, ON M3C 3P2 Canada
(416) 421–8377

Easter Seals & Lehigh Valley Computer Project
P.O. Box 333, 1161 Forty Foot Rd.
Kulpsville, PA 19443
(215) 866–8092

EKEG Electronics Co. Ltd.
P.O. Box 46199, Sta.G
Vancouver, BC V6R 4G5 Canada
(604) 273–4358

E.V.A.S.
P.O. Box 371
Westerly, RI 02981
(800) 872–3827

Extensions for Independence
757 Emory St., Ste. 514
Imperial Beach, CA 92032
(619) 423–7709

Franciscan Children's Hospital & Rehabilitation
Center, Kennedy Day School Program
30 Warren St.
Boston, MA 02135
(617) 254–3800

Franklin Learning Resources
122 Burrs Road
Mt. Holly, NJ 08060
(800) 525–9673

Genovation, Inc.
17741 Mitchell North
Irvine, CA 92741
(714) 833–3355

Harbor Computing Services
P.O. Box 2181
Gig Harbor, WA 98335
(206) 858–9459

Hooleon Corporation
P.O. Box 230
Cronville, AZ 86325
(602) 634–7515

Intellitools
5221 Central Ave., Ste. 205
Richmond, CA 94804
(800) 899–6687

In Touch Systems
11 Westview Rd.
Spring Valley, NY 10977
(914) 354–7431

Jostens Learning Systems, Inc.
Educational Technology,
7878 North 16th St., Ste. 100
Phoenix, AZ 85020
(800) 852–1925

Kay Elemetrics Corp.
12 Maple Ave.
Pine Brook, NJ 07058
(201) 227–2000

Kensington Microwave
2855 Campus Dr.
San Mateo, CA 94403
(800) 535–4242

Koala Acquisitions, Inc.
16055 Caputo Dr., Unit H
Morgan Hill, CA 95037
(408) 776–8181

Kurzweil Applied Intelligence
411 Waverly Oaks Rd.
Waltham, MA 02154
(617) 893–5151

KY Enterprise/Custom Computer Solutions
3039 E. 2nd St.
Long Beach, CA 90803
(310) 433–5244

Lekotek of Georgia, Inc.
1955 Cliff Valley Way, Ste. 102
Atlanta, GA 30329
(404) 633–3430

Life Science Associates
1 Fenimore Rd.
Bayport, NY 11705
(516) 472–2111

Luminaud, Inc.
8688 Tyler Blvd.
Mentor, OH 44060
(216) 255–9082

Lyon Computer Discourse, Inc.
1099 Kinloch Ln.
N. Vancouver, BC V7G 1V8 Canada
(604) 929–8866

MarbleSoft
12301 Central Ave. N.E., Ste. 205
Blaine, MN 55434
(612) 755–1402

Mayer-Johnson Co.
P.O. Box 1579
Solana Beach, CA 92075
(614) 481–2489

Microsystems Software, Inc.
600 Worcester Rd., Ste. B2
Framingham, MA 01701
(508) 626–8511

Micro Video Corp.
210 Collingwood, Ste. 100,
P.O. Box 7357
Ann Arbor, MI 48107
(800) 537–2182

PC-SIG, Inc.
1030 D.E. Duane Ave.
Sunnyvale, CA 94086
(408) 730–9291

Personal Data Systems, Inc.
P.O. Box 1008
Campbell, CA 95009
(408) 866–1126

Phonic Ear, Inc.
3880 Cypress Dr.
Petaluma, CA 94954
(800) 227–0735

Pointer Systems, Inc.
One Mill St.
Burlington, VT 05401
(800) 537–1562

Polytel Computer Products Corp.
1287 Hammerwood Ave.
Sunnyvale, CA 94089
(800) 245–6655

Prentke Romich Co.
1022 Heyl Rd.
Wooster, OH 44691
(216) 262–1984

Psychological Software Services, Inc.
6555 Carrollton Ave.
Indianapolis, IN 46220
(317) 257–9672

R.E.A.C.H., Inc.
890 Hearthstone Dr.
Stone Mountain, GA 30083
(404) 292–8933

Regenesis Development Corp.
1046 Deep Cove Rd.
North Vancouver, BC V7G 1S3 Canada
(604) 929–6663

Royal Data Systems
Rt. 14, Box 230
Morganton, NC 28655
(800) 843–9750

SkiSoft Publishing Corp.
1644 Massachusetts Ave., Ste. 79
Lexington, MA 02173
(800) 662–3622

Street Electronics Corp.
6420 Via Real
Carpinteria, CA 93013
(805) 684–4593

Talking Computers, Inc.
4301 N. Fairfax Dr., Ste. 1034
Arlington, VA 22203
(703) 241–8224

TASH Inc. (Technical Aids & Systems for the
Handicapped)
70 Gibson Dr., Unit 12 Markham, ON L3R 4C2 Canada
(416) 475–2212

Technology for Language and Learning
P.O. Box 327
East Rockway, NY 11518–0327
(516) 625–4550

TeleSensory
455 N. Bernado Ave.
Mountain View, CA 94039–7455
(415) 960–0920

Toys for Special Children, Inc.
385 Warburton Ave.
Hastings on Hudson, NY 10706
(914) 478–0960

UCLA Microcomputer Team
1000 Ventura Ave., Rm. 23–10
Los Angeles, CA 90024
(213) 825–4821

Unicorn Engineering, Inc.
5221 Central Ave., Ste. 205
Richmond, CA 94804
(415) 528–0670

Voice Connection
17835 Skypark Circle, Ste. C
Irvine, CA 92714
(714) 261–2366

Western Center for Microcomputers in
Special Education
1259 El Camino Real, Ste. 275
Menlo Park, CA 94025
(415) 326–6997

Words+, Inc.
P.O. Box 1229
Lancaster, CA 93584
(800) 869–8521

World Communications
245 Tonopah Dr.
Fremont, CA 94539
(415) 656–0911

Xerox Imaging Systems, Inc.
9 Centennial Dr.
Peabody, MA 01960
(800) 343–0311

Zygo Industries, Inc.
P.O. Box 1008
Portland, OR 97207
(800) 234–6006

Software

When identifying and selecting educational software for students with special educational needs, it is critical that the programs acquired be **integrated** into the existing special education curriculum. Specifically, software should not be used in isolation; rather, it should be regarded as an integral material for activities used in teaching skills in the curriculum. As noted earlier, this **curriculum correspondence** is necessary if technology-based learning activities are to benefit students.

The number of software programs that may be of use in remedial and special education settings is nothing short of enormous. What follows is a listing of several **software sources** from which programs and/or program information can be obtained. Both commercial and public domain sources are provided. Please note that many of the public domain sources charge nominal membership fees, disk fees, and/or catalog fees.

Public Domain Software Sources

ADVANTAGE COMPUTING
24285 Sunnymead Blvd.
Ste. 212
Monreno Valley, CA 92388
(800) 828–4666; (714) 924–5889 in CA

ALL MICRO SOFTWARE
P.O. Box 1175
Cardiff, CA 92007
(619) 931–2520

BEST BITS AND BYTES
P.O. Box 8245
Van Nuys, CA 9140
(800) 245–BYTE; (818) 764–9503 in CA

BOSTON COMPUTER SOCIETY
One Kendall Square
Cambridge, MA 02139
(617) 252–0600 ($35 membership fee)

DYNACOMP INC.
Dynacomp Office Bldg.
178 Phillips Rd.
Webster, NY 14580
(800) 828–6772; (716) 265–4040 in NY

MICRO STAR
1105 Second Street
Encinitias, CA 90024
(800) 444–1343

NATIONAL SOFTWARE LABS
3767 Overland Ave., #112
Los Angeles, CA 90034
(213) 559–5456

PC-SIG
1030–D East Duane Ave.
Sunnyvale, CA 94086
(408) 730–9291

PEOPLE'S CHOICE
P.O. Box 171134–P
Memphis, TN 38187
(800) 999–0741; (901) 763–0741 in TN

PUBLIC DOMAIN EXCHANGE
2074–C Walsh Ave, #770
Santa Clara, CA 95051
(800) 331–8125; (408) 496–0624

PUBLIC DOMAIN LIBRARY OF THE DUNCAN
INSTITUTE
Box 138CS
18 Duncan Dr.
New Port Richey, FL 33552
(813) 848–8111

PUBLIC DOMAIN ON FILE
Facts on File
460 Park Ave. South
New York, NY 10016
(800) 322–8755

PUBLIC DOMAIN SOFTWARE LIBRARY
Special Education Technology Training Center,
Department of Special Education,
University of Kentucky, Lexington, KY 40506–0001
(606) 257–4713

PUBLIC SOFTWARE LIBRARY
P.O. Box 37705–PG
Houston, TX 77235–5705
(713) 721–5205
(713) 721–6104

REASONABLE SOLUTIONS
2101 West Main St.
Medford, OR 97501
(800) 876–3475

SHARE-NET
P.O. Box 12368, Dept. G
Oklahoma City, OK 73157
(405) 524–5233

SOFTWARE EXCITEMENT
P.O. Box 3072
Central Point, OR 97502
(800) 444–5457

SOFTWARE OF THE MONTH CLUB
511–104 Encinitas Blvd.
Encinitas, CA 92024
(619) 931–8111

Commercial Software Vendors

What follows is a listing of several commercial software vendors who special-
ize in courseware for students with special learning needs. Most of these vendors
have catalogs or brochures that explain their products. In the interest of saving
space, these producers are *not* cataloged in the comprehensive listing of Resource
Producers found in Appendix A.

Academic Software, Inc.
331 W. 2nd St. at Broadway
Lexington, KY 40507
(606) 233–2332

Academic Therapy Publications
20 Commercial Blvd.
Novato, CA 94947
(415) 883–3314

Access Unlimited
3535 Briarpark Dr., Ste. 102
Houston, TX 77042–5235
(713) 781–7441; (800) 848–0311

ACS Software
University of WA, Dept. of Speech
and Hearing Sciences JG-15
Seattle, WA 98195
(206) 543–7974

Advanced Ideas Inc.
680 Hawthorne Dr.
Tibourn, CA 94024
(415) 425–5086

Ahead Designs
1827 Hawk View Dr.
Encinitas, CA 92024
(619) 942–5860

Aicom Corp.
1590 Oakland Rd.
San Jose, CA 95131
(408) 453–8251; (408) 453–8255

Aims Media
9710 DeSoto Ave.
Chatsworth, CA 91311–4409
(818) 773–4300; (800) 367–2467

Al Squared
1463 Hearst Dr.
Atlanta, GA 30319
(404) 233–7065

American Guidance Services
Publisher's Building
Circle Pines, MN 56223
(612) 786–4343; (800) 328–2560

American Printing House for the Blind
P.O. Box 6085
Louisville, KY 40206–0085
(502) 895–2405; (502) 895–2405 FAX

Amidon Publications
1966 Benson Ave.
St. Paul, MN 56116
(612) 690–2401; (800) 328–6502

Aquaris Instructional
P.O. Box 819
Indian Rocks Beach, FL 34635
(813) 595–7890; (800) 338–2644

Aristo Computers Inc.
6700 S.W. 105th Ave., Ste. 307
Beaverton, OR 97005
(503) 626–6333

Arkenstone, Inc.
1185 Bordeaux Dr., Ste. D
Sunnyvale, CA 94089
(408) 752–2200; (800) 444–4443

Artesian Software
10011 Lewis Ave.
Temperance, MI 48182
(313) 856–3490

Artic Technologies
55 Park St., Ste. 2
Troy, MI 48083
(313) 588–7370; (313)588–2650

A\V Concepts Corp.
30 Montauk Blvd.
Oakdale, NY 11769
(516) 567–7227

Ballard and Tighe, Inc.
480 Atlas St.
Brea, CA 92621
(800) 321–4332

Blissymbolics Communication International
250 Ferrand Dr., Ste. 200
Don Mills, ON M3C 3P2 Canada

Wm. K. Bradford Publishing Co.
310 School St.
Acton, MA 01720
(508) 263–6996; (800) 421–2009

BrainTrain, Inc.
727 Twin Ridge Lane
Richmond, VA 23235
(804) 320–0105; (800) 446–5456

Bright Star Technology, Inc.
1450 114th Ave. S.E., Ste. 200
Bellevue, WA 98044
(206) 451–3697

Britannica Software
345 Fourth St.
San Francisco, CA 94107

Broderbund Software, Inc.
500 Redwood Blvd., P.O. Box 6121
Novato, CA 94948–6121
(415) 382–4400; (800) 521–6263

C & C Software
5713 Kentford Circle
Wichita, KS 67208
(316) 682–2699; (800) 752–2086

Cambridge Developmental Laboratory
Special Times Special Education Software
86 West Street
Waltham, MA 02154
(800) 637–0047

Career Evaluation Systems, Inc.
6050 W. Touchy
Chicago, IL 60648
(312) 774–1212

Castle Special Computer Services, Inc.
9801 San Gabriel N.E.
Albuquerque, NM 87111–3530
(505) 293–8379

CE Software, Inc.
P.O. Box 66580
West Des Moines, IA 50525
(515) 224–1995

Joseph C. Clancy
97 Manchester Rd.
Newton Highlands, MA 02161
(617) 969–2614

CLASS Adaptive Technologies
16 Haverhill St.
Andover, MA 01810

Communication Skill Builders
P.O. Box 42050
Tucson, AZ 85733
(603) 323–7500

ComputAbility Corp.
40000 Grand River, Ste. 109
Novi, MI 48375
(313) 477–6720

Compu-Teach
14924 21st Dr. S.E.
Mill Creek, WA 98012
(800) 448–3224

Computer Tutor, Inc.
1001 15th Pl.
Plano, TX 75704
(214) 423–2772; (800) 472–0071

Computers to Help People, Inc.
1221 W. Johnson St.
Madison, WI 53715–1046
(608) 257–5917

Conover Company
P.O. Box 155
Omro, WI 54963
(800) 933–1933

Continental Press, Inc.
520 E. Bainbridge St.
Elizabethtown, PA 17022
(800) 847–0656 (PA); (800) 233–0759

R.J. Cooper and Associates
24843 DelPrado, Ste. 283
Dana Point, CA 92629
(714) 240–1912

Creative Learning, Inc.
P.O. Box 829
North San Jaun, CA 95960
(916) 292–3001; (800) 842–5360

Cross Educational Software
504 E. Kentucky Ave., P.O. Box 1536
Ruston, LA 71270
(318) 255–8921

CUE SoftSwap
P.O. Box 271704
Concord, CA 94527–1704
(415) 685–7289

Curriculum Associates, Inc.
5 Esquire Rd.
North Billerica, MA 08162
(508) 667–8000

Data Command, Inc.
P.O. Box 548
Kankakee, IL 60901
(800) 528–7390

Dataflo Computer Services, Inc.
HC 32, Box 1
Enfield, NH 03748
(603) 448–2223

Davidson & Associates, Inc.
19840 Pioneer Ave.
Torrance, CA 90503
(213) 534–4070; (800) 545–7677

Didtech Software, Ltd.
3812 William St.
Burmaby, BC V5C 3H9 Canada
(604) 299–4435; (800) 665–0667

DLM Teaching Resources
One DLM Park
Allen, TX 75002
(212) 248–6300; (800) 527–5030

Dunamis, Inc.
3620 Hwy. 317
Suwanee, GA 30174
(404) 932–0845; (800) 828–2443

Easter Seals & Lehigh Valley Computer Project
P.O.Box 333, 1161 Forty Foot Rd.
Kulpsville, PA 19443
(215) 866–8092

EBSCO Curriculum Materials
P.O. Box 1943
Birmingham, AL 35201
(205) 991–6600 ext. 208

Edmark Corp.
P.O. Box 3903
Bellevue, WA 98009–3903
(206) 746–3900; (206) 746–0301 (TTY);
(800) 426–0856

Educational Activities, Inc.
P.O. Box 392
Freeport, Long Island, NY 11520
(516) 223–4666; (800) 645–3739

Educational Program Consultants
51 Cleveland Ave.
Milltown, NJ 08850
(908) 745–9675

Electronic Courseware Systems, Inc.
1210 Lancaster Dr.
Champaign, IL 61821
(217) 359–7099

Enable/Schneier Communication Unit
1603 Court St.
Syracuse, NY 13208
(315) 455–7591

Exceptional Children's Software
P.O. Box 487
Hays, KS 67601
(913) 625–9281

First Byte
19840 Pioneer Ave.
Torrance, CA 90503
(800) 523–2983

Focus Media
839 Stewart Ave., P.O. Box 865
Garden City, NY 11530
(516) 794–8900; (516) 794–8920 FAX

Functional Assessment and Training Consultants
9009 N. Plaza, Ste. 138
Austin, TX 78753
(512) 836–12222

Gameco Industries:
Materials for the Exceptional Student
P.O. Box 310R23
Big Spring, TX 79721–1911
(800) 351–1404

Growing Minds Software
P.O. Box 3704
Ontario, CA 91761–0791
(714) 391–2252

HACH
P.O. Box 10849
Winston-Salem, NC 27108
(800) 624–7968

Hartley Courseware, Inc.
P.O. Box 431
Dimondale, MI 48821
(157) 646–6458; (800) 247–1380

Heartsoft, Inc.
P.O. Box 691381
Tulsa, OK 74169–1381
(800) 285–3475

Houghton Mifflin School Division
One Memorial Dr.
Cambridge, MA 02178
(617) 725–5022; (800) 992–5121

Humanities Software
P.O. Box 950
Hood River, OR 97031
(800) 245–6737

IBM Educational Systems
P.O. Box 2150
Atlanta, GA 30301–2150
(800) 426–2133; (800) 284–9482 TDD

IEP
Rt. 671, P.O.Box 546
Fork Union, VA 23055
(804) 842–2077

Imaginart
307 Arizona St.
Bisbee, AZ 85603
(800) 828–1376

Innocomp
33195 Wagon Wheel Dr.
Solon, OH 44139
(216) 248–6206; (216) 248–0375 FAX

Institut Nazareth et Louis-Braille
1111, St-Charles ouest
Longueil, PQ J4K 5G4 Canada
(514) 463–1710; (514) 463–0243 FAX

Instructional/Communications Technology, Inc.
10 Stepar Pl.
Huntington Station, NY 11746
(516) 549–3000; (800) CALL-ICT

K-12 MicroMedia Publishing
6 Arrow Rd.
Ramsey, NJ 07446
(201) 825–8888; (800) 922–0401

Kidsview Software
P.O. Box 98
Warner, NH 03278
(603) 927–4428

KidTech
21274 Oak Knoll
Tehachapi, CA 93561
(805) 822–1633; (805) 823–1138

Kinder Magic Software
1680 Meadowglen Ln.
Encinitas, CA 92024
(619) 632–1193

Jay Klein Productions
1695 Summit Point Ct.
Colorado Springs, CO 80919
(719) 591–9815

Krell Software
Flowerfield Bldg. #7, Ste. 1D
St. James, NY 11780
(516) 584–7900; (800) 245–7355

Language Analysis Lab
Waisman Ctr., 1500 Highland Ave.,
University of Wisconsin
Madison, WI 53705
(608) 263–5145

Laureate Learning Systems, Inc.
110 E. Springs St.
Winooski, VT 05404
(802) 655–4755; (800) 562–6801

Learning Company
6493 Kaiser Dr.
Fremont, CA
(415) 792–2101; (800) 852–2255

Learning Tools, Inc.
Box 1642
Sebastopol, CA 95473–1642
(404) 641–9954; (800) 333–9954

Learning Well
2200 Marcus Ave.
New Hyde Park, NY 11040
(516) 326–2101; (800) 646–9954

Lekotek of Georgia, Inc.
1955 Cliff Valley Way, Ste. 102
Atlanta, GA 30329
(404) 633–3430

Looking Glass Learning Products, Inc.
276 Howare Ave.
Des Plaines, IL 60018–1906
(800) 545–5457

MarbleSoft
12301 Central Ave. N.E., Ste. 205
Blaine, MN 55434
(612) 755–1402

Marshware, Inc.
P.O. Box 8082
Shawnee Mission, KS 66208
(816) 523–1059; (800) 821–3303

MCE, A Division of Lawrence Productions
1800 S. 35th St.
Galesburg, MI 49078
(616) 665–7075; (800) 421–4157

MECC
3490 Lexington Ave. N.
St. Paul, MN 55126
(612) 481–3611; (800) 228–3504

Merit Software
13635 Gamma Rd.
Dallas, TX 75244
(214) 385–2353

Microcomputer Curriculum Project
P.O. Box 622
Cedar Falls, IA 50613–0622
(800) 552–6227

Micro-Ed
P.O. Box 24750
Edina, MN 55424
(612) 929–2242

Milliken Publishing Co.
P.O. Box 21579
1100 Research Blvd.
St. Louis, MO 63132
(314) 991–4220

Mindplay
3130 N. Dodge Blvd.
Tucson, AZ 85716
(602) 332–6365; (800) 221–7911

Mindscape, Inc.
1345 Diversey Pkwy.
Chicago, IL 60614
(312) 525–1500

Morning Star Software
P.O. Box 5364
Madison, WI 53705
(608) 233–5056; (800) 533–0445

Optimal-Ed Learning Materials
P.O. Box 50489
Henderson, NV 89016
(702) 736–0706

Optimum Resource, Inc.
10 Station Pl.
Norfolk, CT 06058
(800) 327–1473

Parrot Software
P.O. Box 1139
State College, PA 16804
(814) 237–7282; (800) PARROT-1

PEAL Software
P.O. Box 8188
Calabasas, CA 91372
(818) 883–7849

Pelican Software, Inc.
768 Farmington Ave.
Farmington, CT 06032
(203) 674–8221; (800) 822–DISK

Personal Data Systems, Inc.
P.O. Box 1008
Campbell, CA 95009
(408) 866–1126

Psychological Software Services, Inc.
6555 Carrollton Ave.
Indianapolis, IN 46220
(317) 257–9672

Pugliese, Davey and Associates
5 Bessom St., Ste. 175,
P.O. Box 4700
Marblehead, MA 01945–4000
(617) 639–1930; (612) 224–2521

Quest Systems, Inc.
P.O. Box 102
Pittsburgh, KS 66762
(316) 232–2626; (316) 231–5811

Queue, Inc.
338 Commerce Dr.
Fairfield, CT 06430
(203) 333–7268; (800) 232–2224

Research Design Associates
10 Boulevard Ave.
Greenlawn, NY 11740
(516) 754–5280; (800) 654–8715

Tom Snyder Productions
90 Sherman St.
Cambridge, MA 02140
(617) 876–4433

Society for Visual Education, Inc.
1345 Diversey Pkwy.
Chicago, IL 60614
(312) 525–1500; (800) 829–1900;
(312) 525–9474 FAX

South West Ed Psych Services
2001 W. Silvergate Dr.
Chandler, AZ 85224–1201
(602) 253–6528

Spin-A-Test Publishing Co.
3177 Hogarth Dr.
Sacramento, CA 93013
(805) 369–2032

James Stanfield, Co.
P.O. Box 41058
Santa Barbara, CA 93140
(800) 421–6534

J.E. Stewart
18518 Kenlake Pl. N.E.
Seattle, WA 98155
(206) 486–4510

Sunburst Communications
39 Washington Ave.
Pleasantville, NY 10570
(914) 769–5030; (800) 628–8897

Sunset Software
9277 E. Corrine Dr.
Scottsdale, AZ 85260
(602) 451–0753

TASH Inc.(Technical Aids & Systems for the
Handicapped)
70 Gibson Dr., Unit 12 Markham, ON L3R 4C2 Canada
(416) 475–2212; Telex 06–986766 TOR

Teacher Support Software
1035 N.W. 57th St.
Gainesville, FL 32605
(800) 228–2871

Teach Yourself By Computer Software
3400 Monroe Ave.
Rochester, NY 14618
(716) 381–5450

Technical Perspectives, Inc.
3108 Kristin Ct.
Garland, TX 75044
(800) 594–3779

Technology for Language and Learning
P.O. Box 327
East Rockway, NY 11518–0327
(516) 625–4550

Tell'em Ware
1714 Olson Way
Marshalltown, IA 50158
(515) 752–9667

Terrapin Software, Inc.
400 Riverside St.
Portland, ME 04103
(207) 878–8200

Tiger Communication System, Inc.
155 E. Broad St., #325
Rochester, NY 14604
(716) 454–5134

Trace Research and Development Center
Rm. S-151 Waisman Ctr.,
1500 Highland Ave.
University of Wisconsin
Madison, WI 53705
(608) 262–6966; (608) 263–5408

UCLA Intervention Program for Handicapped Children
1000 Veteran Ave., Rm.23–10
Los Angeles, CA 90024
(301) 825–4821

Unicorn Engineering, Inc.
5221 Central Ave., Ste. 205
Richmond, CA 94804
(415) 528–0670

Vocational and Rehabilitation Research Institute
3304 33rd St. N.W.
Calgary, AB T2L 2A6 Canada
(403) 284–1121

Vysion, Inc.
30777 Schoolcraft Rd.
Livonia, MI 48150
(313) 542–3300; (800) 521–1350

Wings for Learning, Inc.
1600 Green Hills Rd.,
P.O. Box 660002
Scotts Valley, CA 95067–0002
(408) 438–5502; (800) 321–7511; (408) 438–4214

Words+, Inc.
P.O. Box 1229
Lancaster, CA 93584
(800) 869–8521

References

Church, G., & Glennen, S. (1992). *The handbook of assistive devices*. San Diego, CA: Singular.

Edyburn, D. (1989). *Applications of microcomputers in the BD classroom*. Reston, VA: Center for Special Education Technology.

Evans, S. S., & Evans, W. H. (1992). Assessment in special education. In L. Bullock (Ed.), *Exceptionalities in children and youth* (pp. 68–90). Boston: Allyn & Bacon.

Patton, J., Blackbourn, J., Kauffman, J., & Brown, G. (1989). *Exceptional children in focus*. New York, NY: Merrill/Macmillan.

section VI : *Partnerships for Lifelong Success*

In this section we highlight the vast array of resources and materials associated with promoting lifelong learning and success for both (a) individuals with disabilities and (b) professionals who deliver services to students with disabilities. Two major categories of resources are housed in this diverse section: Transitions to Work and Postsecondary Education Settings, and Collaborative Consultation with Parents, Families, and Colleagues.

Transitions to Work and Postsecondary Education Settings

Adolescents with disabilities continue to have difficulties making the transition from school settings to the workplace and postsecondary educational settings. With unemployment rates estimated between 30 and 70 percent and drop-out rates among those with disabilities alarmingly high, many have characterized this lack of postschool success as a national crisis. According to Gajar, Goodman, and McAfee (1993), underachievement, dropping-out of school, lack of appropriate career/vocational/counseling programs, limited work experiences, and limited parental involvement have resulted in serious under- and unemployment among those with disabilities. The resources that follow highlight some of the models that have been applied successfully in the delivery of instruction related to transition.

AVAILABLE RESOURCES: Transitions
Generic Textbooks

Clark, G., & Kolstoe, O. (1990). *Career development and transition education for adolescents with disabilities*. Boston: Allyn & Bacon.

Gajar, A., Goodman, L., & McAfee, J. (1993). *Secondary schools and beyond: Transition of individuals with mild disabilities*. New York, NY: Merrill/Macmillan.

Kokaska, C., & Brolin, D. (1985). *Career education for handicapped individuals*. New York, NY: Merrill/Macmillan.

Trapani, C. (1990). *Transition goals for adolescents with learning disabilities*. Boston: Little, Brown.

Resource Books

Baumgart, D. (1990). *Career education: A curriculum manual for students with handicaps*. Gaithersburg, MD: Aspen.

This comprehensive manual shows the reader how to start up and run a successful community-based vocational education program for students with mild, moderate, or severe handicaps. Step-by-step, goal-by-goal, it moves from concept to thank-you letters. Everything is included—administrative forms, questionnaires, goals, and checklists, even for students who are nonreaders. Guidelines, timetables, and supporting materials are also provided.

Bragman, R. (1992). *Employment for individuals with disabilities: What every job-seeker with a disability needs to know.* Indian Rocks Beach, FL: Phillip Roy.

> This sourcebook provides an overview of the transition process, methods to identify job requirements, and strategies to match individuals with appropriate occupations. Useful supplements of selected assessment instruments and state resource profiles are also provided.

Brinckerhoff, L., Shaw, S., & McGuire, J. M. (1993). *Promoting postsecondary education for students with learning disabilities: A handbook for practitioners.* Austin, TX: PRO-ED.

> A practical handbook that assists practitioners to deliver effective support services for students with LD who seek educational opportunities beyond high school. Numerous charts and appendices make this a useful resource.

Calkins, C., & Walker, H. (1990). *Social competence for workers with developmental disabilities.* Baltimore: Paul H. Brookes.

> Designed for those involved in job placement for persons with developmental disabilities, this hands-on manual provides step-by-step procedures for the social success of persons with developmental disabilities in integrated job settings. The book provides detailed guidance on employment-related assessment, social competence, intervention selection, and agency evaluation.

Corbett, J., & Barton, L. (1993). *A struggle for choice: Students with special needs in transition to adulthood.* New York, NY: Routledge.

> This book analyzes the employment opportunities, education, training choices, and community participation as they relate to students with special educational needs. The authors take a distinctive socio-political perspective and explore the issues in terms of class, race, gender, and economic issues.

Gardner, J., Chapman, M., Donaldson, G., & Jacobson, S. (1988). *Toward supported employment*. Baltimore: Paul H. Brookes.

> This text is a clear, easy-to-follow guide that provides hands-on information for facilitating the change from a segregated work activity program to a supported work program. It introduces the key elements of the change, identifies change-related variables that must be controlled, and defines the roles and responsibilities of management and integral staff.

Kravets, M., & Wax, I. (1993). *The K & W guide to colleges and the learning disabled student*. Deerfield, IL: Kravets, Wax, & Associates.

> This is a reference/resource book for students, parents, and professionals that provides detailed explanations of special programs, services, and entrance requirements in an easy-to- read and comprehensive format.

Mcloughlin, C., Garner, J., & Callahan, M. (1987). *Getting employed, staying employed: Job development and training for persons with severe handicaps*. Baltimore, MD: Paul H. Brookes.

> This manual provides specific strategies for securing employment for persons with severe disabilities. It features current service delivery structures, strategies for development, and employment training techniques within community settings.

Meers, G. D. (1987). *Handbook of vocational special needs education*. Gaithersburg, MD: Aspen.

> This information base for decision-makers regarding programming for disadvantaged and handicapped students includes discussions of federal legislation, curriculum modification techniques, work experience and cooperative placement programs, support services, vocational assessment, career education, the role of parents and advocates for vocational training, and the role of the administrator of special needs programs.

Moon, M., Inge, K., Wehman, P., Brooke, V., & Barcus, J. (1990). *Helping persons with severe mental retardation get and keep employment*. Baltimore: Paul H. Brookes.
> The authors provide a comprehensive, data-based overview of philosophical issues, successful instructional strategies, and employment outcomes for high school-age youth and adults with severe mental retardation involved in supported employment. This provides guidelines for implementation, case studies, and numerous forms and checklists based on actual applications of supported employment in a variety of settings.

Muklewicz, C., & Bender, M. (1988). *Competitive job-finding guide for persons with handicaps.* Austin, TX: PRO-ED.
> The bulk of this book is devoted to strategies for helping people with disabilities make the transition to employment. Topics include assessing work readiness, removing employment barriers, selecting appropriate jobs, strategies for obtaining employment, and adjusting to employment.

Peterson's Guide (1992). *Peterson's colleges with programs for students with learning disabilities*. Princeton, NJ: Author.
> This is a comprehensive guide with advice and detailed profiles on nearly 1,000 two- and four- year college programs for students with LD. Current facts about each school's program and specific LD support services are provided. Information is also provided on admission requirements and suggestions are given for making the most of campus visitations.

Powell, T., et al. (1991). *Supported employment: Providing opportunities for persons with disabilities*. White Plains, NY: Longman.
> The authors present practical information for implementing a supported employment program for individuals with disabilities. Issues related to career planning, instructional strategies, and health are addressed.

Rusch, F. R. (1990). *Supported employment: Models, methods, issues.* Sycamore, IL: Sycamore.

> This is an edited text that provides critical information for the implementation of supported employment programs. One major special section of the book is devoted to the transition from school to work.

Rusch, F. R., DeStefano, J., Chadsey-Rusch, J., Phelps, L., & Szymanski, E. (1992). *Transition from school to adult life: Models, linkages, and policy.* Sycamore, IL: Sycamore Publishing.

> This edited resource text addresses far-reaching and complex issues related to school reform, model program development and evaluation, transition to college, state-level policy planning and development, and cultural and language issues.

Scheiber, B., & Talpers, J. (1987). *Unlocking potential: College and other choices for learning disabled people: A step-by-step guide.* Bethesda, MD: Adler & Adler (Distributed by Woodbine House).

> This concise guide provides information and ideas for prospective college students with learning disabilities and their families, as well as high school and college counselors. Topics covered include deciding whether college is the right choice, choosing courses, making accommodations in the classroom, study skills, and obtaining needed support services.

Sowers, J., & Powers, L. (1991). *Vocational preparation and employment of students with physical and multiple disabilities.* Baltimore, MD: Paul H. Brookes.

> Key issues such as mobility, accessibility, and communication in the context of employment preparation for persons with severe developmental and physical disabilities are covered in this text, as are adaptive strategies for establishing relationships with employers and teaching on-the-job communication skills.

Thomas, J., & Thomas, C. (1991). *Directory of college facilities & services for people with disabilities.* Phoenix: Oryx Press.

> This directory contains information about the physical facilities and services for students with disabilities at more than 1,600 colleges and universities in the United States and Canada.

Wehman, P. (1992). *Life beyond the classroom: Transition strategies for young people with disabilities.* Baltimore, MD: Paul H. Brookes.

> The text acts as a guide to planning, designing, and implementing successful transition programs for students with disabilities. Using clear-cut models and approaches, the author applies his strategies to all major areas of disability and to all facets of the transition process—initiation of the transition program, job development, training, and final placement. Practitioners, special education instructors, community service providers, students, vocational rehabilitation counselors, and disability advocates are the intended readers of this text.

Wehman, P., & McLaughlin, P. *Vocational curriculum for developmentally disabled persons.* Austin, TX: PRO-ED.

> Practitioners and teachers in activity centers, special and vocational educational programs, and rehabilitation facilities all benefit from this illustrated book which presents a logically sequenced array of work skills that provides a continuum of jobs for the developmentally disabled trainees. Each skill is presented with instructions and materials needed, task analysis, teaching procedures, and implementation guidelines.

Wircenski, J. L. (1982). *Employability skills for the special needs learner: An integrated program of reading, math, and daily living skills.* Gaithersburg, MD: Aspen.

> This integrated program of reading, math, and daily living skills helps handicapped and disadvantaged youth make the transition from school to work. It includes ready-to-use lesson plans and answer sheets, and emphasizes personal organization, getting along with others, following direc-

tions, developing a sense of pride, accepting criticism, and making decisions.

Curriculum Guides/Comprehensive Programs/Kits

EBSCO Transition Skills Centers. Birmingham, AL: EBSCO Industries.

> This comprehensive resource contains diverse training modules related to success in the workplace. EBSCO also markets a number of other comprehensive curricula and kits which focus on the transitional and career needs of individuals with special education needs.

Life Centered Career Education. (1989). By D. Brolin and Associates. Reston, VA: Council for Exceptional Children.

> CEC markets a comprehensive program in which life skills are infused into traditional subject matter areas. Twenty-one competencies and 97 subcompetencies in daily living skills, personal/social skills, and occupational guidance and preparation are presented along with activities and teaching strategies. Materials associated with this program include a trainer's manual with accompanying videotape, a curriculum manual, and two activity books.

The Prevocational Assessment and Curriculum Guide. By D. Mithaug, D. Mar, & J. Stewart. Seattle: Exceptional Education.

> This is an empirically validated method for developing training programs for persons preparing for sheltered employment. The program's four major functions are: to assess and identify the training needs of handicapped people; to analyze behavior and skills deficits; to prescribe training goals; and to evaluate client performance by administering the instrument. Skills assessed include: attendance, endurance, independence, production, learning, behavior, communication skills, social skills, grooming, and toileting skills. Materials in the kit include a teacher's manual, skills inventories, a curriculum guide, and summary profile sheets.

The Transition Skills Guide: An Integrated Curriculum with Reading and Math Materials. (1992). By J. Wircenski. Gaithersburg, MD: Aspen.

> This is an integrated curriculum designed to meet the needs of students identified as at-risk learners. The guide contains 78 transition skill lessons divided into seven sections: values clarification skills, socialization skills, communication skills, decision making skills, team building skills, financial management skills, and job procurement/retention skills. Teacher lesson plans complete with performance objectives, content outline, and learning activities are provided for each lesson. Student learning activities focus on transition, reading, and math. The binder format allows for easy duplication, and record keeping is facilitated through the use of student profile sheets reflecting the various components of the 78 lessons.

Organizations, Advocacy Groups, Clearinghouses, and Agencies

> The **Arkansas Research & Training Center in Vocational Rehabilitation** markets a large number of resources (e.g., assessment devices, employment development interventions, resource manuals, inservice development programs) centering on the development of employability skills and job opportunities for individuals with disabilities. **Write:** Media and Publications Section, Hot Springs Rehabilitation Center, P.O. Box 1358, Hot Springs, AR 71902 or **Phone:** (501) 624–4411.

> The **Association of Persons in Supported Employment (APSE)** provides support and information to people who implement supported employment (e.g., job coaches, enclave and mobile crew supervisors, small business entrepreneurs, etc.). The organization also publishes a newsletter, **The Advance.**

The **Association on Handicapped Student Services Programs in Postsecondary Education (AHSSPPE)** is a national non-profit organization of members from over 600 institutions of higher education. It promotes full participation of individuals with disabilities in college life. Information sharing is a key element of the goal to upgrade the quality of services available to students with disabilities. The organization sponsors an annual conference and publishes a bimonthly newsletter, **Alert,** and the **AHSSPPE Journal. Write:** AHSSPPE, P.O. Box 21192, Columbus, OH 43221 or **Phone:** (614) 488–4972 (Voice/TDD).

The **Center on Postsecondary Education for Students with Learning Disabilities** offers technical assistance on developing support services for students with learning disabilities for colleges and postsecondary programs throughout the country. Program staff provide training for administrators and postsecondary service providers through inservice presentations and degree programs on campus. Center staff are also engaged in on-going research and writing/dissemination on issues related to postsecondary students with LD. The organization publishes the **Postsecondary LD Network News** three times per year, which includes information on conferences, resources, and "best practices" for services providers. **Write:** Center on Postsecondary Education for Students with Learning Disabilities, The University of Connecticut, U-64, 249 Glenbrook Road, Storrs, CT 06269–2064 or **Phone:** (203) 486–4036.

Division of Career Development and Transition (DCDT) of CEC encourages interdivisional and interagency utilization of effective career development and transition concepts. The organization publishes a journal, **Career Development and Exceptional Individuals,** twice yearly, and a newsletter, **DCDT Times** quarterly. **Write:** DCDT, CEC, 1920 Association Drive, Reston, VA 22091 or **Phone:** (703) 620–3660.

The **HEATH Resource Center** is a national clearinghouse which collects and disseminates information about disability issues in postsecondary education. The center identifies and describes educational and training opportunities as well as promoting and recommending strategies for the full participation by individuals with disabilities in postsecondary programs. HEATH publishes a newsletter three times a year as well as a host of other resource papers, monographs, and directories. **Write:** HEATH, One Dupont Circle, Suite 800, Washington, DC 20036 or **Phone:** (800) 544–3284.

The **National Association of Vocational Education Special Needs Personnel (NAVESNP)** is an organization of secondary and postvocational education professionals concerned with the education of disadvantaged students and students with disabilities or other special needs. The organization publishes the **NAVESNP Journal** and sponsors five regional subgroups. **Write:** NAVESNP, c/o Athens Technical Institute, U.S. Highway 29 North, Athens, GA 30610 or **Phone:** (404) 549–2362.

The **National Council on Independent Living (NCIL)** is a national association that disseminates information about independent living matters and relevant legislation through its membership network. It can provide referral to a local program for consumers, practical information for professionals, and advice to persons interested in starting an independent living center. **Write:** NCIL, 310 S. Peoria St., Suite 201, Chicago, IL 60607 or **Phone:** (312) 226–1006.

President's Committee on Employment of People with Disabilities is a public/private partnership of national and state organizations and individuals working together to improve the lives of individuals with disabilities by increasing their opportunities for employment. The committee serves in an advocacy role and provides a variety of types of technical information. Contact the committee for a full listing of useful publications. **Write:** President's Committee, 1331 F Street, N.W., Washington, DC 20004–1107. **Phone:** (202) 376–6200; TDD (202) 376–6219.

Collaborative Consultation with Parents, Families, and Colleagues

The instructional and social/emotional needs of students with disabilities make the delivery of educational and habilitative services a team effort. To maintain this team effort it is important for professionals involved in delivering services to develop a **transdisciplinary orientation.** Such an orientation not only encourages a close working relationship among parents, general educators, and the many related service professionals involved with students, it also helps ensure that relevant information, knowledge, and intervention techniques are transferred and generalized across disciplines and individuals. Clearly, the close collaboration among special educators, general educators, and parents can stimulate the development of novel approaches to the challenges faced by students with disabilities. The resources that follow present a number of strategies for promoting and maintaining collaboration.

AVAILABLE RESOURCES:
Collaborative Consultation
Generic Textbooks

> Morsink, C., Thomas, C. C., & Correa, V. (1991). *Interactive teaming: Consultation and collaboration in special programs*. New York, NY: Merrill/Macmillan.

> Turnbull, A. P., & Turnbull, H. R. (1990). *Families, professionals, and exceptionality: A special partnership*. New York, NY: Merrill/Macmillan.

Resource Books

> Buscaglia, L. (1983). *The disabled and their parents*. Thorofare, NJ: Slack.

Various aspects related to the counseling of individuals with disabilities and their families are addressed. The book includes contributions from a number of noteworthy authors divided into six "challenge" sections: (a) the overall challenge, (b) as the researcher sees the challenge, (c) the family meets the challenge, (d) the disabled person meets the challenge, (e) the counselor meets the challenge, and (f) the challenge for tomorrow.

Featherstone, Helen. (1982). *A difference in the family: Life with a disabled child*. New York: Penguin.

This classic, written by a parent/educator whose son had severe disabilities, offers a thoughtful, in-depth look at the positive and negative effects a child with disabilities can have on the family.

Fine, M. (1991). *Collaboration with parents of exceptional children*. Brandon, VT: CPPC.

Intended for both students and practicing professionals, this text explores how professionals and parents can form an effective partnership to meet the needs of students with disabilities.

Lobato, D. J. (1990). *Brothers, sisters, and special needs: Information and activities for helping young siblings of children with chronic illnesses and developmental disabilities*. Baltimore, MD: Paul H. Brookes.
Leader's companion packet for brothers, sisters and special needs. Baltimore, MD: Paul H. Brookes.

Young children, ages 3–8, with siblings with chronic illnesses and developmental disabilities have their needs addressed in this curriculum and activity guide. The accompanying packet is used by the professionals and parents as they conduct the sibling workshop programs designed to provide background on issues facing young siblings in the family and to provide recommendations for meeting sibling needs.

Meyer, D., Vadasy, P., & Fewell, R. (1990). *Living with a brother or sister with special needs: A book for sibs*. Seattle: University of Washington Press.

> This is a book for brothers and sisters of children with disabilities that provides straight talk on a number of issues relating to nature and causes of disabilities. It also addresses many of the common feelings, problems, and concerns shared by siblings.

Powell, T., & Gallagher, P. (1992). *Brothers & sisters—A special part of exceptional families*. Baltimore, MD: Paul H. Brookes.

> Siblings of children and adults with developmental disabilities share their daily experiences at home, in school, and in the community. Coupled with these insights, the authors discuss current research findings on siblings' needs, adjustment patterns, and family-oriented services available in the community. Families of exceptional individuals gain practical strategies for strengthening family relationships.

Pueschel, S., Bernier, J., & Weidenman, L. (1988). *The special child: A sourcebook for parents of children with developmental disabilities*. Baltimore, MD: Paul H. Brookes.

> Parents of special children get answers in this easy-to-understand home reference—answers concerning prognoses and treatments and answers concerning the roles of the professionals, diagnostic tests, medical treatments, educational strategies, legal issues, and counseling in the treatment, education, and success of their special children.

Routburg, M. (1986). *On becoming a special parent: A mini-support group in a book*. Chicago, IL: Parent/Professional Publisher.

> This practical handbook has been written for parents of children with extra needs by a mother of young girl with severe brain damage. Through hints and easy-to-read suggestions, parents learn to deal with the everyday struggles of living with the special child.

Murphy, J. (1982). *Home care of handicapped children series*. Lyons, CO: Carol Lutey.

This series of guidebooks, designed for individuals (teachers, parents, paraprofessionals, child care workers, related service personnel) who care for or educate children ages 3–12 in a home setting, provides general information in the areas of basic child health, learning, play, safety measures, and practical hints related to specific handicapping conditions. Eleven separate volumes, each related to a specific handicapping condition, are available. Specific areas covered are: asthma, autism, cleft palate, cystic fibrosis, diabetes, epilepsy, hearing impairment, hemophilia, mental retardation, orthopedic handicaps, and visual impairment.

Seligman, M., & Darling, R. (1992). *Ordinary families, special children: A systems approach to childhood disability*. New York, NY: Guilford.

The authors address the effect of childhood disability on the family from a multisystems perspective, providing professionals with a better understanding of the contextual world of these families and describing systems-based therapeutic modalities that can be used to help them.

Shea, T., & Bauer, A. (1991). *Parents and teachers of children with exceptionalities: A handbook for collaboration*. Boston: Allyn & Bacon.

This is a comprehensive text which first describes a model for parent/teacher collaboration and then illustrates specific activities which promote the collaborative enterprise. Special issues which influence the collaborative relationship are explored in several chapters and an extensive reference/resource list is provided.

Simon, Robin. (1987). *After the tears: Parents talk about raising a child with a disability*. Orlando, FL: Harcourt Brace Jovanovich.

In this brief book, parents share their emotions and suggestions about coping with a child with a disability from infancy to adulthood.

Singer, G., & Irving, L. (1992). *Support for caregiving families: Enabling positive adaptation to disability.* Baltimore, MD: Paul H. Brookes.

> Families of individuals with developmental disabilities are offered practical information about the array of family support services and are provided with goals, tactics, and techniques useful to them in this edited volume. Empirical evaluation studies on model programs are also offered.

Stein, S. B., & Frank, D. (1991). *About handicaps: An open family book for parents and children together.* New York, NY: Walker and Co.

> This is an easy-to-read and wonderfully illustrated book that assists parents in explaining disabilities to children. This is just one of many books published by Walker and Co. that puts disabilities and other problems related to "life" in a format understandable to children. Other titles include: *What do you mean I have a learning disability, Somebody called me a retard today . . . and my heart felt sad, About phobias,* and *On dying.*

Thompson, M. (1992). *My brother, Matthew.* Rockville, MD: Woodbine House.

> This illustrated tale provides a realistic, compassionate look at a family dealing with the needs of a child with a disability and the effects that disability has on the family. The story encourages siblings to share their emotions and reassures them that their role in the family is important.

Webster, E. J., & Ward, L. M. (1993). *Working with parents of young children with disabilities.* San Diego, CA: Singular.

> This text is designed to assist professionals to work more effectively with parents. Individual chapters address parents' reactions to a diagnosis, the ongoing crises they experience with their child, guilt experiences, and parents' need for confirmation from professionals. Anecdotes from group therapy sessions are included in every chapter.

Comprehensive Programs/Kits

Collaboration in Schools: An Inservice and Preservice Curriculum for Teachers, Support Staff, and Administrators. Austin, TX: PRO-ED.

> The authors offer a complete curriculum in providing inservice and preservice training experiences for classroom teachers, special education teachers, support staff, and school administrators through collaborative consultation and effective teaming. In this manner, all educators jointly responsible for the education of exceptional and at-risk students collaborate and coordinate in an effective and complete system. The curriculum concentrates on the prevention of serious learning/behavioral problems in at-risk students, and it improves the coordination of instruction and remediation for already identified exceptional students.

Multimedia

"Somedays' child: A focus on special needs children and their families." Portland, OR: Educational Productions.

> In this 30–minute video, three families share their experiences in caring for their special needs children. One of the major issues addressed by the video is how parents' observations, feelings, and concerns must be an essential part of program planning. Other related video titles of interest produced by Educational Productions are: **"What about me: Brothers and sisters of children with disabilities"** and **"A place for me: Planning for the future.**

Organizations, Advocacy Groups, and Agencies

The **Family Resource Center on Disabilities (FRCD),** formerly the Coordinating Council for Handicapped Children, seeks to improve services for all children with disabilities. FRCD offers information and referral services, family support services, transition services, special education rights training, and training opportunities for parent leaders. Parents and professionals across the nation can receive training manuals and pamphlets from FDRC such as *How to organize an effective parent/advocacy group and move bureaucracies,* which is a 100–page handbook that gives step-by-step directions on how to organize a parent group from scratch; *How to get services by being assertive,* which demonstrates positive assertiveness techniques for staffings, IEP meetings, due process hearings, and other special education meetings; and *Special education manual,* which provides up-to-date federal and state special education rules under one cover. Pamphlets cover such titles as "Does Your Child Have Special Education Needs?", "How to Participate Effectively in Your Child's IEP Meeting," and "Your Child's School Records." Pamphlets are available in English and Spanish. **Write:** FRCD, 20 E. Jackson Blvd., Room 900, Chicago, IL 60604 or **Phone:** (312) 939–3513.

The PACER Center, Parent Advocacy Coalition for Educational Rights, sponsors workshops, develops model programs, trains parents and professionals, and distributes publications and other resources with the goal of helping children with disabilities reach their full potential through education. The Center publishes the **Pacesetter Newsletter,** for parents interested in special education issues, and the **Pacer Advocate,** a newsletter for readers with an interest in legislation and court rulings affecting special education and disability issues.

Parent Educational Advocacy Training Center (PEATC) provides educational consultation services and conducts parent training courses which are open to anyone able to attend from across the country. Participants in the three- or four-day courses come in mixed pairs (i.e., parent/teacher or parent/VR counselor) and agree to return to their community and teach the curriculum just learned. Among the courses are "Next Steps: Planning for Employment," "Supported Employment Opportunities," and "World of Work." PEATC also publishes a quarterly newsletter, **The PEATC Press.**

appendix A : *Publishers, Producers, and Suppliers*

Note: Addresses for sources of assistive technology and software are given in Section V, pages 231–60.

Abingdon Press, 201 Eighth Ave. South, Nashville, TN 37202 **Phone:** (800) 251–3320

Academic Success Press, Inc., P.O. Box 2567, Pompano Beach, FL 33072

Academic Therapy Publications, 20 Commercial Blvd., Novato, CA 94949–6191 **Phone:** (800) 422–7249

T.M. Achenbach, University Associates in Psychiatry, One South Prospect St., Burlington, VT 05401–3456 **Phone:** (802) 656–8313

Addison-Wesley Publishing Co., Menlo Park, CA 94025 **Phone:** (800) 227–1936

AGS. *See* American Guidance Services

Allied Publishing Company, P.O. Box 337, Niles, MI 49120

Allyn & Bacon, 160 Gould St., Needham Heights, MA 02194–2310 **Phone:** (800) 852–8024

American Disability Channel, 1777 N.E. Loop 410, Suite 1410, San Antonio, TX 78217 **Phone:** (512) 824–SIGN/824–1666 TDD

American Federation for the Blind, c/o American Book Center, Brooklyn Navy Yard, Building #3, Brooklyn, NY 11205 **Phone:** (718) 935–9647

American Guidance Services, Circle Pines, MN 55014–1796 **Phone:** (800) 328–2560

Ann Arbor Programs, Academic Therapy Publications, 20 Commercial Blvd., Novato, CA 94949–6191 **Phone:** (800) 422–7249

Annick Educational, 15 Patricia Ave., Willowdale, Ontario, Canada M2M 1H9 **Phone:** (416) 221–4802

Ann Morris Enterprises, Inc., 890 Fams Court, East Meadow, NY 11554 **Phone:** (516) 292–9232

The Arc, National Headquarters, 500 E. Border St., Suite 300, P.O. Box 300649, Arlington, TX 76010 **Phone:** (202) 785–3388

Arena Press, 20 Commercial Boulevard, Novato, CA 94949–6191 **Phone:** (800) 422–7249

Aspen Publishers, Inc., 200 Orchard Ridge Dr., Gaithersburg, MD 20878 **Phone:** (800) 638–8437

Attainment Company, Inc., 504 Commerce Parkway, Verona, WI 53593 **Phone:** (800) 327–4269

Barnell-Loft, 958 Church St., Baldwin, NY 11510

BFA Educational Media, Phoenix Films, 2349 Chaffee Dr., St. Louis, MO 63146 **Phone:** (800) 221–1274

John F. Blair, Publisher, 1406 Plaza Dr., Winston-Salem, NC 27103–1470

Book-Lab, 500 74th St., North Bergen, NJ 07047 **Phone:** (800) 654–4081

R.R. Bowker, 121 Chanlon Rd., New Providence, NJ 07974 **Phone:** (800) 521–8110

Paul H. Brookes Publishing Co., P.O. Box 10624, Baltimore, MD 21285–0624 **Phone:** (800) 638–3775

Brookline Books, P.O. Box 1046, Cambridge, MA 02238 **Phone:** (800) 666–BOOK

Wm. C. Brown Publishers, 2460 Kerper Blvd., Dubuque, IA 52001

Bubba Press, 2100 Cactus Ct., Walnut Creek, CA 94595

Capitol Publications Inc., 1101 King St., P.O. Box 1453, Alexandria, VA 22313–2053 **Phone:** (800) 327–7203

Carolrhoda Books, Inc., 241 First Ave. North, Minneapolis, MN 55401 **Phone:** (800) 328–4929

Chelsea Curriculum Publications, School Division, P.O. Box 5186, Yeadon, PA 19050 **Phone:** (800) 362–9786

Chronimed Publishing, Ridgedale Office Center, 13911 Ridgedale Dr., Minnetonka, MN 55343 **Phone** (612) 541–0239

Clancy, J., Software and Resources, 97 Manchester Rd., Newton Highlands, MA 02161–1132 **Phone:** (617) 969–2614

Communication/Therapy Skill Builders, 3830 E. Bellevue, P.O. Box 42050–T91, Tucson, AZ 85733 **Phone:** (602) 323–7500

Constructive Playthings, 1127 East 119th St., Grandview, MO 64030–1117 **Phone:** (800) 255–6124

Continental Press, 520 East Bainbridge St., Elizabethtown, PA 17022 **Phone:** (800) 233–0759

Cornerstones, Inc. 1440 San Juline Circle, St. Augustine, FL 32095 **Phone:** (800) 745–8212

Corwin Press, Inc., P.O. Box 2526, Thousand Oaks, CA 91319–8526 **Phone:** (805) 499–9774

Council for Exceptional Children, 1920 Association Dr., Reston, VA, 22091–9494 **Phone:** (703) 620–3660

CPPC, 4 Conant Square, Brandon, VT 05733 **Phone:** (800) 433–8234

Creative Communicating, P.O. Box 3358, Park City, UT 84060

Creative Publications, 5040 W. 111 St., Oak Lawn, IL 60453 **Phone:** (800) 624–0822

Creative Teaching Press, Inc., P.O. Box 6017, Cypress, CA 90630–0017 **Phone:** (800) 444–4CTP

Cuisenaire Co. of America, P.O. Box 5026, White Plains, NY 10602–5026 **Phone:** (800) 237–3142

Curriculum Associates, Inc., 5 Esquire Rd., N. Billerica, MA 01862–2589 **Phone:** (800) 225–0248

Delmar Publishers, Inc., Two Computer Dr. West, Albany, NY 12212

Demos Publications, Inc., Suite 201, 386 Park Ave. South, New York, NY 10016

Didax Inc., Educational Resources, One Centennial Dr., Peabody, MA 01960

DLM, P.O. Box 4000, Allen, TX 75002 **Phone:** (800) 527–4747

Dutton/New American Library, 375 Hudson St., New York, NY 10014 **Phone:** (212) 366–2000

DVS Home Video, P.O. Box 64428, St. Paul, MN 55164–0428 **Phone:** (800) 736–3099, ext. 31

EDC Publishing, P.O. Box 470663, Tulsa, OK 74147 **Phone:** (800) 475–4522

Edmark, P.O. Box 3218, Redmond, VA 98073 **Phone:** (800) 426–0856/ (206) 861–7179 TDD

Educational Activities, Inc., P.O. Box 87, Baldwin, NY 11510 **Phone:** (800) 645–3739

Educational Development Corporation, 10302 E. 55th Pl., Tulsa, OK 74146 **Phone:** (800) 331–4418

Educational Performance Associates, Publishers, 600 Broad Ave., Ridgefield, NJ 07657 **Phone:** (201) 941–1425

Educational Productions Inc., 7412 SW Beaverton Hillsdale Highway, Suite 210, Portland, OR 97225 **Phone:** (800) 950–4949

Educators Publishing Service, Inc., 75 Moulton St., Cambridge, MA 02138 **Phone:** (617) 547–6706

EPIE, P.O. Box 839, Water Mill, NY 11976 **Phone:** (516) 283–4922

ETR Associates, P.O. Box 1830, Santa Cruz, CA 95061–1830 **Phone:** (800) 321–4407

Exceptional Education, P.O. Box 15308, Seattle, WA 98115

Exceptional Teaching Aids, 20102 Woodbine Ave., Castro Valley, CA 94546 **Phone:** (510) 582–4859

Fearon/Janus/Quercus, 500 Harbor Blvd., Belmont, CA 94002 **Phone:** (800) 877–4283

Feeling Good Associates, 77–6502 Marlin Rd., Kailua-Kona, HI 96740 **Phone:** (808) 326–4192

Films for the Humanities, Inc., P.O. Box 2053, Princeton, NJ 08543–2053 **Phone:** (800) 257–5126

Fisher-Price, 620 Girard Ave., East Aurora, NY 14052 **Phone:** (800) 433–5437

Gallaudet University Press, 800 Florida Ave., NE, Washington, DC 20002–3695 **Phone:** (800) 451–1073

Gamco Industries, Inc., P.O. Box 310R23, Big Spring, TX 79721–1911 **Phone:** (800) 351–1404

Gateway Educational Co., P.O. Box 6868, Orange, CA 92613 **Phone:** (800) 222–3334

Golden Books and Games, Western Publishing Co., 1220 Mound Ave., Racine, WI 53404 **Phone:** (414) 633–2431

Good Morning Teacher! Publishing Company, P.O. Box 1200, Palo Alto, CA 94302 **Phone:** (415) 424–9471

Guilford Publications, Inc., 72 Spring St., New York, NY 10012 **Phone:** (800) 365–7006

Hamilton Associates, Starry Night Distributors, 26 Appletree Lane, Latham, NY 12110 **Phone:** (800) 255–0818

Hamilton Publication, P.O. Box 3222, Boulder, CO 80307 **Phone:** (303) 499–3183

Harcourt Brace Jovanovich, 6277 Sea Harbor Dr., Orlando, FL 32887 **Phone** (800) 225–5425

HarperCollins College Publishers, 10 E. 53rd St., New York, NY 10022 **Phone:** (800) 242–7737

Hawthorne Educational Services, Inc., 800 Gay Oak Dr., Columbia, MO 65201 **Phone:** (800) 542–1673

Holcomb's Educational Materials, 3205 Harvard Ave., Cleveland, OH 44105 **Phone:** (800) 362–9907

Holiday House, Inc., 425 Madison Ave., New York, NY 10017 **Phone:** (212) 688–0085

Henry Holt and Company, Books for Young Readers, 115 West 18th St., New York, NY 10011 **Phone:** (800) 488–5233

Hubbard, P.O. Box 104, Northbrook, IL 60062

Human Kinetics Publishers, Inc., 1607 N. Market St., Box 5076, Champaign, IL 61825–5076 **Phone:** (217) 351–5076

Imaginart Communications Products, 307 Arizona St., Bisbee, AZ 85603 **Phone:** (800) 828–1376

Indiana University Audio-Visual Center, Bloomington, IN 4705–5901 **Phone:** (800) 552–8620

International Reading Association, 800 Barksdale Rd., P.O. Box 8139, Newark, DE 19714–8139 **Phone:** (302) 731–1600

International Universities Press, Inc., 59 Boston Post Rd., Madison, CT 06443–1524

Jalmar Press, 45 Hitching Post Dr., Building 2, Rolling Hills Estates, California 90274–5169 **Phone:** (310) 547–1240 or (800) 662–9662

Jamestown Publishers, P.O. Box 9168, Providence, RI 02940 **Phone:** (401) 351–1915

Jossey-Bass Publishers, 350 Sansome St., San Francisco, CA 94104

Kaplan School Supply Corporation, 1310 Lewisville-Clemmons Rd., P.O. Box 609, Lewisville, NC 27023–0609 **Phone:** (800) 334–2014

KIDSRIGHTS, 3700 Progress Blvd., Mount Dora, FL 32757 **Phone:** (800) 892–KIDS

Kimbo Educational, P.O. Box 477, 10 North Third Ave., Long Branch, NJ 07740 **Phone:** (908) 229–4949 or (800) 631–2187

Kravets, Wax, & Associates, Inc., P.O. Box 187, Deerfield, IL 60015–0187

Lakeshore Learning Materials, 2695 E. Dominguez St., Carson, CA 90749 **Phone:** (800) 421–5354

Learner Managed Designs, Inc., 2201–K W. 25th St., Lawrence, KS 66047 **Phone:** (913) 842–6881

Lerner Publications Company, 241 First Ave. North, Minneapolis, MN 55401–9906 **Phone:** (800) 328–4929

LML, Inc., 3222 Greenmead Rd., Baltimore, MD 21207 **Phone:** (410) 922–7747

Longman Publishing Group, Addison-Wesley Publishing Co., 10 Bank St., White Plains, NY 10606 **Phone:** (800) 447–2226

Longwood Division, Allyn & Bacon, 111 10th St., Des Moines, IA 50309 **Phone:** (800) 848–4400, ext. 92

Love Publishing Company, 1777 S. Bellaire St., Denver, CO 80222–4306 **Phone:** (303) 757–6912 or (303) 757–2579

LRP Publications, 747 Dresher Rd., Suite 500, Department 450, P.O. Box 980, Horsham, PA 19044–0980 **Phone:** (800) 341–7874, ext. 347.

LS&S Group, P.O. Box 673, Northbrook, IL 60065 **Phone:** (800) 568–4789

Carol L. Lutey Publishing, Box 3434 North Star Route, Lyons, CO 80540

Macmillan Children's Book Group, 866 Third Ave., New York, NY 10022 **Phone:** (800) 257–5755

Magination Press, A Division of Brunner/Mazel, Inc., 19 Union Square West, 8th Floor, New York, NY 10003 **Phone:** (800) 825–3089

Math Teachers Press, Inc., 5100 Gamble Dr., Suite 398, Minneapolis, MN 55416 **Phone:** (612) 545–6535; (800) 852–2435

MaxiAIDS, 42 Executive Blvd., Farmingdale, NY 11735 **Phone:** (800) 522–6294

Merrill/Macmillan, 866 Third Ave., New York, NY 10022 **Phone:** (800) 228–7854

Mosby, 11830 Westline Industrial Dr., St. Louis, MO **Phone:** (800) 325–4177

National Association of the Deaf, 814 Thayer Ave., Silver Spring, MD 20910–4500 **Phone:** (301) 587–1788; TDD (301) 587–1791

National Braille Press, Inc., 88 St. Stephen St., Boston, MA 02115 **Phone:** (617) 266–6160

National Crisis Prevention Institute, 3315–K North 124th St., Brookfield, WI 53005

National Professional Resources, Inc., 25 South Regent St., Port Chester, NY **Phone:** (914) 937–8879

Newmarket Press, 18 E. 48 St., New York, NY 10017 **Phone:** (212) 832–3575

New Readers Press, 1320 Jamesville Ave., Box 131, Syracuse, NY 13210 **Phone:** (315) 422–9121; (800) 448–8878

Open Court Publishing Company, 315 Fifth St., Peru, IL, 61354 **Phone:** (800) 435–6850

Oryx Press, 4041 N. Central at Indian School Rd., Phoenix, AZ 85012 **Phone:** (800) 279–6799.

Oxford University Press, 200 Madison Ave., New York, NY 10016 **Phone:** (800) 451–7556

Parent/Professional Publisher, P.O. Box 59730, Chicago, IL 60645

Penguin, 375 Hudson St., New York, NY 10014 **Phone:** (212) 366–2000.

Peterson's Guides, Box 2123, Princeton, NJ 08542–2123 **Phone:** (800) 338–3282

Phoenix Learning Resources, 2345 Chaffee Rd., St. Louis, MO 63146 **Phone:** (800)221–1274

Phonic Ear Inc., 3880 Cypress Dr., Petaluma, CA 94954–7600 **Phone:** (707) 769–1110

Planned Parenthood Shasta-Diablo, 1291 Oakland Blvd., Walnut Creek, CA 94596 **Phone:** (510) 935–4066

Poetry Alive, P.O. Box 9643, Ashville, NC 28815 **Phone:** (800) 476–8172.

Practical Press, P.O. Box 455, Moorhead, MN 56561–0455 **Phone:** (218) 236–5244

Prentice-Hall, Englewood Cliffs, NJ 07632 **Phone:** (800) 288–4745

PRO-ED, 8700 Shoal Creek Blvd., Austin, TX 78758–6897 **Phone:** (512) 451–3246

Psychological Corporation, Harcourt Brace Jovanovich, Inc., 555 Academic Ct., San Antonio, TX 78783–3954 **Phone:** (800) 228–0752

R & E Publishers, P.O. Box 2008, Saratoga, CA 95070

Research Press, Dept. G., P.O. Box 9177, Champaign, IL
    61826 **Phone:** (217) 352–3273

Resources for Industry, R.D. #3, Box 12, Prospect Ave,
    Walton, NY 13856 **Phone:** (607) 865–7184

Resources for Rehabilitation, 33 Bedford St., Suite 19A,
    Lexington, MA 02173 **Phone:** (617) 862–6455

Rigby, P.O. Box 797, Crystal Lale, IL 60039–0797 **Phone:**
    (800) 822–8661

Riverside Publishing Company, 8420 Bryn Mawr, Chi-
    cago, IL 60631 **Phone:** (800) 767–TEST

Routledge, Inc., 29 West 35th St., New York, NY 10001–
    2299 **Phone:** (212) 244–6412

Phillip Roy, P.O. Box 130, Indian Rocks Beach, FL 34635
    Phone: (813) 593–2700; (800) 255–9085

Saxon Publishers, 1320 W. Linsey, Norman, OK 73069
    Phone: (800) 284–7019

Science Research Associates (SRA), 155 North Wacker
    Dr., Chicago, IL 60606 **Phone:** (312) 984–7000

Singular Publishing Group, 4284 41st St., San Diego, CA
    92105–1197 **Phone:** (800) 521–8545

Slack Incorporated, 6900 Grove Rd., Thorofare, NJ
    08086–9447 **Phone:** (609) 853–5991

Slosson Educational Publications, Inc., P.O. Box 280,
    East Aurora, NY 14052 **Phone:** (800) 828–4800

Society for Visual Education, Inc., 1345 Diversey Parkway, Chicago, IL 60614–1299 **Phone:** (800) 624–1678

Southern Illinois University Press, P.O. Box 3697, Carbondale, IL 62902–3657 **Phone:** (618) 453–2281

Springer-Verlag Publishers, 536 Broadway, New York, NY 10012–3955 **Phone:** (212) 431–4370

James Stanfield Company, Inc., P.O. Box 41058, Santa Barbara, CA 93140 **Phone:** (800) 421–6534

Stevenson Learning Skills, Inc., 85 Upland Rd., Attleboro, MA 02703

Success by Design, Inc., P.O. Box 957033, Hoffman Estates, IL 60195 **Phone:** (800) 327–0057

Sycamore Publishing Company, P.O. Box 133, Sycamore, IL 60178 **Phone:** (815) 756–5388

Syracuse University Press, 1600 Jamesville Ave., Syracuse, NY 13244–5160 **Phone:** (315) 443–2597

T.F.H. Ltd., 4449 Gibsonia Rd., Gibsonia, PA 15044 **Phone:** (412) 444–6400

T.J. Publishers, 817 Silver Spring Ave., Suite 206, Silver Spring, MD 20910–4617

Teachers College Press, 1234 Amsterdam Ave., New York, NY 10027 **Phone:** (800) 488–2665

Temple University Press, Broad and Oxford Streets, Philadelphia, PA 19122

Charles C. Thomas, 2600 South First St., Springfield, IL 62794–9265 **Phone:** (800) 258–8980

Troll Associates, 100 Corporate Dr., Mahwah, NJ 07430

Turman Publishing Company, 1319 Dexter Ave. North, Seattle, WA 98109 **Phone:** (206) 282–1650 (Call collect to order)

United Educational Services, P.O. Box 1099, Buffalo, NY 14224 **Phone** (800) 458–7900.

University of Alaska Press, Gruening Building, 1st floor, Fairbanks, AK 99775 **Phone:** (907) 474–6389

University of Minnesota Press, 2037 University Ave. Southeast, Minneapolis, MN 55414 **Phone:** (800) 388–3863

University of Washington Press, P.O. Box 50096, Seattle, WA 98145–5096 **Phone:** (206) 543–8870

University Press of America, 4720 Boston Way, Lanham, MD 20706 **Phone:** (800) 462–6420

Vantage Press Inc., 516 W. 34th St., New York, NY 10001

Variety Pre-Schoolers' Workshop, 47 Humphrey Dr., Syosset, NY 11791–4098 **Phone:** (800) 933–VPSW

Visible Ink Incorporated, 40 Holly Lane, Rosyln Heights, NY 11577

VORT Corporation, P.O. Box 60880–K, Palo Alto, CA 94306 **Phone:** (415) 322–8282

Wadsworth Inc., 7625 Empire Dr., Florence, KY 41042

George Wahr Publishing Co., 3041/2 S. State St., Ann Arbor, MI 48104 **Phone:** (313) 668–6097

Walker and Company, 720 Fifth Ave., New York, NY 10019 **Phone:** (800) AT-WALKER

Waterfront Books, 98 Brookes Ave., Burlington, VT 05401

Weekly Reader Corporation, 245 Long Hill Rd., Middletown, CT 06457 **Phone:** (800) 446–3355

Western Psychological Services, 12031 Wilshire Blvd., Los Angeles, CA 90025 **Phone:** (800) 648–8857

Westport Publishers, Inc., 4050 Pennsylvania, Suite 310, Kansas City, MO 64111 **Phone:** (800) 347–BOOK

Wilmor Distribution Center, 2912 Reach Rd., Williamsport Industrial Park, Williamsport, PA 17701

Wisconsin Department of Public Instruction, Publication Sales, Drawer 179, Milwaukee, WI 53293–0179 **Phone:** (800) 243–8782

Woodbine House, 5615 Fishers Lane, Rockville, MD 20852 **Phone:** (301) 468–8800; (800) 843–7323

The Wright Group, 19201 120th Ave., N.E., Bothell, WA 98011–9518

Wright Group, 10949 Technology Pl., San Diego, CA 92127

Xerox Imaging Systems, Adaptive Technology Products, 9 Centennial Dr., Peabody, MA 01960 **Phone:** (508) 977–2000

Zephyr Press, P.O. Box 13448, Tucson, AZ 85732–3449 **Phone:** (602) 322–5090

appendix B : *Review* : *Forms*

If we have overlooked any resources that you think should be included in **The Special Education Sourcebook,** please use these review forms to make recommendations. Send completed review forms to Dr. Michael S. Rosenberg, c/o Woodbine House, 5615 Fishers Lane, Rockville, MD 20852.

REVIEW FORM—ORGANIZATIONS

Section/Subsection of Sourcebook:

_____

Name, Address, Phone Number of Organization:

_____

_____

_____

Geographical Areas Served:

_____

Description of Services Provided:

_____

_____

Special Notes or Issues:

_____

_____

REVIEW FORM—PUBLISHERS & PRODUCERS

Section/Subsection of Sourcebook:

_____

Type of Resource (Book, Video, Journal, etc.):

_____

Title and Author of Resource:

_____

Publication Date:

_____

Name, Address, Phone Number of Publisher/Producer:

_____

_____

_____

Abstract or Description of Resource:

_____

_____

_____

Special Notes or Issues:

_____

_____

Title Index

A

B

C

F

G

H

I

R

S

Author Index

Organization Index

Subject Index

About the authors

Michael S. Rosenberg earned his Ph.D. in Special Education from The Pennsylvania State University. He is Professor and Chair of the Special Education Department at Johns Hopkins University. Irene Edmond-Rosenberg has a masters in Public Administration from The Pennsylvania State University. She is an Assistant Professor of English at Baltimore City Community College and a freelance writer.